The Media, the Public and the
Financial Crisis

Mike Berry

The Media, the Public and the Great Financial Crisis

palgrave
macmillan

Mike Berry
Cardiff University
Cardiff, UK

ISBN 978-1-137-49972-1   ISBN 978-1-137-49973-8   (eBook)
https://doi.org/10.1007/978-1-137-49973-8

Library of Congress Control Number: 2018964420

Cover illustration: Jaromir Chalabala / EyeEm / Getty Images
Cover design: Tom Howey

This Palgrave Macmillan imprint is published by the registered company Springer Nature Switzerland AG
The registered company address is: Gewerbestrasse 11, 6330 Cham, Switzerland

Acknowledgements

Firstly, I would like to thank my colleagues at Cardiff University's School of Journalism, Media and Culture who provided encouragement and support during the production of this book: Stuart Allan, Cindy Carter, Stephen Cushion, Lina Dencik, Inaki Garcia-Blanco, Jenny Kidd, Kerry Moore, Karin Wahl-Jorgensen and Andrew Williams. Particular thanks are due to Justin Lewis and Jenny Kitzinger who read chapter drafts and offered invaluable advice on how sections of this book could be improved. I am also indebted to Glyn Mottershead and Richard Sambrook for helping to arrange interviews with journalists.

I would also like to thank academics at other departments who have been supportive of my work. James Curran, Aeron Davis, Natalie Fenton and Des Freedman at Goldsmiths, Jen Birks, Neal Curtis, Tracey Potts and Colin Wright at Nottingham, Laura Basu at Utrecht and Emma Briant at Essex. Thanks too to Nottingham University for providing the small grant that allowed me to carry out the focus group research. I owe a special debt of gratitude to my former supervisor, Greg Philo at Glasgow University, for my initial research training but also for years of support, encouragement and advice.

I would also like to express my gratitude to the journalists and economists whose insights and specialist knowledge were very useful in the production of this book. From the news media thank you to Dan Atkinson, Aditya Chakrabortty, Evan Davis, Larry Elliott, Kevin Maguire, George Pascoe-Watson, Robert Peston, Hugh Pym, Damian Reece and Kevin Schofield. From the economics profession thanks to Panicos Demetriades, Michael Hudson and Howard Reed. I would also like to thank Simon Wren-Lewis who has generously looked at drafts of chapters and offered advice on various aspects of macroeconomics. I am also indebted to Karel Williams and the other academics working at CRESC at the University of Manchester whose work on finance and Britain's economic model is cited regularly throughout the book.

The staff at Palgrave Macmillan have been supportive over the many years that it has taken to write this book. In particular I would like to thank Heloise Harding, Martina O'Sullivan, Lucy Spinger, Lucy Batrouney, Mala Sanghera-Warren and Carolyn Zhang all of whom have shown remarkable fortitude, patience and good humour in the face of countless missed deadlines.

Some of the material in Chap. 2 appears in Mike Berry (2013) 'The Today Programme and the Banking Crisis', *Journalism* 14(2): 253–70. Chapter 4 contains material from Mike Berry (2015) 'The UK Press and the Deficit Debate', *Sociology*, 50 (3): 542–559, and Mike Berry (2016) 'No Alternative to Austerity: How BBC Broadcast News Reported the Deficit Debate', *Media, Culture and Society*, 38 (6): 844–863.

Finally I would like to dedicate this book to my partner Louise and my daughter Delilah. Both have been remarkably patient and supportive through the long days and nights that it has taken to complete this book.

CONTENTS

List of Figures

LIST OF TABLES

INTRODUCTION

When the British banking system was rescued in October 2008 there was much talk of a 'crisis of capitalism' and even newspapers not generally seen as bastions of radicalism—such as the *Financial Times*—were featuring articles advising readers to brush up on their Karl Marx (Kennedy 2009). 'Banker bashing' dominated the headlines with 'villains' such as 'Fred the Shred' Goodwin of the Royal Bank of Scotland held up to public scorn and ridicule. The title of a book by the journalist Paul Mason (2009) *Meltdown: The End of the Age of Greed* seemed to capture the belief shared by many that the crisis marked a turning point in British capitalism. Yet within a year, a government White Paper had stepped back from major structural reforms to finance such as breaking up the banks judged 'too big to fail'. Meanwhile, the debate over bank reform had become eclipsed by discussion of Britain's budget deficit where by early 2010 a public consensus had solidified in favour of cuts to public spending in order to 'balance the books' (Yougov 2010). That consensus would last through the 2010 and 2015 General Elections playing a pivotal role in consecutive Conservative General Election victories (Ashcroft 2010; Hunter 2015). That the public would twice elect a party committed to cuts to the welfare state appeared to challenge a wide body of academic research which had consistently found that governments struggle to reduce spending in the face of public opposition (Pierson 1994, 1996, 2004; Mahoney 2000; Palier 2001; Taylor-Gooby 2001; Starke 2006).

Ten years on from the near collapse of the British banking system, the consequences of the Great Financial Crisis (GFC) continue to reverberate.

Economic growth remains anaemic despite an unprecedented period of ultra-aggressive monetary policy. The rejection of fiscal stimulus in favour of unconventional monetary policy—in the form of quantitative easing—has sharply widened wealth and income inequalities, which have been further exacerbated by unprecedented cuts to Britain's welfare state (*Financial Times* 2016; Ryan 2017). Such policies—which have been mirrored in the United States and parts of the Eurozone—have had profound political consequences. These include intense political polarisation and the growth of populist parties. From UKIP in Britain to the Front National in France, the Northern League in Italy and Donald Trump's Republican Party, austerity has helped boost political movements which espouse openly racist and/or anti-democratic attitudes (Judis 2016; Wolf 2017; Elliott 2017).

Whilst many books have been written about what caused the GFC and how to 'fix finance', none until now has examined the role of the mass media in influencing the formation of public opinion on the crisis. This book marks a first attempt to address this by connecting news reports with structures of audience understanding and belief. To achieve this the book focuses on the three elements of the 'circuit of communication'—the production, content and reception of media messages—because only by studying these simultaneously can the process of communicative power be fully understood (Miller and Philo 2002; Philo et al. 2015). The production of news is investigated through interviews with leading journalists and news editors which examine the various factors that structure news accounts. News itself is explored using a series of extensive content analyses of print and broadcast coverage, whilst audience reception processes are unpacked using focus group discussions with the general public supplemented by reference to large scale polling data.

As this book will demonstrate, the media helped to establish of a set of public beliefs about what caused the GFC and how it could be addressed. In the initial phase of the crisis when much of the British banking system was part-nationalised, the media influenced who was seen as responsible for the crisis, whether the bank rescue plans were viewed as an appropriate response and what could be done to reform the sector. This shaping of public opinion was a function of both what appeared in news reports but also the perspectives and arguments that were excluded. A key consequence was that the media functioned to channel the very real public anger than existed at the time into largely symbolic issues—like restricting

Fred Goodwin's pension pot—whilst leaving the deep structural faults in the banking system and its problematic relationship to Britain unbalanced economic model, largely unexamined.

The media was also critical in establishing key elements of public belief in the later stages of the GFC as the banking crisis and subsequent recession led to a rise in public debt and deficits. Media narratives about the dangers of public debt and deficits helped create public support for austerity policies which did substantial damage to Britain's economy and social fabric. However, it is important to recognise that the media were also implicated in much longer processes of political and economic socialisation which affected how the public understood the debates around the deficit and the turn to austerity. Over many years the Press helped to create a climate of opinion that was suspicious of public investment and hostile to welfare and migrants. Although the primary short term political casualty of these media narratives was the Labour party, over the longer term they fostered the growth of anti-state, anti-welfare and anti-migrant attitudes which contributed to the rise of populism and the Brexit vote.

Although the primary focus of the book is on how news reporting influenced public knowledge and attitudes towards the GFC, a number of other themes run through the book. One is how economic journalism is constructed. So the book's penultimate chapter examines the various pressures, constraints and intellectual assumptions that influence the production of economic news. Another is the debate over what economic journalism should cover. As this book shows most mainstream economic journalism centres on a narrow range of headline macroeconomic indicators. However, what is often missing is both the distributional composition of these aggregate indicators and the shifts in the underlying structure of the economy. So broadcast news rarely talks about the composition of wealth in the economy or the high levels of regional economic polarisation. Little is said about—or linkages made between—the deterioration of working conditions in the labour market, the reliance on personal debt as a core motor of economic growth, the UK's chronic balance of payments problems or how our reliance on a large finance sector may produce financial 'Dutch Disease' which damages other parts of the economy (Blakely 2018). This inability to connect with—and crucially explain—the lived economy of most citizens, not only hinders a public debate on how the economy might be improved but it also leaves people vulnerable to false and misleading explanations for Britain's economic problems.

STRUCTURE OF THE BOOK

The core purpose of this book is to examine how the media reported the GFC, why it was reported in that manner and what consequences for public knowledge and opinion flowed from identifiable patterns in news coverage. To achieve this the book is laid out in the following way.

In order to provide context to the GFC, Chap. 1 presents a brief history of the major structural changes to the British economy since 1979 and how these were related to political decisions taken by both Conservative and Labour governments. These policy shifts led to finance becoming increasingly dominant in the economy—at the expense of other sectors—in a process that has been dubbed 'financialisation' (Krippner 2005; Epstein 2005; Palley 2007; Freeman 2010; Engelen et al. 2011; Dolphin 2013; Shaxson and Christensen 2014; Kay 2015; Lagna 2016; Davis and Walsh 2016; Blakeley 2018). They also led to the creation of a new economic model based on a system of 'privatised Keynesianism' where economic growth became increasingly reliant on rising consumer debt underpinned by the rapid growth in derivatives markets (Crouch 2009). The chapter then traces the development of the GFC from the initial failure of the American sub-prime lender New Century Financial in April 2007 to the near collapse of the British banking system in October 2008. It concludes by examining how the financialisation of the British economy was mirrored by the increasing penetration of financial sector actors into the spheres of lobbying, politics and the media.

The next two chapters concentrate on how the banking crisis was reported and the impact of news accounts on public knowledge and opinion. Chapter 2 begins by examining why the banks collapsed before laying out the range of debate on managing the failed institutions and long-term reforms to the sector. The chapter then discusses the methodological background to the study before presenting the analyses of national newspaper and BBC radio news (*Today programme*) during 2008 and 2009. These content studies pointed to significant differences between press and broadcast coverage but also major areas of overlap. In particular, press and broadcast coverage was unanimous in presenting the view that there was 'no alternative' to the part-nationalisations and focused much of their attention on the issue of bankers' bonuses. Chapter 3 explores how the banking crisis was understood by audiences through a series of focus groups conducted in Glasgow, the Midlands and the South East of England over the summer of 2009. These indicated that many people struggled to understand the crisis but also that the media were important in establishing important aspects of audience belief such as the view that the part-nationalisations had been the 'only option' and that the key issue was reforming bankers' pay structures. The chapter concludes by discussing what happened to the reform process post-2009.

The following three chapters focus on the deficit and the turn to austerity: exploring the range of debate among economists, how the media represented the spectrum and balance of arguments and how this, in turn, played a role in influencing public knowledge and attitudes. Chapter 4 examines how the media debate over Britain's budget deficit developed during the first nine months of 2009. It starts by examining what caused the rise in the deficit before evaluating Britain's public finances within both historical and international contexts. It then looks at the range of debate among economists on how serious a problem the deficit represented and the options for managing it. Next, comes the findings of content analyses of press and broadcast (BBC News at 10) coverage of deficit reporting which found a very strong emphasis on the alleged dangers of public deficits and strong endorsement of austerity policies. Chapter 5 presents the findings of a series of focus groups which examine public knowledge and attitudes towards the deficit. Once again the research suggests that the media were critical in establishing core elements of audience belief particularly in relation to perceptions of what caused the rise in the deficit, how serious a problem it represented and how it should be addressed. Chapter 6 further unpacks public attitudes to the deficit and austerity by examining how key audiences beliefs identified in the focus groups—that much of Labour's extra public spending had been wasted, and that welfare payments and immigration were key drivers of deficit spending—were related, in part, to long-term patterns of media socialisation. This involves an examination of further samples of press content stretching back to the turn of the millennium considered alongside other factors that may have contributed to the construction of public knowledge and attitudes in these areas.

Chapter 7 draws on interviews with senior economic correspondents and news editors to explore the factors that structured the production of GFC news. In these interviews a variety of issues were raised that are rooted in patterns of media ownership, political economy and the sociology of newswork. These include sourcing, commercial pressures, proprietorial influence and political partisanship. The book concludes in Chap. 8 by pulling together the findings from the production, content and reception studies and considering their implication for a range of groups including news organisations and political parties.

REFERENCES

Ashcroft, M. (2010). *What Future for Labour?* Available at: http://lordashcroft-polls.com/2010/09/what-future-for-labour/. Accessed 9 July 2018.

Blakeley, G. (2018). *On Borrowed Time: Finance and the UK's Current Account Deficit.* IPPR. Available at: http://www.ippr.org/research/publications/on-borrowed-time. Accessed 10 July 2018.

Crouch, C. (2009). Privatised Keynesianism: An Unacknowledged Policy Regime. *British Journal of Politics and International Relations, 11,* 382–399.

Davis, A., & Walsh, C. (2016). The Role of the State in the Financialisation of the UK Economy. *Political Studies, 64*(3), 666–682.

Dolphin. (2013). *Don't Bank On It: The Financialisation of the UK Economy.* Available at: https://www.ippr.org/publications/dont-bank-on-it-the-financialisation-of-the-uk-economy. Accessed 9 July 2018.

Elliott, L. (2017, March 26). Populism Is the Result of Global Economic Failure. *Guardian.* Available at: https://www.theguardian.com/business/2017/mar/26/populism-is-the-result-of-global-economic-failure. Accessed 9 July 2018.

Engelen, E., Eturk, I., Froud, J., Johal, S., Leaver, A., Moran, M., Nilsson, A., & Williams, K. (2011). *After the Great Complacence.* Oxford: Oxford University Press.

Epstein, G. (Ed.). (2005). *Financialization and the World Economy.* Cheltenham: Edward Elgar Publishing.

Financial Times. (2016). *S&P: QE 'Exacerbates' Inequality.* Available at: https://www.ft.com/content/b4e604c8-b61a-362e-b741-a78f7009a569. Accessed 9 July 2018

Freeman, R. (2010). It's Financialisation! *International Labour Review, 149*(2), 163–183.

Hunter, P. (2015). *Red Alert: Why Labour Lost and What Needs to Change.* Smith Institute. Available from: https://smithinstitutethinktank.files.wordpress.com/2015/07/red-alert-why-labour-lost-and-what-needs-to-change.pdf. Accessed 9 July 2018.

Judis, J. B. (2016). *The Populist Explosion: How the Great Recession Transformed American and European Politics.* New York: Columbia Global Reports.

Kay, J. (2015). *Other People's Money: Masters of the Universe or Servants of the People.* London: Profile Books.

Kennedy, P. (2009, March 12). Read the Big Four to Know Capital's Fate. *Financial Times.*

Krippner, G. R. (2005). The Financialization of the American Economy. *Socio-Economic Review, 3*(2), 173–208.

Lagna, A. (2016). Derivatives and the Financialisation of the Italian State. *New Political Economy, 21*(2), 167–186.

Mahoney, J. (2000). Path Dependence in Historical Sociology. *Theory and Society,* *29*, 507–548.

Mason, P. (2009). *Meltdown: The End of the Age of Greed.* London: Verso.

Miller, D., & Philo, G. (2002). Circuits of Communication and Power: Recent Developments in Media Sociology. In M. Holborn (Ed.), *Developments in Sociology* (pp. 1–22). Ormskirk: Causeway Press.

Palier, B. (2001). Beyond Retrenchment: Four Problems in Current Welfare State Research and One Suggestion How to Overcome Them. In J. Clasen (Ed.), *What Future for Social Security? Debates and Reforms in National and Cross-national Perspective* (pp. 105–119). The Hague: Kluwer Law.

Palley, T. (2007). *Financialization: What It Is and Why It Matters* (Working Paper No 525). New York: Levy Economics Institute. Available at: http://papers.ssrn.com/sol3/papers.cfm?abstract_id=1077923. Accessed 9 July 2018.

Philo, G., Miller, D., & Happer, C. (2015). Circuits of Communication and Structures of Power: The Sociology of the Mass Media. In M. Holborn (Ed.), *Contemporary Sociology* (pp. 444–470). London: Polity Press.

Pierson, P. (1994). *Dismantling the Welfare State? Reagan, Thatcher, and the Politics of Retrenchment.* Cambridge: Cambridge University Press.

Pierson, P. (1996). The New Politics of the Welfare State. *World Politics, 48*(2), 143–179.

Pierson, P. (2004). *Politics in Time: History, Institutions, and Political Analysis.* Princeton: Princeton University Press.

Ryan, F. (2017, November 17). Now It's official: The Less You have, the More Austerity Will Take From You. *Guardian.* Available at: https://www.theguardian.com/commentisfree/2017/nov/17/austerityminorities-women-disabled. Accessed 16 Oct 2018.

Shaxson, N., & Christensen, J. (2014). *The Finance Curse: How Oversized Financial Sectors Attack Democracy and Corrupt Economics.* London: Commonwealth.

Starke, P. (2006). The Politics of Welfare State Retrenchment: A Literature Review. *Social Policy and Administration, 40*(1), 104–120.

Taylor-Gooby, P. (2001). Sustaining State Welfare in Hard Times: Who Will Foot the Bill? *Journal of European Social Policy, 11*(2), 133–147.

Wolf, M. (2017, June 27). The Economic Origins of the Populist Surge. *Financial Times.*

YouGov. (2010). *Economy.* Available at: https://d25d2506sfb94s.cloudfront.net/today_uk_import/YG-Archives-Pol-Channel4Economy-100329.pdf. Accessed 10 July 2018.

CHAPTER 1

The Rise and Fall of British Finance

This chapter examines the background to the GFC. It focuses on how regulatory and tax policies introduced by both Conservative and Labour governments fostered the development of financial innovation in the City of London, radically changing the structure of the British economy. The chapter also examines why political elites chose to favour the interests of finance over other sectors of the economy. In part, this was a consequence of extensive lobbying by the sector but it was also because financial innovation came to underpin a new growth model based on expanding consumer debt which helped to compensate for stagnant wage growth. However as the events of 2008 proved it was a model that was both dangerous and unstable.

THE FINANCIALISATION OF THE UK ECONOMY

Since the dawn of the Imperial Age the City of London has held a central place in Britain's economic life. As Cain and Hopkins (2016) note, the City played a key role in the development of 'Gentlemanly Capitalism' manifested through domestic economic development and the spread of Empire. However, this review will concentrate primarily on the period after 1979 when the finance sector expanded rapidly whilst manufacturing as a share of national output declined (Coates 1995).

The key reason for the rapid expansion of finance was the decision by the Conservative government to progressively remove the regulations

M. Berry, *The Media, the Public and the Great Financial Crisis*, https://doi.org/10.1007/978-1-137-49973-8_1

on banking, capital and credit that had been introduced during and after the Great Depression. Three decisions in particular were to prove pivotal to the growth of the finance sector. The first was to remove exchange controls in 1981. This shifted the balance of power against labour and towards capital as investment was free to flow to areas where it could secure greater returns (Davis and Walsh 2016). It also hindered domestic manufacturing and accelerated financial globalisation—which increased the power of the City. As former City trader David Buik put it, 'by abolishing exchange controls in 1981, Margaret Thatcher pulled the trigger that made London the international financial centre of the world' (cited in Butcher 2013: 3).

The second key decision was to deregulate the provision of consumer credit. The restrictions on higher purchase agreements were abolished, ownership of credit cards expanded and mortgage lending boomed as consumer borrowing tripled during the 1980s (BBC 2013). The final decision was to deregulate the activities of the City through the 'Big Bang' reforms of October 1986. These were in part driven by technological change as in the shift from trading on 'open-outcry' exchange floors to screen based electronic exchanges. However, the Big Bang also altered the structure of the City by abolishing the distinction between stockbrokers, advisers and 'jobbers' (who created the market in shares), and broke up the clubby old boy networks of the Square Mile by allowing foreign firms—primarily large American and European investment banks—to move into the market. As Will Hutton argues, this allowed foreign banks to evade Wall Street's regulations which separated commercial from investment banking activities and banned proprietary trading:

> 'Big Bang' in 1986 allowed the brokers and jobbers on London's stock market to be bought up by American, European and Japanese investment banks so they could do in London what was outlawed in New York by Roosevelt's Glass-Steagall Act, introduced in the aftermath of the credit crunch that caused the Great Depression. They could manage huge investment funds, trade in any kind of financial security both on their own account and for clients, advise on deals and act as large banks – all under the same roof despite the conflicts of interest that were prohibited in New York. London began to rise in the league tables of international finance. The foundations of Anglo-American financial capitalism were being laid – and with them the seeds of its own demise. (Hutton 2008: 9)

The decision by policy makers to favour the interests of the City over manufacturing had a profound effect on the structure of the British economy and patterns of regional development (Hutton 1996; Davis and Walsh 2016). Inward capital flows increased markedly, pushing up sterling, damaging exports and widening the UK's trade deficit. As Tony Dolphin, senior economist at the Institute for Public Policy Research, noted, the bias towards finance 'produced a casualness about the decline of manufacturing and the collapse of all competing sectors which is really quite jaw-dropping' (cited in Stewart and Goodley 2011: 23).

Such structural shifts were accelerated in the mid 1990s with the rise of financial innovation—particularly securitisation and derivative trading. Although securitisation was not a new process—it can be traced back to the late eighteenth century when Dutch capital helped to fund real estate speculation in North America (Frehen et al. 2012)—the late 1990s saw a sharp increase in its use. Securitisation involved the process of taking assets (such as the revenue streams from loans, credit cards or mortgage payments), pooling them and then turning them into securities (or risk weighted tiers of securities) which could then be traded in secondary markets. These new securities were a type of derivative because their value was based on the price of an underlying asset. As Engelen et al. (2011) note, the growth of securitisation and derivatives was at the time seen as a positive development by regulators and financial economists due to four interlinked prospects:

First, that financial innovation would de-risk core financial institutions; second, that it would free up capital in those institutions which would boost returns safely; third, that it would lead to a superior allocation of capital at a system level and produce liquidity in new markets and stimulate growth; and fourth, that it would 'democratize' finance – permitting the extension of loans to those households that had hitherto been excluded from the benefits of cheap credit. (2011: 44)

Between 1998 and 2009 the global value of over the derivatives (OTC) market grew from $80,309 billion to $614,674 billion, equivalent to a rise from about 2.4 times to 10 times global GDP (Engelen et al. 2011: 42). Most of this rise was driven by an increase in interest rate contracts which as Engelen et al. note, reflected 'innovation in other markets, and in particular the rapid expansion of securitization in the 2000s which increased the financial sector's appetite for floating, mainly LIBOR-linked securities'

(2011: 42). New financial products such as the credit default swap (CDS), effectively insurance contracts against loan defaults—although you didn't need to hold the insured loan to buy a CDS so that they could operate as purely speculative instruments—also expanded rapidly during the period, rising from a market of less than a $2,000 billion in 2001 to $62,000 billion by the end of 2007 (Hjort et al. 2013).[1]

A number of factors have been cited for the explosion in financial innovation from the late 1990s. On the supply side the large increase in consumer debt from the 1980s onwards provided the raw materials for the creation of mortgage and other asset backed securities. On the demand side Wall Street and the City of London saw huge influxes of foreign capital from the Petro-states, awash with cash from a commodity boom, and China eager to recycle its trade surpluses and savings glut (Wolf 2010). This wall of money on the 'hunt for yield'—and in America encountering record low interest rates—fuelled the demand for complex products which paid a good coupon rate. Furthermore, the low interest rate environment offered the opportunity for financial firms to gear up and gamble on derivatives. Other factors were also significant such as the role of higher maths graduates ('Quants') in creating the complex models (e.g. Black–Scholes, Capital Asset Pricing Model) which underpinned trading strategies, and the role of tax havens used extensively for tax and regulatory arbitrage (Keeler 2009; Shaxton 2012).

As financial innovation accelerated finance and real estate begun to play an increasingly central role in the British economy. Whilst the UK economy as a whole grew by 3 per cent per annum between 1997 and 2007 the finance sector expanded by an annual rate of 6 per cent (Burgess 2011). Finance grew from less than 6.6 per cent of the economy to 9 per cent, and the real estate sector grew from 12.6 per cent to 16.2 per cent (Giles 2009). Even more dramatic was the increasing share of corporate profits generated by the finance, real estate and insurance (FIRE) sectors. Between 2002 and 2007 companies from oil and mining plus the FIRE sector accounted for more than 70 per cent of all FTSE 100 profits (Engelen et al. 2011). Finance alone accounted for 30 per cent of all FTSE profits during this period when its share of UK employment was static and it accounted for only 8 per cent of UK output (Engelen et al. 2011). Underlying this profit was the high returns on equity that were being generated by investment and retail banks. This was commonly above 15 per cent per annum and at some banks such as Lloyds TSB between 23 per cent and 34 per cent (Engelen et al. 2011). However this profit surge was not the result of high-value innovation—returns on assets were very low typically less than 1 per cent—but instead was primarily achieved by expanding bank balance sheets which increased from 50 per cent of UK GDP in the 1970s to 300 per cent in 2000, to 550 per cent in 2007 (Smaghi 2010). As Haldane notes increased leverage was the key factor in the growth and profitability of the sector:

> During the golden era, competition simultaneously drove down returns on assets and drove up target returns on equity. Caught in this cross-fire, higher leverage became banks' only means of keeping up with the Joneses. Management resorted to the roulette wheel... leverage increased across the financial system as a whole. Having bet the bank on black, many financial firms ended up in the red. (Haldane 2009: 3, cited in Engelen et al. 2011: 108)

One flipside of swelling bank balance sheets was a sharp rise in household indebtedness which increasingly came to underpin the growth in UK GDP, public spending and employment. This temporarily obscured the weaknesses in other parts of the economy, especially the non-financial private sector and in particular manufacturing—which lost two million jobs between 1997 and 2010 (Comfort 2013). Replicating the Thatcher government, growth under New Labour became heavily reliant on consumer demand funded by housing equity release. Between 1997 and 2007 housing equity withdrawal was equal to 103.3 per cent of the growth in UK GDP, slightly less than the 104.2 per cent seen during Mrs. Thatcher's administration (Engelen et al. 2011). By 2014 UK homeowners had borrowed £1.8 trillion, or 125 per cent of total UK GDP, via home equity release (Hutton 2014). Econometric modelling conducted by Oxford Economic Forecasting has attempted to gauge how the economy would have fared without this increase in household indebtedness. Estimating on the basis that the level of debt to disposable income rose from 102 per cent in 1997 to 120 per cent in 2007 (just over a quarter of the rise actually seen) over the ten year period real consumption would have been 8.9 per cent lower, consumer prices would have been 12.5 per cent lower and the UK would have suffered four consecutive years of deflation between 2000 and 2003 (Turner 2008).

The debt fuelled growth after 1997 did however allow New Labour to undertake a major programme of public investment. Spending in areas such as health and education saw sustained real terms increases whilst transfer payments reduced child and pensioner poverty, though poverty rates for childless working age people rose (IFS 2013). Growth in health and education spending also operated as Engelen et al. (2011) note, as an 'undisclosed regional policy' by boosting state and para-state employment in areas outside the South East where private sector job creation was 'weak or failing':

> State and para-state employment expanded right across the national economy, but was particularly critical where private sector job was weak or failing...in London and the South, state and para-state employment accounted for no more than 23–32 per cent of employment growth between 1998 and 2007; while in the Midlands, the North, Wales and Scotland, it accounted for between 38 and 61 per cent of the employment growth over the same period, with most of the rest induced by public expenditure multiplier effects. Increasingly state and para-state employment was crucially important in the old industrial areas like the West Midlands and the North East, where declining manufacturing was not replaced by any other autonomous private sector activity. (Engelen et al. 2011: 216)

On the eve of the 2008 banking crisis the British economy found itself in a precarious position, with its reliance on finance and debt leaving it dangerously exposed to a downturn. It hosted the largest financial centre (as a proportion of GDP) of any major developed nation which was heavily leveraged and involved in risky business practices. Its manufacturing base had fallen as a proportion of GDP to nearly 40 per cent below the Eurozone average (10.1 per cent versus 16.1 per cent) and its productivity and research and development spending lagged behind key EU competitors such as France and Germany (World Bank 2017; ONS 2007). The UK was running a persistently high current account deficit and suffered from extreme regional economic polarisation with much of the area outside London and the South East being heavily dependent on public spending. Just before the crisis, the IMF (2008) estimated that the UK housing market was overvalued by 20–30 per cent whilst household debt, which had become another of the economy's key motors of growth, was at record levels.

As this review has demonstrated a key factor behind the growth of the UK's unbalanced economic model was a finance sector employing a business model which concentrated heavily on the maximisation of shareholder value through commercial and residential real estate lending rather than the provision of 'patient finance' to fund productive capital accumulation (Mazzucato 2011; Engelen et al. 2011).

EXPLAINING POLITICAL SPONSORSHIP OF FINANCIALISATION: PRIVATISED KEYNESIANISM, ELITE STORY TELLING AND REGULATORY CLOSURE

In the previous section I sketched out a broad series of structural changes to the British economy after 1979 which led to it becoming increasingly financialised. This involved the FIRE sector becoming increasingly significant in the economy at the expense of other sectors whilst growth was increasingly underpinned by rising consumer and (financial sector) debt.

This section will consider why both Conservative and Labour governments supported these shifts. This is important both as context but also because it explains the response of key political actors to the GFC. To do so requires the examination of two interlinked issues. The first concerns the fact that financialisation created the space for a new 'policy regime' of 'privatised Keynesianism' which could sustain—temporarily at least—economic growth without the use of classic Keynesian demand management (Crouch 2009). The second focuses on how the financial sector was able to shape the regulatory sphere in its own interests through the use of lobbying and elite story telling.

As Crouch (2009: 382) notes in the post-war era states sought an economic model which reconciled 'the uncertainties and instabilities of a capitalist economy with democracy's need for stability for people's lives and capitalism's own need for confident mass consumers'. This was partly achieved through the creation of strong welfare regimes which worked to foster political stability and acted as a bulwark against the spread of communism. However the standard of living guaranteed by welfare states was below that required to maintain the 'purchasing power…needed to sustain an expanding, consumption-driven economy' (Crouch 2009: 384). To counter this the UK as well as the Scandinavian states, Austria and to a lesser extent the USA instituted a policy of Keynesian demand management:

> In times of recession, when confidence was low, governments would go into debt in order to stimulate the economy with their own spending. In times of inflation, when demand was excessive, they would reduce their spending, pay off their debts and reduce aggregate demand. The model implied large state budgets, to ensure that changes within them would have an adequate macroeconomic effect…The Keynesian model protected ordinary people

from the rapid fluctuations of the market that had brought instability to their lives, smoothing the trade cycle and enabling them gradually to become confident mass consumers of the products of a therefore equally confident mass-production industry. (Crouch 2009: 386)

The inflationary shocks of the 1970s provided the political space for return of 'free market' economic doctrine which had been largely marginalised since the Great Depression. In the UK, organisations such as Institute of Economic Affairs, Adam Smith Institute, Institute of Directors and the Centre for Policy Studies were critical players in establishing the hegemony of neoliberal ideas and the dismantling the post-war Keynesian compact (Desai 1994; Gamble 1994). The new orthodoxy involved 'the absolute priority of near-zero inflation at whatever cost in terms of unemployment, the withdrawal of state assistance to firms and industries in difficulties, the priority of competition, the predominance of a shareholder maximisation as opposed to a multiple stakeholder model of the corporation, the deregulation of markets and the liberalisation of global capital flows' (Crouch 2009: 388). However, the return of free market policies created a conundrum. With no Keynesian demand management and workers experiencing stagnating real income because of the erosion of labour power, globalisation and new technology, how could consumer spending be maintained in Anglo-American economies primarily dependent on domestic consumption? The answer under a regime of privatised Keynesian was for individuals—rather than governments—to take on debt in order to stimulate the economy. This process, underwritten by the growth of derivative trading and the increase in mobile investment funds, created a new growth model supported by successive British governments:

> Eventually governments, especially British ones, began to incorporate privatised Keynesianism into their public policy thinking, though the phrase did not occur to them. While a reduction in the price of oil would be seen as good news (because it reduced inflationary pressure), a reduction in the price of houses would be seen as a disaster (as it would undermine confidence in debt), and governments would be expected to act through fiscal or other measures to get prices rising again... The possibility of prolonged, widespread unsecured debt was in turn made possible through innovations that had taken place in financial markets, innovations which for a long time had seemed to be an excellent example of how, left to themselves, market actors find creative solutions...Through the links of these new risk markets to ordinary consumers via extended mortgages and credit card debt, the

dependence of the capitalist system on rising wages, a welfare state and government demand management that had seemed essential for mass consumer
confidence, had been abolished. The bases of prosperity shifted from the
social democratic formula of working classes supported by government
intervention to the neo-liberal conservative one of banks, stock exchanges
and financial markets. (Crouch 2009: 392)

This approach was to prove attractive to New Labour as it allowed them
to create a new electoral block centred on London and the home counties.
Under first past the post this was a critical element of the electorate that
Labour has struggled to attract during the 1980s and early 1990s (Radice
1992; Radice and Pollard 1993, 1994). However, under a system of privatised Keynesian this group could be won over by the prosperity created
by a booming London based financial sector and the tax-free capital gains
created by consistently rising house prices—which were especially concentrated in London and the home counties (Engelen et al. 2011).

Political elites also supported financialisation due to pressure from
extensive financial sector lobbying and elite story telling. In their account
of the history of UK financial oversight, researchers from CRESC locate
the origins of light touch regulation in the fact that the City emerged in
the period before the formation of the Britain's democratic state
(Engelen et al. 2011; Froud et al. 2011; Johal et al. 2014). In this
absence of legal and democratic oversight the City developed a system of
informal self-regulation which survived the introduction of the universal
suffrage, the growth of the trade union movement and coming to power
of the Labour Party. Froud et al. (2011) argue that one reason why the
City was able to avoid democratic oversight was elite 'story telling' manifested through 'a venerable tradition of constitutional mystification
about 'arm's length control' and such like which justified the unaccount-
ability of elites by implying that the delicate functioning of our institutions would only be upset by the intrusion of majoritarian democratic
forces' (Froud et al. 2011: 4).

The unleashing of the free market after 1979 did not automatically
guarantee the regulatory and tax regimes favoured by City interests so the
sector invested heavily in lobbying by both individual firms and sector
wide alliances (Moran 2006; Froud et al. 2011). At the core of these
efforts were two powerful arguments to justify the maintenance of a permissive regulatory environment. The first drew on the pre-1914 narrative
about the superiorities of self-regulation but was now buttressed by new

theories which emphasised the efficiency and self-regulating character of markets as well as the ability of financial elites to manage risk through new forms of innovation. Engelen et al. (2011) argue that such theories soon became a new 'intellectual superstructure' which came to dominate not only financial economics, accounting and financial law but also politics, media and the regulatory sphere:

> At the intellectual root of blindness lay the rise within the economics profession of theories of efficient markets that ascribed to market processes and institutions a superior capacity (superior to regulators) to monitor, measure and anticipate risk. These theories conquered large parts of the profession and were central to the accounts of the working of finance which was taught in leading business schools. Equally significant, the connection between academic economists, market practices and regulatory styles in the period leading up to the crisis had a concretely structural form. In the generation before the great crash, financial economics - especially through business school education and in the role of professional economists in consultancies and in research departments of financial institutions - became an important component of corporate life. This corporatization of a discipline which had hitherto been organized in relatively autonomous academic hierarchies was important in reinventing the media-visible and publically engaged economist, who was no longer a professor against the backdrop of a book case but the 'chief economist' of a giant investment bank captured against the background of a dealing room. (Engelen et al. 2011: 136–137)

Even debacles like the collapse of Barings in 1995, which ought to have discredited the model of light touch regulation, had little impact. When the new tripartite regulatory regime was introduced by New Labour in 1997 there appeared to be movement towards a 'more formal publically controlled system' but the 'strength of the historically entrenched regulatory ideology, and the strength of the interests in the markets, ensured that the [newly created] FSA was rapidly colonized by that old ideology' (Engelen et al. 2011: 143).

The second powerful narrative that was deployed to head off closer regulation was the argument that the City represented the cornerstone of a new post-industrial economic model. With manufacturing in decline, financial services could use its comparative advantage to become a national champion—as long as the regulatory environment was sufficiently unobtrusive:

What was to replace all this manufacturing might? The narrative that developed was to the effect that the deregulation of London as a financial centre had created an alternative economic dynamic, had given the UK a comparative advantage in building a post-industrial service economy, the great motor of which would be the financial services sector, especially its heart in the City. At the height of the Great Moderation, policymakers such as the Chancellor of the Exchequer, and leading voices of City interests, were united in expressing and believing in this story. The account had an important corollary. If the City was an economic powerhouse, it was a powerhouse which had to operate in a fiercely competitive global financial services industry, against many rival centres. It could only operate successfully if light-touch regulation allowed maximum flexibility in the pursuit of enterprise and creativity. (Johal et al. 2014: 412)

As Engelen et al. (2011: 143–144) note, this narrative was a 'deliberate creation of organisations like the City of London Corporation with its annual reports extolling the contribution of finance to London and the wider economy as well as sector-specific reports like those from the British Private Equity and Venture Capital Association. Furthermore the narrative was 'powerful because it was promoted by the heft of a new lobbying and PR machine…and served to align the calculations of different elites (in markets, in the core executive and the regulatory agencies)' (Engelen et al. 2011: 144).

THE FALL OF FINANCE

The first sign of the impending crisis was the bankruptcy of the US mortgage lender New Century Financial in April 2007 (BBC 2007). It had lent heavily to the subprime market and suffered substantial losses following the downturn in the US housing market in the second half of 2006. Three months later two highly levered hedge funds owned by the US investment bank Bear Stearns, which had also invested heavily in mortgage backed securities, collapsed (Bland 2007). On 9 August 2007, stock markets around the world plunged following the announcement that BNP Paribus had suspended withdrawals from three of its investment funds which had invested in subprime because of the 'complete evaporation of liquidity in certain market segments of the US securitization market' (Peston 2007). By this stage the US housing market was in free fall and the value of mortgage backed securities, which were widely dispersed across the international financial system and underpinned the asset base of many institutions, had fallen sharply in value—though by how much it was impossible to estimate because the market for the securities had vanished. Widespread fear over the solvency of institutions led to banks restricting lending to the corporate and household sectors. The credit crunch had begun.

The following month the freezing up of the interbank lending markets claimed their first British victim. Northern Rock, a Newcastle based bank which had expanded aggressively following its conversion from a building society and floatation on the stock exchange in 1997, found itself suffering a liquidity squeeze. The bank had become heavily reliant on the wholesale money markets and securitisation of its mortgage book to fund lending. However, with the contraction of the interbank lending market and the collapse of the market for mortgage backed securities Northern Rock found it impossible to roll over its short term borrowing and begun to run out of funds. On 13 September, members of the Tripartite Authority (Treasury, Bank of England and the FSA) met at the Treasury to finalise the details of a bailout which was due to be announced the next morning (Pym 2014). However, news of the rescue plan leaked out before the announcement could be made, and a run started on the bank. By lunchtime of 14 September queues were building up around Northern Rock branches across the country as panicked customers rushed to withdraw their savings. The run continued for three days until the government announced that all deposits in the banks would be guaranteed. Over the next five months the Government tried repeatedly to engineer a private takeover of Northern Rock before conceding defeat on 17 February 2008 and fully nationalising the bank. In the meantime, another former building society, Alliance and Leicester, came close to bankruptcy in November 2007 before being bailed out with a secretive £3 billion life line from the Bank of England (Watt and Riley-Smith 2015). The following year the bank was bought by the Spanish bank Santander in a £1.2 billion deal.

As 2008 progressed more banks struggled to stay afloat. In March 2008 the giant American investment bank Bear Stearns was taken over by JP Morgan Chase following a liquidity crisis and an almost complete collapse in its share price. However it was September 2008 when the crisis reached a peak as banks across the globe teetered on the edge of insolvency. On 8 September the American government nationalised Freddie Mac and Fanny Mae, who between them underwrote half the US mortgage market (Elliott 2008). The following week on 15 September the American investment bank Lehman Brothers filed for bankruptcy following enormous losses on mortgage backed securities. On 17 September the US government intervened to prevent the collapse of AIG, the world largest insurance company. Five days later US Treasury Secretary Hank Paulson, in an attempt to stem the crisis, unveiled a $700 billion rescue plan to buy up toxic bank assets. During September and October 2008 more banks in America and Europe would either collapse or be saved in costly state bailouts. These included Merill Lynch, Washington Mutual and Wachovia in the USA, and Fortis, UBS and the Anglo-Irish Bank in Europe. In the UK the government persuaded Lloyds to take over HBOS to save it from collapse whilst Bradford and Bingley was nationalised and its branch network and depositor base sold to Santander. The autumn of 2008 saw the most serious financial crisis since the Great Depression, leading to intense debate on how the international financial system came so close to systemic failure.

THE FINANCIALISATION OF THE CIRCUIT OF COMMUNICATION

The financialisation of the economy during this period was mirrored by major structural and ideological transformations in media systems and the range of information that was available to audiences. Philo et al.'s (2015) 'circuit of communication' model which connects the 'diverse range of agencies facilitating the flow of information' in a system of media production, content and reception offers a useful framework for exploring these changes. The four components of the circuit are *public and private institutions which supply information to the media; the media themselves; stratified audience groups;* and *decision makers in a wide range of political, regulatory and corporate spheres.* Digital media—whether in the form of blogs, alternative news sites or social media—function as a parallel stream of information which can reinforce or challenge what appears in the traditional mass media.

Power is frequently exercised through the interpenetration of different elements of the circuit. So for instance, City institutions are important suppliers of information to the media, key media sources and also influential decision makers in the regulatory field. At the same time all elements of the circuit independently interact in forms of communication that are not linear. For example, the media and the public are at times cut out of the circuit—or as Dinan and Miller put it a 'short-circuit' operates—where institutions and/or decision makers talk amongst themselves through processes such as lobbying (Dinan and Miller 2008, 2012). At other times specialist media may be used as an inter-elite channel which excludes the great bulk of the public, as for instance happens with much investor-focused financial news and PR (Davis 2000). The model is therefore more complex than many liberal pluralist or (neo) Marxist models which tend to see information flows moving in a straight line from information suppliers to the media to audiences who then respond by influencing elites.

In terms of *decision making* the move since the 1980s to remove democratic controls on capital have seen corporations play an increasingly central role in governance. This has been the result of the exercise of power in newly privatised areas of the economy and through the increased role of lobbying (Balanya et al. 2000; Beder 2006; Carroll 2010; Monbiot 2000; Traynor 2014; Stavinoha 2016). Facilitating this has been the growth of what Wedel (2011) describes as a 'show elite' of government advisers, private sector consultants, think tankers and lobbyists. This group, whose loyalties and interests are opaque, have attached themselves to key nodes of power in order to 'naturalise' the role of finance and work to build its interests into government policy (Happer 2016; Miller and Dinan 2003; Froud et al. 2012; Davis 2017; Davis and Williams 2016). This process of regulatory capture has been strengthened by the counter-flow of politicians and regulators to the boards of major financial organisations creating conflicts of interest (Warwick Commission 2009; Miller and Dinan 2009; Cave 2013; Thomas 2017). Government has also seen itself—at both the state and local level—being increasingly drawn into the activities of the financial markets as its political and economic fortunes have become connected to financial innovation and the vicissitudes of the markets (Lagna 2016; Financial Times 2017). Furthermore, the increased dependence of political parties on corporate donations from the City—which contributed half of all Conservative funding at the 2010 General Election—has also strengthened the influence of finance (Watt and Treanor 2011).

Meanwhile the finance sector has played an increasingly significant role as *supplier of information to the media*. One of the early drivers of this shift was the Conservative privatisation of state assets in the 1980s. In order to ensure the success of this programme the government invested heavily in public relations. The privatisation programme and the Conservative government's focus on 'enterprise culture' and a 'shareholding democracy' meant that reporting of the financial markets became a progressively more central aspect of news reports. As Philo (1995) notes this also brought to prominence a new class of 'expert'—the City analyst—who became an important commentator not just on the markets but also on the broader macroeconomy:

> By the end of the 1980s, financial and City news had become central areas of media reporting, especially on television. This was one consequence of the dominance of Conservatives and their promotion of the merits of share ownership, entrepreneurs and business dealing in general. Consequently movements in the City were routinely reported and 'experts' from merchant banks and finance houses were consulted for their apparently neutral opinions on the latest trade or financial news. This gave them an important status as 'impartial' commentators. (Philo 1995: 413)

Such processes accelerated in the 1990s as consumers were increasingly drawn into the activities of the financial markets through further privatisations, the demutualisation of building societies as well as the purchase of homes, pensions and new products such as payment protection insurance (Fine 2013; Robertson 2016; Engelen et al. 2011). This generated an increased market for financial news, manifested in the proliferation of finance and money supplements in national newspapers which were underwritten by a threefold rise in global spending on financial products (Greenfield and Williams 2001). This kind of journalism rarely asked critical questions about the growth of finance and it tended to restrict its watchdog role to individual cases of corporate malfeasance (Tambini 2010; Doyle 2006; Fahy et al. 2010). As Mills's (2015) interviews with BBC staff demonstrated this period also saw a major cultural shift at the BBC with the Corporation moving to markedly expand its coverage of the City and the financial markets whilst downgrading alternative perspectives from organised labour.

This is not to say that the media has become completely closed off to alternative perspectives. It remains contested terrain with the degree of openness dependent on a complex matrix of factors. A central issue is ownership, with the bulk of the national press under the control of proprietors who have long supported free markets and deregulation, whilst being strongly opposed to organised labour (Greenslade 2004). Despite this, such publications are subject to powerful commercial imperatives which means that at times even staunchly Conservative newspapers feel the need to respond to public anger by criticising aspects of the free market. Broadcast media are subject to regulations concerning impartiality and balance and many journalists feel a responsibility to speak up for the 'public interest' (Harding 2012). Nevertheless, as Happer (2016: 443) notes: 'the interdependency both materially and ideologically of financial experts, policy-makers and journalists means that the trend towards the 'preferred' stories and explanations as well as the closing of alternatives is well supported.'

In the next chapter I will continue the story of the banking crisis and discuss how broadcast and print media reported its most intense phase.

Note

1. The use of speculative or 'naked' CDS contracts are alleged to have been central to some of the most controversial events of the financial crisis. Most notoriously, Goldman Sachs was accused of creating and then selling toxic mortgage backed securities as sound investments to its clients whilst simultaneously betting against those same securities using CDS contracts (Morgenson and Story 2009).

References

Balanya, B., Doherty, A., Hoedeman, O., Ma'anit, A., & Wesselius, E. (2000). *Europe Inc. Regional and Global Restructuring and the Rise of Corporate Power*. London: Pluto.

BBC. (2007). *Top US Lender in Chapter 11 Move*. Available at: http://news.bbc.co.uk/1/hi/business/6519051.stm. Date accessed 9 July 2018.

BBC. (2013). *Margaret Thatcher: How Her Changes Affected Your Finances*. Available at: http://www.bbc.co.uk/news/business-22064354. Date accessed 9 July 2018.

Beder, S. (2006). *Suiting Themselves: How Corporations Drive the Global Agenda*. London: Earthscan.

Bland, B. (2007, July 18). Bear Stearns Hedge Funds Wiped Out. *Daily Telegraph*. Available at: http://www.telegraph.co.uk/finance/markets/2812344/Bear-Stearns-hedge-funds-wiped-out.html. Date accessed 9 July 2018.

Burgess, S. (2011). Measuring Financial Sector Output and Its Contribution to UK GDP. *Bank of England Quarterly Bulletin Q3*. Available at: http://www.bankofengland.co.uk/publications/Documents/quarterlybulletin/qb110304.pdf. Date accessed 9 July 2018.

Butcher, S. (2013). *Six Things Margaret Thatcher Did for Britain's Bankers*. Available at: http://news.efinancialcareers.com/uk-en/138421/six-things-margaret-thatcher-did-for-the-city/. Date accessed 9 July 2018.

Cain, P. J., & Hopkins, A. G. (2016). *British Imperialism*. London: Routledge.

Carroll, W. (2010). *Corporate Power in a Globalizing World.* Toronto: Oxford University Press.

Cave, T. (2013). *More than a Lobby: Finance in the UK.* Available at: https://www.opendemocracy.net/ourkingdom/tamasin-cave/more-than-lobby-finance-in-uk. Date accessed 9 July 2018.

Coates, D. (1995). UK Underperformance: Claim and Reality. In D. Coates & J. Hillard (Eds.), *UK Economic Decline: Key Texts* (pp. 3–24). London: Prentice Hall.

Comfort, N. (2013). *The Slow Death of British Industry: A 60-Year Suicide, 1952–2012.* London: Biteback Publishing.

Crouch, C. (2009). Privatised Keynesianism: An Unacknowledged Policy Regime. *The British Journal of Politics and International Relations, 11,* 382–399.

Davis, A. (2000). Public Relations, Business News and the Reproduction of Corporate Elite Power. *Journalism, 1*(3), 282–304.

Davis, A. (2017). The New Professional Econocracy and the Maintenance of Elite Power. *Political Studies, 65*(3), 594–610.

Davis, A., & Walsh, C. (2016). The Role of the State in the Financialisation of the UK Economy. *Political Studies, 64*(3), 666–682.

Davis, A., & Williams, K. (2016). Introduction: Elites and Power After Financialization. *Theory, Culture and Society, 34*(5–6), 3–26.

Desai, R. (1994). Second Hand Dealers in Ideas: Think Tanks and the Thatcherite Hegemony. *New Left Review I, 203,* 27–64.

Dinan, W., & Miller, D. (2008). Transparency in EU Decision Making, Holding Corporations to Account: Why the ETI Needs Mandatory Lobbying Disclosure. In *Corruption and Democracy: Political Finances – Conflicts of Interest – Lobbying – Justice.* Strasbourg: Council of Europe.

Dinan, W., & Miller, D. (2012). Sledgehammers, Nuts and Rotten Apples: Reassessing the Case for Lobbying Self-Regulation in the United Kingdom. *Interest Groups and Advocacy, 1*(1), 105–114.

Doyle, G. (2006). Financial News Journalism: A Post-Enron Analysis of Approaches Towards Economic and Financial News Production in the UK. *Journalism, 7*(4), 433–452.

Elliott, L. (2008, September 9). Saving Fannie and Freddie Was Nationalisation Pure and Simple. *Guardian.* Available at: https://www.theguardian.com/commentisfree/2008/sep/09/freddiemacandfanniemae.subprimecrisis. Date accessed 9 July 2018.

Engelen, E., Eturk, I., Froud, J., et al. (2011). *After the Great Complacence.* Oxford: Oxford University Press.

Fahy, D., O'Brien, M., & Poti, V. (2010). From Boom to Bust: A Post-Celtic Tiger Analysis of the Norms, Values and Roles of Irish Financial Journalists. *Irish Communications Review, 12,* 5–20.

Financial Times. (2017). *Local Councils Are Set to Lose the Property Game* [Editorial]. Available at: https://www.ft.com/content/a1d92484-2a91-11e7-bc4b-5528796fe35c. Accessed 9 July 2018.

Fine, B. (2013). *Towards a Material Culture of Financialisation* (FESSUD: Working Paper Series No. 15). Available from: http://fessud.eu/working-papers/. Accessed 9 July 2018.

Frehen, R., Rouwenhorst, K. G., & Goetzmann, W. N. (2012). Dutch Securities for American Land Speculation in the Late Eighteenth Century. In E. N. White, K. Snowden, & P. Fishback (Eds.), *Housing and Mortgage Markets in Historical Perspective*. Chicago: University of Chicago Press.

Froud, J., Moran, M., Nilsson, A., & Williams, K. (2011). Opportunity Lost: Mystification, Elite Politics and Financial Reform in the UK. *Socialist Register, 47*, 98–119.

Froud, J., Moran, M., Nilsson, A., & Williams, K. (2012). Stories and Interests in Finance: Agendas of Governance Before and After the Financial Crisis. *Governance, 25*(1), 35–59.

Gamble, A. (1994). *The Free Economy and the Strong State; The Politics of Thatcherism*. Basingstoke: Macmillan.

Giles, C. (2009, December 2). Manufacturing Fades Under Labour. *Financial Times*. Available at: https://www.ft.com/content/f32a3392-df7a-11de-98ca-00144feab49a. Accessed 9 July 2018.

Greenfield, C., & Williams, P. (2001). Finance Advertising and Media Rhetoric. *Southern Review, 34*(4), 44–66.

Greenslade, R. (2004). *Press Gang: How Newspapers Make Profits from Propaganda*. London: Pan.

Happer, C. (2016). Financialisation, Media and Social Change. *New Political Economy, 22*(4), 437–449.

Harding, P. (2012). Journalists Need a Workable Definition of 'the Public Interest'. *BBC Website*. Available at: http://www.bbc.co.uk/blogs/collegeofjournalism/entries/56efff05-2996-3c18-bf14-116a2c267627. Accessed 9 July 2018.

Hjort, V., Mahadevan, S., & Sheets, A. (2013, November 4). Five Years After Lehman: The Changes in Credit Markets Since the Crisis Began, *The Hedge Fund Journal*. Available at: http://www.thehedgefundjournal.com/content/five-years-after-lehman. Accessed 9 July 2018.

Hutton, W. (1996). *The State We're in: Why Britain Is in Crisis and How to Overcome It*. London: Vintage.

Hutton, W. (2008, October 5). This Terrifying Moment Is Our One Chance for a New World. *Observer*.

Hutton W. (2014, January 19). Britain Is Scared to Face the Real Issue – It's All About Inequality. *Observer*.

Institute for Fiscal Studies (IFS). (2013). *Labour's Record on Poverty and Inequality.* Available at: https://www.ifs.org.uk/publications/6738. Accessed 9 July 2018.

International Monetary Fund. (2008, October). *World Economic Outlook (WEO) Financial Stress, Downturns, and Recoveries.* Available at: http://www.imf.org/external/pubs/ft/weo/2008/02/pdf/text.pdf. Accessed 9 July 2018.

Johal, S., Moran, M., & Williams, K. (2014). Power, Politics and the City of London After the Great Financial Crisis. *Government and Opposition, 49*(3), 400–425.

Keeler, R. (2009). *Tax Havens and the Financial Crisis.* Available at: http://dollarsandsense.org/archives/2009/0509keeler.html. Accessed 9 July 2018.

Lagna, A. (2016). Derivatives and the Financialisation of the Italian State. *New Political Economy, 21*(2), 167–186.

Mazzucato, M. (2011). The Entrepreneurial State. *Renewal, 19*(3/4), 1–11.

Miller, D., & Dinan, W. (2003). Global Public Relations and Global Capitalism. In D. Demers (Ed.), *Terrorism, Globalization and Mass Communication* (pp. 193–214). Spokane: Marquette Books.

Miller, D., & Dinan, W. (2009, May 4–5). *Revolving Doors, Accountability and Transparency - Emerging Regulatory Concerns and Policy Solutions in the Financial Crisis, (GOV-PGC-ETH-2009-2).* Paper Prepared for the OECD and the Dutch National Integrity Office Organized Global Forum on Public Governance 'Building a Cleaner World: Tools and Good Practices for Fostering a Culture of Integrity', Paris.

Mills, T. (2015). *The End of Social Democracy and the Rise of Neoliberalism at the BBC.* Thesis Submitted at the University of Bath.

Monbiot, G. (2000). *Captive State: The Corporate Takeover of Britain.* London: Macmillan.

Moran, M. (2006). The Company of Strangers: Defending the Power of Business in Britain, 1975–2005. *New Political Economy, 11*, 453–478.

Morgenson, G., & Story, L. (2009, December 23). Banks Bundled Bad Debt, Bet Against It and Won. *New York Times.*

ONS. (2007). International Comparisons of Productivity: The Current and Constant PPP Approach. *Economic & Labour Market Review, 1*(8). Available at: http://webarchive.nationalarchives.gov.uk/20160106035853/http://www.ons.gov.uk/ons/rel/elmr/economic-and-labour-market-review/no%2D%2D8%2D%2Daugust-2007/international-comparisons-of-productivity%2D%2Drecommended-uses-of-the-current-and-constant-ppp-approach.pdf. Accessed 9 July 2018.

Peston, R. (2007). US Exports Poison. Peston's Picks. *BBC Blog.* Available at: http://www.bbc.co.uk/blogs/thereporters/robertpeston/2007/08/09. Accessed 9 July 2018.

Philo, G. (1995). Political Advertising and Public Belief. *Media, Culture and Society, 15*, 407–418.

Philo, G., Miller, D., & Happer, C. (2015). Circuits of Communication and Structures of Power: The Sociology of the Mass Media. In M. Holborn (Ed.), *Contemporary Sociology* (pp. 444–470). London: Polity Press.

Pym, H. (2014). *Inside the Banking Crisis*. London: Bloomsbury Press.

Radice, G. (1992). *Southern Discomfort*. London: Fabian Society.

Radice, G., & Pollard, S. (1993). *More Southern Discomfort*. London: Fabian Society.

Radice, G., & Pollard, S. (1994). *Any Southern Comfort?* London: Fabian Society.

Robertson, M. (2016). (De)constructing the Financialised Culture of Owner-Occupation in the UK, with the Aid of the 10Cs. *New Political Economy, 22*(4), 398–409.

Shaxton, N. (2012). *Treasure Islands: Tax Havens and the Men Who Stole the World*. London: Vintage.

Smaghi, L. B. (2010, April 15). *Has the Financial Sector Grown too Big?* Speech at the Nomura Seminar, The Paradigm Shift After the Financial Crisis, Kyoto. Available at: https://www.ecb.europa.eu/press/key/date/2010/html/sp100415.en.html. Accessed 10 July 2018.

Stavinoha, L. (2016). Losing the Media Battle, Waging the Policy War: The Pharmaceutical Industry's Response to the Access to Medicines Crisis in the Global South. *Global Media and Communication, 12*(3), 275–294.

Stewart, H., & Goodley, S. (2011, October 9). Big Bang's Shockwaves Left Us with Today's Big Bust. *Observer*.

Tambini, D. (2010). What Are Financial Journalists for? *Journalism Studies, 11*(2), 158–174.

Thomas, R. (2017). Regulators and the Revolving Door. *Committee on Standard in Public Life Blog*. Available at: https://cspl.blog.gov.uk/2017/02/08/regulators-and-the-revolving-door/. Accessed 10 July 2018.

Traynor, I. (2014). 30,000 Lobbyists and Counting: Is Brussels Under Corporate Sway? *Guardian*. Available at: https://www.theguardian.com/world/2014/may/08/lobbyists-european-parliament-brussels-corporate. Accessed 10 July 2018.

Turner, G. (2008). *The Credit Crunch: Housing Bubbles, Globalisation and the Worldwide Economic Crisis*. London: Pluto Press.

Warwick Commission. (2009). *The Warwick Commission on International Financial Reform: In Praise of Unlevel Playing Fields*. Warwick: University of Warwick. Available at: https://www2.warwick.ac.uk/research/warwickcommission/financialreform/report/uw_warcomm_intfinreform_09.pdf

Watt, H., & Riley-Smith, B. (2015, January 7). Labour Plans Were 'Ill-Conceived and Misguided' During Financial Crisis. *Daily Telegraph*. Available at: http://www.telegraph.co.uk/news/politics/labour/11329049/Labour-plans-were-ill-conceived-and-misguided-during-financial-crisis.html. Accessed 10 July 2018.

Watt, N., & Treanor, J. (2011, February 8). Revealed: 50% of Tory Funds Come from City. *Guardian*. Available at: https://www.theguardian.com/politics/2011/feb/08/tory-funds-half-city-banks-financial-sector. Accessed 10 July 2018.

Wedel, J. (2011). *The Shadow Elite: How the World's New Powerbrokers Undermine Democracy, Government and the Free Market*. New York: Basic Books.

Wolf, M. (2010). *Fixing Global Finance*. London: Yale University Press.

World Bank. (2017). *Manufacturing, Value Added (% of GDP)*, World Bank National Accounts Data, and OECD National Accounts Data Files. Available at: https://data.worldbank.org/indicator/NV.IND.MANF.ZS. Accessed 10 July 2018.

CHAPTER 2

The Banking Crisis: Content Studies

INTRODUCTION

On the afternoon of 7 October 2008, whilst attending a meeting of European finance ministers in Brussels, the Chancellor Alistair Darling received a call from Tom Killop, the Chairman of Royal Bank of Scotland (RBS). 'Chancellor, my bank is going to run out of money within a few hours, what are you going to do about it?', Killop asked (cited in Pym 2014: 119–120). RBS, at the time the world's largest company (Jones 2009), whose balance sheet equated to 125 per cent of UK GDP, was experiencing a 'virtual' run as corporate clients fearing for the institution's solvency withdrew billions of pounds of funds on deposit. Darling knew that only the Bank of England, the UK's lender of last resort, could save RBS and so he immediately flew back to London on a private jet for a meeting with Mervyn King. However, there was a problem. The Bank of England's remit prevented it from lending to an insolvent institution and the Bank had concluded that although RBS's immediate need was for funding it lacked the capital to survive (Wilson et al. 2011).

Plans for the recapitalisation of the banking sector, which had been under preparation for weeks—but faced stiff resistance from bank executives—were agreed in principle that evening, allowing the Bank of England to immediately provide liquidity support to RBS. The following morning the Chancellor announced the broad outlines of a plan which involved three elements—recapitalisation, the provision of liquidity and the introduction of a loan guarantee scheme. By the end of the week, the

© The Author(s) 2019
M. Berry, *The Media, the Public and the Great Financial Crisis*,
https://doi.org/10.1007/978-1-137-49973-8_2

Bank of England had made £85 billion of new lending to the UK banking system, yet the markets remained gripped by panic with Friday seeing stock market falls that 'appeared relentless and irreversible' (Pym 2014: 144). Over the weekend of 11–12 October 2008 politicians, Bank of England executives, members of the FSA, Treasury officials and their banking advisors finalised the bailouts with the heads of Britain's major banks in meetings at the Treasury. On Monday October 13, the Chancellor announced the full details of the plan. RBS would receive £20 billion of taxpayers' money and Lloyds/HBOS £17 billion. In exchange the state would take a 60% stake in RBS and a 40% stake in Lloyds/HBOS. The government also agreed to provide an extra £200 billion in liquidity support and a £200 billion loan guarantee facility. In exchange for government support, the top executives at RBS and HBOS were dismissed, curbs on executive pay were introduced and dividend payments were suspended until the share price of the rescued institutions recovered. Although the banking sector would require further bailouts in 2009, the night of 7 October 2008 was the point at which the British banking system came closest to systemic failure. In his memoirs, Gordon Brown's press aide, Damian McBride, recounted the sense of panic felt by the prime minister that evening:

> We've just got to get ourselves ready in case it goes wrong tomorrow. And I mean really wrong…if the banks are shutting their doors, and the cashpoints aren't working, if people go to Tescos and their cards aren't being accepted, the whole thing will just explode. If you can't buy food, or petrol or medicine for your kids, people will just start breaking the windows and helping themselves…it'll be anarchy. I'm serious… we'd have to think: do we have curfews, do we put the army on the streets, how do we get order back? (cited in Pym 2014: 133)

This chapter will examine how the crisis itself was narrated by the press and broadcast media. Particular attention will be focused on how the media explained the crash, how the bank rescue plans were evaluated and what long terms solutions were put forward to reform the sector. However, before presenting the primary empirical data the chapter will first sketch out the different explanations as to what caused the crisis and the range of debate on possible reforms.

Why Did It Happen?

Why the banking system failed is complex as different institutions made different mistakes. Bradford and Bingley, for instance, expanded heavily in the risky buy-to-let and self-certification mortgage markets, so that when the markets turned in 2007 the Bank found itself facing mounting losses. RBS, on the other hand, overpaid for the Dutch Bank ABN AMRO which was later revealed to be full of toxic debt. However, as the House of Commons Treasury Committee (2009) report into the crisis concluded, underlying most of these failures were three common factors. One was an increasing reliance on the wholesale money markets for funding. In their rush to expand many UK banks had become increasingly dependent on borrowing from the money markets. When these money markets seized up due to concerns about the solvency of finance sector institutions, British banks were unable to roll over their liabilities. A second factor underlying the crisis was the increase in leverage amongst UK banks. In the decade leading up to the crash the banking sector saw a sharp increase in leverage ratios—assets in relation to equity—and this was the most important factor which distinguished those banks that failed from those that survived. As Mervyn King noted in his evidence to the Select Committee:

> Most financial crises in the past have been characterised by excessive lever-age, borrowing, debt, and that has been true here too … 40 years ago if you had asked any of the clearing banks … what fraction of their balance sheet was in liquid short-term assets they would have said about a third and the answer now is 1%. There has been a massive change in the balance sheet structure of our banking system and it is not surprising, therefore, that you make more money in banking doing that because you are using the assets in a riskier form and most years that generates a higher return, but it means that when things go wrong the costs are so much higher, so excessive leverage is the common theme. (House Of Commons 2009: 37–38)

A third factor underlying the crash was the failure of risk management in the face of increasing financial complexity. Key to this was a belief that securitisation—where banks increasingly packaged up their mortgages and sold them on to investors—had reduced systemic risk. This 'originate and dis-tribute model' was believed to have made the financial system more secure as risk would be more widely distributed. However as Turner noted things did not work out this way:

> It was argued that securitised credit intermediation could reduce risks for the whole banking system, since while some of the credit risk would be held by the originating bank and some by other banks acting as investors, much would be passed through to end non-bank investors. Credit losses would therefore be less likely to produce banking system failure. But that is not what happened. Because when the music stopped ... the majority of the holdings of the securitised credit, and the vast majority of the losses which arose, did not lie in the books of end investors intending to hold the assets to maturity, but on the books of highly leveraged banks and banklike institutions. (House of Commons 2009: 33)

This problem was amplified by increasing complexity of many of the new financial products created by securitisation which meant that it was impossible to conduct effective risk pricing. Furthermore, the rise of synthetic products linked to the value of the housing market meant that the impact of non-performing loans became multiplied many times over throughout the financial system.

Behind these proximate causes of the crisis it has been suggested were a number of other factors. These included:

1) The failure of regulatory authorities and key politicians to supervise the finance sector. Prior to the crisis in both the US and Great Britain regulatory controls such as Glass-Steagall had been progressively relaxed. Furthermore, regulation had failed to keep with financial innovation and the growth of the shadow banking system. Some have argued that authorities had become subject to 'regulatory capture' partly through the operation of the 'revolving door' between firms and regulators (Warwick Commission 2009; Miller and Dinan 2009).

2) The failure of many in the economics profession whose models underpinned the forecasts made by decision makers in government, regulatory authorities, central banks as well as key institutions such as the IMF and OECD. Most macroeconomists failed to predict the crisis and believed that financial innovation had reduced systemic risk. In 2006 the IMF argued that financial innovation had 'increased the resilience of the financial system' and reduced the chances of

bank failures (cited in Turner 2016: 242). Critics have suggested that the dominant economic models were deficient in two key areas. First, they relied on assumptions about the efficiency of markets (Efficient Markets Hypothesis) and the rationality of economic agents (Rational Expectations Hypothesis) which were unrealistic and lacked an evidential base (Stiglitz 2010; Skidelsky 2014; Economist 2009; Orrell 2010). Secondly, they paid insufficient attention the role of the finance, money and the banking system whilst assuming that most lending funded productive investment rather than speculation (Pettifor 2016; Smith 2010; Harvey 2012; Keen 2017).

3) Failures by credit ratings agencies who gave toxic securities AAA ratings. This was due to both inadequate risk pricing models and endemic conflicts of interests where the agencies were being paid by the banks and companies they were rating (Utzig 2010). Former head of Moody's, William Harrington, claimed that senior management used 'intimidation and harassment' to persuade their analysts to produce ratings wanted by the company's clients'. 'The goal', he argued, was 'to mould analysts into pliable corporate citizens who cast their committee votes in line with the unchanging corporate credo of maximising earnings of the largely captive franchise' (Neate 2011: 6–7).

4) Remuneration structures in the banking industry. It has been argued that the bonus system operating in many investment banks incentivised short-run risk taking whilst potentially exposing their employers and other stakeholders to substantial losses over the longer run (FSA 2009). In effect, an asymmetrical reward system was in operation where employees picked up the upside when trades worked out, but when they went bad most of the downside risk was borne by shareholders, depositors, creditors and the taxpayer.

5) The effects of 'shareholder value' as the central corporate objective from the 1990s combined with a weak system of corporate governance. Pressure on finance companies to deliver at least 15% return on equity for shareholders provided a strong incentive for banks to expand their balance sheets using borrowing rather than equity, expand real estate lending, and undertake high-stakes acquisitions and mergers such as RBS' takeover of ABN Amro (Engelen et al. 2011).

6) Auditors, particularly from the 'Big Four' who failed to spot the flaws in the business models of banks—like Northern Rock—who went bankrupt shortly after being given a clean bill of health (Sikka 2009).

Some commentators argued that the crisis had structural causes. For instance some maintained that the financial crisis was closely connected to deregulation and capital market liberalisation (e.g. Glyn 2007; Keen 2017; Pettifor 2006; Turner 2008). Economists such as Keen (2017) and Pettifor (2006) argued that the financial crisis, particularly in the UK and America, was at root a private debt crisis and the key problem was that the banks had been allowed to create vast quantities of private and corporate debt primarily to fuel asset speculation. These economists argued that the deleveraging of this debt would lead to a decade or more of economic stagnation. Others such as Smaghi (2010) argued that a key driver of asset bubbles and financial instability was global imbalances. The trade surpluses produced by countries such as China had been lent back to the deficit countries helping to underpin debt fuelled consumption and real estate booms.

HOW TO RESPOND TO THE CRISIS?

This section will review the range of debate on possible responses to the failure of the banking system. These can be separated into immediate and long-term responses. Immediate responses involved how to deal with the banks that were facing bankruptcy whilst the long-term responses concerned the reforms necessary to prevent a repeat of the crisis and help return the economy to growth after the downturn.

The government decided to part-nationalise the stricken banks and not exercise direct control over their activities. Instead it created an 'arm's length' body (UKFI) composed of senior City figures whose goal was to secure 'shareholder value' and return the banks to the market as soon as possible. However there were other options that were available to the government. These included:

1) *Let the banks go bankrupt.* This proposal was put forward by Lilico (2009) who argued that the government should have let insolvent banks go bust. Depositors, he argued, should have had first claim on the assets of insolvent institutions but bondholders should have borne the consequences of risk taking. Echoing Schumpeter's calls for 'creative destruction' Lilico argued that governments should further deregulate the banking industry whilst ensuring that the market punished poor business practices and investment decisions.

2) *Fully nationalise the banks and then return them to the market as soon as possible* (Krugman 2008; Buiter 2009a; Stephens 2009; Stiglitz in Evans-Pritchard 2009). Temporary nationalisation of the banking system was the approach that Sweden took in the early 1990s when it faced a systemic solvency crisis in its banking sector following financial deregulation and the collapse of subsequent asset price bubbles. This approach would have involved losses to share and bond holders but would have avoided the situation of 'zombie' banks[1] that the Japanese found themselves in during the 1990s following the collapse of an unprecedented property bubble. Some years after the crisis, two key figures in the bank rescue plans—Paul Myners and Adair Turner—argued that it would have been better if the part-nationalised banks had been fully nationalised (Pym 2014).

3) *Fully nationalise the banks and keep some or all of them in the state sector.* Those who argued for this policy pointed to evidence that state banks offer more stability than private banks—especially if regulation of the private banking system is weak—and that a large state presence in banking is sometimes associated with higher rates of economic growth, more productive investment and less risky speculation (Tasch 2015; Andrianova et al. 2009; Brown 2015). During the crisis, John McDonnell (2008) called for the banks to be nationalised and transformed into institutions which funnelled long-term investment into areas such as new green technology and infrastructure investment. 'The taxpayer', he argued, 'through the government, should now be forcing through an agenda with control of the board: offering full transparency and stakeholder democracy for customers and the workforce.' Such changes, it was argued, would focus productive investment into SMEs, rebalance the economy, improve the resilience of the UK banking sector, protect banking jobs and support social inclusion. In sum, it was argued that a greater presence for public banks would help to overcome the tendency for UK banking to concentrate primarily on real estate lending and thus help to rectify some of the key structural weaknesses in the economy.

In terms of longer term reforms to the sector a number of policies have been advocated. These include:

- Restricting bonuses (Stiglitz 2008). Some argued that delaying the payment of bonuses to make them contingent on long-term trading positions would discourage risk taking.
- The creation of a new global financial architecture (Winnett 2008; Sachs 2008). Gordon Brown, in particular, argued that a New Bretton Woods system needed to be instituted with increased transparency and the IMF given the role of a global central bank with a responsibility for overseeing the health of the global economy.
- Strengthen banks' capital buffers. The Basel II Accords which set down minimal capital adequacy, liquidity and leverage ratios were widely seen to have been inadequate. After the banking crisis the Basel III Accords were introduced which strengthen bank's capital requirements.
- Measures to tackle global imbalances. Stiglitz (2006) argued that the measures proposed by the Keynes more than six decades previously based on a new reserve system and new international currency could be instituted to reduce the scale of global trade deficits/surpluses.
- Reduce the size of individual banks (Elliott et al. 2008; Buiter 2009b). Many banks during the crisis were judged to be 'too big to fail' in that if they collapsed they would through their interconnectedness to other institutions pose a threat to the whole banking system. Having smaller banks that could be allowed to fail or separating investment from retail banking could remove the possibility of moral hazard and costly state bailouts.
- Setting up an inspection regime for derivatives and other complex financial products with the riskiest products potentially being banned (Elliott et al. 2008; Eichengreen 2008; Stiglitz 2008; Chang 2008).
- Clamping down on tax havens which were used for regulatory and taxation arbitrage (Chang 2008; Murphy, 2008; Stiglitz 2008; Elliott et al. 2008).
- Increased regulation of the shadow banking system (Chang 2008; Roubani 2008; Koenig 2008; Sachs 2008). This part of the financial sector which comprises institutions such as hedge funds, private equity, structured investment vehicles and securitisation companies are largely unregulated and were used extensively by investment banks to avoid oversight.
- The introduction of a financial transactions tax to curb market volatility (Chang 2008; Sachs 2008; Stiglitz 2008).

- Increased regulation of ratings agencies and auditors. Some commentators have suggested replacing the main ratings agencies with a publicly accountable not-for-profit body. (e.g. Chang 2008; Hunt, 2008).
- Measures to restrict the 'revolving door' which sees politicians and regulators move onto the boards of major financial institutions (e.g. Andrianova et al. 2009; Beattie 2008; Foley 2008).
- Much stricter restrictions on the creation of credit plus the introduction of capital controls (Elliott et al. 2008). Some of these options were later examined in research by the Bank of England and FSA (Jones and Masters 2011).
- Measures to reduce inequality. Turner (2008) argues wage compression driven by globalisation, outsourcing and the weakening of labour bargaining power has been the driving force behind credit and asset bubbles and that to prevent a reoccurrence of the crisis measures must be introduced to reduce inequality. This was a position also taken in an IMF working paper by Kumhof and Rancière (2010).

Having laid out the background to the crisis and the range of policy responses this chapter will now briefly discuss methodology before examining the contours of press and broadcast reporting.

RESEARCH METHODS: CONTENT ANALYSIS

The media are key to the exercise of power in modern societies. They can set the agenda for what are seen as the most important stories of the day but they can also restrict the information that is available for viewers to understand events and issues. The method employed in this book to analyse content is called *Thematic Analysis*. This is a method which has been used extensively in areas such as industrial news, food scares and risk (Glasgow Media Group 1976, 1980, 1982; Philo 1999), conflict reporting (Philo and Berry 2004, 2011; Lewis 2004) and military spending (Lewis and Hunt 2011; Lewis 2008). The method is based on the assumption that in any contested area there will be competing ways of explaining events or issues. These explanations are linked to particular interests which seek to explain the world in ways that justify their own position. So for instance, in the 1970s a series of studies investigated the reporting of the debates over the failings of the British economy (Glasgow Media Group 1976, 1980, 1982). At the time Britain was widely seen to be falling behind its main competitors. In this public controversy the trade unions pointed to management failings in the organisation of industry and low levels of capital investment. These meant that machinery often broke down and production was less efficient than in other countries. In contrast, those on the right blamed trade unions and industrial unrest. The research first mapped the range of opinion in the debate and the evidence that underpinned various positions. These were identified from published materials such as books, reports, articles as well as other accounts which appeared in the mass media. The research then examined which accounts and explanations were featured in television news bulletins and which were absent. The research found that the problems of manufacturing were primarily presented as being due to trade unions and industrial disputes, while alternative explanations were downgraded in coverage. This could be seen, for instance, in the construction of news headlines which frequently mentioned strikes and the problems that were allegedly causing, but never referenced issues around management and investment. If some explanations were present on the news and some were absent it seemed likely that this would affect what TV audiences understood and believed.

More recently an evolving strand of research has employed both interviews with journalists and audience group research to unpack the entire 'circuit of communication' from the production of news to its reception amongst audiences (Miller et al. 1998; Philo and Berry 2004, 2011). For instance, research which examined reporting of the Israel-Palestine conflict revealed how lobbying and public relations influenced the construction of news accounts which had powerful effects on public understanding of the conflict. This book adopts a similar approach by combining thematic analysis of news bulletins with audience studies and interviews with journalists.

Newspaper Sample

The newspaper coverage in this chapter is drawn from two samples. The first consists of two weeks of weekday coverage (6 October 2008–17 October 2008) during the period when the bank bailouts were initially announced (8 October 2008), and then enacted (13 October). During this period there was an intense media focus on both how the banks got into difficulties and the bank rescue plans. It therefore represents the period when these issues were most heavily discussed in the media. The second sample consists of a week's weekday coverage (6 July 2009–10 July

2009) during the period when the government released a White Paper on financial reform. This represented the period when discussion of reforms to the finance sector were particularly prominent in the press.

The sample consisted of six newspapers: the *Guardian*, *Telegraph*, *Mail*, *Mirror*, *Sun* and *Daily Record*. The newspapers were chosen on the basis that they represented the variety of left and right opinion in the broadsheet, mid-market and tabloid press. The *Daily Record*, a Scottish newspaper, was included because some of the focus groups were conducted in Scotland and a number of participants cited the newspaper as a key news source.

The first sample was generated from a Nexis search using the keyword bank*. This generated a total of 2533 news articles (*Guardian* 700, *Telegraph* 520, *Mail* 594, *Mirror* 282, *Sun* 271 and *Record* 166) over the ten-day sample period. These were then manually sifted to first remove all the Irish editions of the newspapers. They were then sifted again and the only articles retained were those that either (a) identified an actor(s) responsible for the crisis or provided an explanation for why it happened, (b) offered commentary on the bailout, or (c) discussed possible long-term reforms to the sector. This left a total of 367 articles—121 in the *Guardian*, 88 in the *Telegraph*, 59 in the *Mail*, 35 in the *Sun*, 33 in the *Mirror* and 31 in the *Record*.

Newspapers in the sample were then analysed to identify:

1) Who or what was identified as responsible for the crisis.
2) What caused the crisis.
3) The sources who were featured in news accounts (direct speech only).
4) Evaluations of the bank bailouts.
5) Criticisms of the bailouts.
6) Alternatives to the bailouts.
7) Long-term reforms to the sector.

The second sample was generated from a Nexis search using the keywords bank* AND reform OR white paper. This generated a total of 35 news articles (15 in *Guardian*, 12 in the *Telegraph*, five in the *Mail*, two in the *Mirror*, one in the *Sun* and none in the *Record*) over the five day sample.

Broadcast News Sample

Three samples of Radio 4's *Today programme* were examined. The first, which only analysed patterns of source access, consists of six weeks of coverage starting on 15 September 2008, the day Lehman Brothers went bankrupt, and ending on 31 October 2008, two and a half weeks after the conclusion of the British banking rescue. The second sample covered the same period as the print sample (6 October 2008–17 October 2008) and examined broadly the same features of coverage. Thus, the three main areas of interest were (a) who was cited as being responsible for the crisis and why did the banks fail, (b) who were the sources framing the parameters of debate, and (c) what was the range of debate on the bailouts and possible reforms to the sector? The third sample encompassed the first seven months of 2009. This time frame was chosen because it represented the period when the debates around potential reforms to the sector were most prominent in the media. It was possible to examine a much broader sample of broadcast coverage because the BBC website provided précis of individual segments of the *Today programme* which cut down the time needed to locate relevant content. Because this précis only covered the second two hours of the programme (7:00am–9:00am) only these parts were coded.[2]

The *Today programme* was chosen for three reasons. Firstly, at the time it attracted an audience of approximately seven million listeners per day which made it the most popular news programme in broadcasting (BBC 2011). Secondly, its audience has a heavy concentration of professionals and opinion formers, and, thirdly, it is widely seen as significant in setting news and political agendas in other parts of the media. In 2005, MPs voted it the most influential programme in broadcasting (BBC 2005).

The audio broadcasts were downloaded from the BBC website archive and Box of Broadcasts and only segments which covered the banking crisis and issues connected to the crisis were coded.

NEWSPAPER FINDINGS: SAMPLE 1 (6 OCTOBER 2008–17 OCTOBER 2008)

Who and What Caused the Crisis?

At the centre of most crises are debates over blame and responsibility. Within social science these are commonly referred to as issues of 'problem

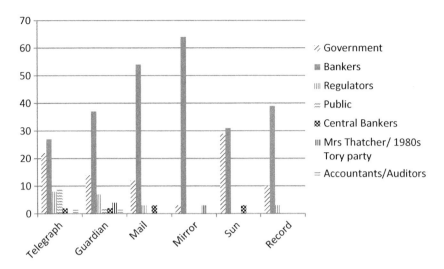

Fig. 2.1 Attribution of responsibility for the banking crisis (percentage of articles citing top seven actors)

Table 2.1 Additional actors cited (percentage of articles citing each actor)

Telegraph	Pension funds/investors 1.1%, 1.1% Non-executive directors,
Guardian	Pension funds/investors 0.8%, 0.8% Rating agencies, 0.8%, 'Quants'/trading software 0.8%,

attribution' (e.g. Entman 1993; Iyengar 1991). In the newspaper coverage there were significant variations in how different titles attributed responsibility and explained the reasons behind the crisis. There were also major differences between newspapers in terms of how many actors were identified as responsible, with the two broadsheets (*Guardian* ten actors and *Telegraph* nine actors) citing a much greater range of culpable parties than the tabloids (*Mail* four actors, *Sun*, *Mirror* and *Record* all three actors) (Fig. 2.1 and Table 2.1).

Across the sample bankers (in 39.5 per cent of articles) were the group most frequently identified as being responsible for the crisis. Criticism of bankers was most prominently voiced by journalists, columnists, politicians and members of the public with the most virulent criticism appearing in the tabloids. A common approach was to contrast the treatment of members of the public or businesses who had fallen on hard times with the 'largesse' meted out to bankers. In other articles tabloids treated bankers to the approach that they traditionally reserve for refugees (Philo et al. 2013) and those on benefits (Golding and Middleton 1983) by arguing that those reliant on the public purse are living the high life. A *Sun* article entitled 'bankers £2m bash with stars' spoke of Lloyds TSB bankers who had been 'bailed out by taxpayers' billions...guzzling champagne...and whooping it up on a £2 million weekend bender' (*Sun*, 14 October 2008). Another article focused on the activities of RBS 'fat cats':

> Fat cat execs at failed RBS enjoyed a secret £150k junket at a five-star hotel yesterday just days after a £15 billion bail-out...They enjoyed a free bar all night, guzzling port, cognac, champagne and 150 bottles of fine wine. The menu included sashimi salmon, beef wellington with Madiera jus, white chocolate and lime delice and petit fours. RBS director David Manson told execs to have fun even though 'we let a lot of shareholders down'. (*Sun*, 16 October 2008)

In the *Mail* Max Hastings called for those responsible to be 'name and shamed':

> What is different about the banking disaster is that, while we realise that some of the fattest cats in the City and Wall Street have screwed up our lives, we still know few of their names, and less still about how they did it. We are told that Sir Fred Goodwin is an obvious candidate for sacking, because his direction of Royal Bank of Scotland has been the most conspicuously reckless. But there are hundreds of equally guilty men and women, who have not yet been identified...Who were these lunatics, taking home millions every year for conducting their businesses in a fashion which, if you and I did likewise in our own lives, would have ruined us in quick time?...Nobody is going to say: 'We shouldn't be looking for scapegoats.' We want scapegoats. (*Mail*, 10 October 2008)

Hastings also argued that there was 'no means of recovering from these people any part of the fortunes', and calls for bank executives to repay bonuses were rare with only a single article in the *Record* (17 October 2008) and *Mirror* (9 October 2008) advocating this. However, there were six letters from members of the public—two in the *Record* (13 and 14 October 2008) and *Sun* (13 and 15 October 2008) and one in the

Guardian (16 October 2008) and *Mail* (7 October 2008)—which argued that bankers should be stripped of their bonuses. Across the media there were also few calls for criminal investigations to be launched against bank executives. The only exceptions were two articles in the *Guardian* (6 October 2008 and 13 October 2008) and one in the *Sun* (7 October 2008).

Whilst the bankers were primarily held responsible for the crisis, the Labour government were blamed in approximately one in six articles. The *Telegraph* and *Sun* were much more likely to pin responsibility on the Labour government than other newspapers in the sample. Some of this may have been driven by political partisanship—the *Telegraph* is a Tory supporting newspaper and the *Sun* at this point was shifting its allegiance from New Labour back to the Conservatives. There was markedly less criticism in the *Mail* which may have been because of the alleged closeness between the *Mail* editor Paul Dacre and Gordon Brown (Robinson 2008). Both the *Telegraph* and *Sun* featured articles which argued that Labour had failed to adequately regulate the banks and expressed outrage that Brown was being lauded for his bailout plan. For instance, a *Sun* article argued:

> IT'S sickening to hear Gordon Brown hailed as the brilliant saviour of the global economy… Yesterday's bank nationalisation will get chapters in history books yet has not been debated once in Parliament despite being a colossal burden on us taxpayers. We are all meant to accept it as a miraculous deal, and to thank God for clever old Gordon. Pass the bucket. It was Brown's reckless ten years as Chancellor that created the bubble that has burst with a big bang louder than a hundred Hiroshimas. (*Sun*, 14 October 2008)

And in the *Telegraph*:

> The PM should not be revelling; he should be showing some humility and accepting a share of the blame. His almost pathological inability to do either is not a source of comfort: it is profoundly disturbing. While the eventual outcome will not, I suspect, involve gratitude to Gordon Brown or any other politician, it will include public revulsion at the largely Labour political class that brought this country so low. The search will be on for those most worthy of blame, and near the head of the queue will be the current PM…. Labour over-spent, over-borrowed and failed to regulate adequately. (*Telegraph*, 10 October 2008)

However even within the *Telegraph* there were some articles which presented a more favourable view of Labour and its bank rescue plan. The most prominent of these cited comments made by the US economist Paul Krugman, who had just been awarded the Nobel Prize for Economics. Krugman was also given his own comment piece in the *Telegraph* on 14 October 2008 where he praised the Brown government for exhibiting a 'combination of clarity and decisiveness [that] has not been matched by any other Western government'.

Although the *Guardian* featured less criticism of Brown than the *Telegraph* it too at times included some strongly worded rebukes of the government's economic policy. In one comment piece its economic editor argued that the bank bailouts were only necessary 'because 11 years of grotesque government toadying to the City has left Britain in a parlous position and there was no alternative but to resort to concepts expunged from the New Labour lexicon' (*Guardian*, 13 October 2008).

Whilst Gordon Brown was subject to substantial criticism in some parts of the press, the traditionally Labour supporting *Mirror* and *Record* were mostly supportive. The *Mirror*, in particular, offered fulsome praise for Gordon Brown's handling of the crisis. A leading article titled 'Real Man of Vision' argued:

> The international verdict on Gordon Brown is stunning, the Prime Minister hailed as a visionary statesman. With even right-wing US President George Bush forced to copy the Prime Minister's bank rescue plan, Mr Brown's global standing has never been higher. The lavish tributes make a mockery of political point-scoring in Britain where opponents who denounce him for party gain expose their ignorance of economics. (*Mirror*, 15 October 2008)

Whereas virtually all the blame in the tabloids focused on the bankers or politicians, the two broadsheets highlighted a wider range of actors. So the role of auditors in signing off company accounts and failing to warn against excessive lending were highlighted in two articles in both the *Guardian* and *Telegraph*. Both broadsheets also identified the role of investors and pension funds in pressurising bank CEOs to produce unrealistic returns and claimed that central bankers has allowed interest rates to remain too low for too long. There were also some interesting differences between coverage in the two broadsheets. The *Telegraph* was much more likely to blame the public for the banking crisis. One in eleven *Telegraph* articles contained arguments which blamed the crisis on consumers taking on too much debt:

But behind the headlines is a story about how so many of us have walked blindly into this crisis and have been partly to blame for its eruption...the whole decade of debt, never mind deposits, reveals the collective suspension of our critical faculties in pursuit of instant gratification. Consumers piled on huge amounts of credit without understanding the risk of doing so, or at least refusing to acknowledge the risk. We've been through a collective hysteria that allowed us only to see reward. (*Telegraph*, 10 October 2008)

This tendency to blame the public may be attributed to traditional small 'c' conservative values which stress the importance of personal responsibility, thrift and 'living within your means'. Since this approach wasn't taken by other right of centre newspapers it may also reflect that the *Telegraph*'s more affluent readership were less likely to have over-extended themselves through credit and so such criticism would not have been taken as an attack on their readership. In contrast, the *Guardian* alone amongst newspapers featured four articles and a letter which blamed Mrs Thatcher's decision to deregulate the finance sector. It also featured a single article which discussed the role of credit ratings agencies and another which highlighted the role of maths graduates employed to build trading models and the impact of high frequency trading software.

In terms of what has actually caused the crisis, 25 different factors were identified across the sample. The *Guardian* cited 23 separate factors, the

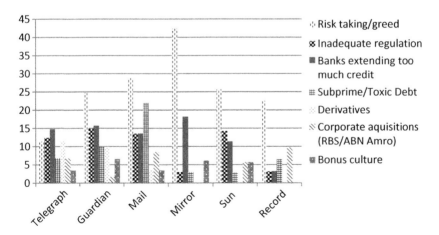

Fig. 2.2 Top seven explanations for the banking crash (percentage of articles featuring each explanation)

Telegraph 22, the *Mail* 14 and the three 'red tops' six each. The top seven most cited factors which accounted for the overwhelming majority of explanations can be seen in Fig. 2.2. The additional factors are listed in Table 2.2.

By far the most popular explanation for the crisis (appearing in just under a quarter of articles) was that it had been created by the recklessness, risk taking or greed of bankers. This explanation accounted for more than half of all explanatory statements in the *Mirror, Sun* and *Record* illustrating that these newspapers *tended to frame the causes of the crisis in terms of individual moral failings rather than broader social or structural factors*. In the *Guardian* and *Mail,* approximately a quarter of articles mentioned greed or risk taking but in the *Telegraph* only about one in 10. The role of 'greed' in particular was prominently highlighted in headlines:

Table 2.2   Additional factors cited (percentage of articles citing each actor)

Daily Telegraph	10.2% public taking on too much debt; 9.1% leverage; 5.7% inadequate capital ratios; 4.5% ultra-low interest rates; 3.4% faulty auditing;2.3% incorrect risk pricing; 2.3% overreliance on wholesale money markets; 2.3% deregulation; 1.1% government failure to control money supply; 1.1% banks packaging and selling toxic debt; 1.1% global trade imbalances; 1.1% removing regulatory powers from The Bank of England; 1.1% complexity; 1.1% pension funds or investors demanding high returns; 1.1% inadequate supervision by non-executive directors.
Guardian	4.1% deregulation; 4.1% inadequate capital ratios; 2.5% overreliance on wholesale money markets; 2.5% complexity; 2.5% global trade imbalances; 1.7% incorrect risk pricing; 1.7% leverage; 1.7% Public taking on too much debt; 1.7% banks packaging and selling toxic debt; 0.8% breakdown of Bretton Woods system; 0.8% regulatory arbitrage in tax havens; 0.8% interest rates too low; 0.8% removing regulatory powers from The Bank of England; 0.8% faulty auditing; 0.8% pension funds or investors demanding high returns; 0.8% inequality.
Daily Mail	6.8% overreliance on wholesale money markets; 5.1% leverage; 3.4% interest rates too low; 1.7% banks packaging and selling toxic debt; 1.7% regulatory arbitrage in tax havens; 1.7% incorrect risk pricing; 1.7% inadequate capital ratios
Daily Mirror	6.1% banks packaging and selling toxic debt;
Sun	None
Daily Record	3.2% overreliance on wholesale money markets;

MAKE ALL THESE GREEDY BANKERS FEEL THE PAIN (*Mirror,* 9 October 2008)

SNOUT ON YOUR EARS: END OF MEGA-BONUS CULTURE FOR GREEDY CITY BANKERS (*Mirror,* 9 October 2008)

Why greedy bankers should feel my pain (*Sun,* 10 October 2008)

Greed speeded the bankers' downfall (*Telegraph,* 15 October 2008)

GREED THAT FUELLED A CRASH; As £37bn of your money is spent nationalising banks, it's revealed City bonuses last year were £17bn. (*Mail,* 14 October 2008)

Brown may be today's saviour, but only by cleansing the City of greed and restoring trust will he find redemption (*Guardian,* 14 October 2008)

The next most widely cited explanation was banks extending too much credit which appeared in 13.8 per cent of articles. This explanation which emphasised links between the sharp rise in mortgage and credit card debt, the housing bubble and banks getting into financial difficulties was mentioned in all newspapers and represented a factor that, as will be discussed in the section looking at audience beliefs, resonated strongly with members of the public. Many articles were highly critical of the finance sector and regulators for not supervising mortgage lending more closely. The *Mail's* City editor Alex Brummer commented on the fate of Northern Rock:

But there are useful points from the Newcastle bank's trading update...it is interesting, if not surprising, to see that an astonishing 50pc of the bank's 125pc 'Together' mortgages are in arrears. This confirms that in the last days Adam Applegarth and the regulator, the Financial Services Authority, appear to have lost touch with reality...Decisive action against the former Rock directors ought to be part of the confidence-building exercise for the banking system. The public needs to know that those who drove financial institutions to the edge are paying a price and not simply collecting their handsome pensions. (*Mail,* 15 October 2008)

In the *Guardian,* Polly Toynbee extended the blame to Gordon Brown and Mrs Thatcher:

Yes indeed it was a new world order. It began with Margaret Thatcher's big bang deregulation and now it has nearly brought the world's economy crashing to destruction. It was a new world order of ballooning borrowing beyond the wildest imaginings of any previous era. Under Brown's stewardship, British citizens were allowed to over-borrow more than anyone in the world, more even than Americans, in a house price and credit card bubble of horrifying dimensions. (*Guardian*, 14 October 2008)

The right of centre newspapers added the charge that Brown had allowed credit creation to expand and under-regulated the City because it provided the tax revenues to raise public spending. The issue of lax regulation was prominent in the broadsheets as well as the *Sun* and the *Mail*, but in the two Labour supporting tabloids criticism of Brown was fairly muted.

Other more technical aspects of the financial crisis—such as the role of derivatives, subprime lending or toxic debt were primarily discussed in the broadsheets and to a much lesser extent the *Mail*. Some articles provided glossaries and explanations for the more technical aspects of the crisis. For instance a *Telegraph* article 'Banks flee jaws of a financial menace' (16 October 2008) explained how credit default swaps worked and discussed their role in the crash. Despite this, major issues such deregulation, complexity, auditing or ultra-low interest rates were only discussed in a handful of articles in the broadsheets or *Mail*. The topic of inequality was mentioned once in the entire sample in a comment piece by Polly Toynbee:

It is the extremes of inequality in the west's most unequal countries that set off this nuclear explosion. Gargantuan bonuses in Wall Street and the City were earned from creating fairy money, imagined to be owned by people too poor to pay anything at all. If the poor had more money, it wouldn't have happened. If mega-bonuses had not inflated share prices and borrowing beyond reason, fantasy capitalism would have been avoided. (*Guardian*, 7 October 2008)

In a similar vein discussion of the role of tax havens in the crisis was confined to a single article in the *Guardian* and one letter in the *Mail*. Structural accounts were also relatively rare. The role of global imbalances linking Western deficits to Asian surpluses appeared in three articles in the *Guardian* and one in the *Telegraph*. Accounts which linked the problems of uneven domestic economic development with the finance driven model of growth supported by both Labour and the Conservatives were confined to a handful of articles in the *Guardian* primarily written by the newspaper's economics editor Larry Elliott:

For the past 20 years, policy-makers in the UK have convinced themselves that the might of the City could compensate for the country's inability to make anything. The notion that the ever widening trade deficit was merely a temporary phase while Britain adjusted to a weightless, virtual, financially-driven future has now been exposed for the grotesque fantasy it always was... the bankruptcy of the City also represents the bankruptcy of New Labour economics, which has been based to an unhealthy degree on a desire to ape the go-getting, deal-making culture of the United States. Labour governments of the past have always had industrial strategies, which have normally been based on the idea that manufacturing matters. Since 1997, ministers have convinced themselves that Britain had a comparative advantage in financial services and that therefore industrial policy should be based on giving the City what the City wants. The light-touch regulation of financial services was but one expression of the almost total obeisance to big capital. (*Guardian*, 8 October 2008)

If the crisis offered an opportunity to step back and reflect on the contribution of the finance sector to Britain's lopsided economic model, it was one that was spurned by all newspapers except the *Guardian*. Instead, the crisis was largely explained—especially in the mass circulation tabloids—as being the result of reckless, greedy bankers and to a lesser extent politicians failing to regulate the system. More developed accounts which implicated a wider range of parties and factors were largely confined to the broadsheets and occasionally the *Mail*. However, even in these broadsheets a more complete picture of what happened could only be gleaned if readers had closely followed the small number of in-depth feature articles and comment pieces which unpacked the underlying complexities.

Who Gets to Speak?

The relationship between reporters and sources is at the heart of journalism and research has consistently pointed to the dominance of high status official sources in news accounts (e.g. Glasgow Media Group 1976, 1980, 1982; Berry 2013; Wahl-Jorgensen et al. 2013). A number of explanations have put forward for this finding. Fishman (1980) argues that reporters hold a normative view of who is qualified to speak on policy issues and in practice this usually means a government official or a representative of another powerful institutional group. Fishman (1980) also argues that journalists over access political actors because such sources are the key supplier of official information needed to construct stories. Other commentators such as Tuchman (1972) suggest that a reliance on official sources protects journalists from lawsuits or accusations of partiality. However, in practice the British press, unencumbered by the impartiality regulations imposed on broadcasting, has free rein to be opinionated and this is reflected in the fact that (a) nearly half of the articles (47.7 per cent) in the sample were opinion (comment, leader or letters) pieces, and, (b) nearly half (46.0 per cent) of all articles featured no sources at all.

As can be seen Fig. 2.3 and Table 2.3, the most prominently cited source category across all newspapers—except the *Telegraph*—was Labour party politicians, principally the Prime Minister and the Chancellor of the Exchequer. This finding is very much in line with previous research which has found that incumbents tend to be significantly more accessed than opposition parties (e.g. Semetko 1996). The dominance of Labour voices was particularly pronounced in the two Labour supporting tabloids where many articles were constructed around a single quotation from the Labour leader. Conservative politicians and the Liberal Democrats were present in all newspapers but to a much lesser degree, whilst the Scottish Nationalist Party was prominent in the *Record* but marginal elsewhere. After politicians, the next most heavily sourced actors were financial sources from the City such as economists, analysts, stock brokers and

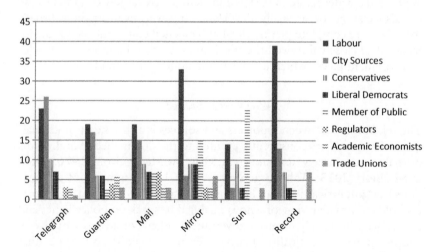

Fig. 2.3 Top eight sources (percentage of newspaper articles featuring each source)

Table 2.3   Additional sources cited (percentage of newspaper articles featuring each source)

Telegraph	4.5% International Monetary Fund; 2.3% Centre for Economics and Business Research; 2.3% British Chamber of Commerce; 1.1% Confederation of British Industry; 1.1% Institute for Fiscal Studies; 1.1%; Trade Unions; 1.1% British Bankers' Association; 1.1% Institute of Directors; 1.1% Association of Chartered Certified Accountants; 1.1% Bank of England; 1.1% Lawyer
Guardian	3.3% Academic (non-economist); 2.5% Confederation of British Industry; 2.5% Tax Justice Network; 1.7% International Monetary Fund; 1.7% UK Shareholder's Association; 1.7% Other Media; 0.8% Scottish Nationalist Party; 0.8% Institute for Fiscal Studies; 0.8% Association of Chartered Certified Accountants; 0.8% Centre for Economics and Business Research; 0.8% Building Societies Association; 0.8% New Economics Foundation; 0.8% Federation of Small Businesses; 0.8% Respect Party; 0.8% Bank of England; 0.8% Resolution Foundation; 0.8% Community Savings Banks Association
Daily Mail	3.4% Institute for Fiscal Studies; 1.7% Scottish Nationalist Party; 1.7% Taxpayers' Alliance
Mirror	3.0% Scottish Nationalist Party; 3.0% Institute of Directors; 3.0% Bank of England
Sun	2.9% Scottish Nationalist Party
Daily Record	19.3% Scottish Nationalist Party; 6.5% Respect Party; 3.2% Pollster

hedge fund managers. This class of expert was particularly prevalent in the *Telegraph*, *Guardian* and *Mail* which was partly a function of the prominence of business, city, money and finance sections in this part of the press. Such sources were typically used to offer opinion on the development of the crisis and how it might be resolved. Academic economists were featured far less frequently, and aside from Paul Krugman they were barely cited at all.

Both the *Sun* and the *Mirror* looked distinct in terms of sourcing in that so much opinion was drawn from extremely brief—often no more than a sentence or two—letters from the general public. On the whole letters tended to reflect newspapers' editorial stance so that letters in the *Sun* and *Mail* were usually critical of Labour whilst those in the *Record* and *Mirror* were supportive. However, there were examples where letters either went against the editorial line or raised significant issues not covered by a newspaper's journalists. For instance, the letters page was the only place in the *Mail* where the role of tax havens in the crisis was raised:

AFTER Wall Street and the City of London, the next step for the Government is to take control of offshore banking, which through the use of unregulated hedge funds based in tax havens has been partly responsible for the financial crisis. The German government's investigation into Liechtenstein earlier this year showed that billions of untaxed funds are hidden away by companies, individuals and possibly organised crime in such 'offshore' accounts. If these funds and the taxes owed on them were repatriated, it would alleviate the financial problems of the banks and provide much-needed tax revenue for the Government, opening the way for a fairer tax system for all. It would also enable more funds to become available for alleviating poverty and helping poor countries develop. (*Mail*, 16 October 2008)

Such brief fragments are unlikely to have a great deal of impact on public opinion, especially when set against the predominant tone and tenor of much of the rest of the *Mail's* reporting, but they are a reminder that even the most partisan newspapers are not always monolithic in their coverage.

The broadsheets cited a much wider selection of actors than the tabloids and the type of sources featured represented the political orientation of each newspaper. So the *Telegraph* was more likely to feature organisations such as the International Monetary Fund, the British Bankers Association and the Institute of Directors, whilst the *Guardian* sourced from more left of centre organisations such as trade unions, the Tax Justice Network and the New Economics Foundation.

Discussion of the Bank Rescue Plans: Costs, Downsides and Alternatives

The initial taxpayer outlay for the October 2008 bailouts was £37 billion which was spent on shares in RBS and Lloyds/HBOS. A further £200 billion was made available for liquidity support and another £200 billion provided as a loan guarantee facility—though it was unclear at the time how much of this would be drawn upon and whether the loan guarantee facility would actually cost the taxpayer anything. Estimating the final cost to the taxpayer was made even more difficult because it would depend on what price the bank shares could be sold for in the future and how quickly the banks could repay their loans to the taxpayer. This didn't deter newspapers who provided wildly varying accounts of how much the rescue plans would cost. For instance, the *Mirror* cited a figure of £50 billion which was then presented as a cost per head of the population:

How much taxpayers' money is really at risk?
At least £50 billion, although the Government could make a profit on this if markets recover. This works out at £820 for every man, woman and child in the UK. (*Mirror*, 13 October 2008)

But the *Mail* provided an estimate more than ten times as large:

Startling figures showed Mr Brown's bank bailout will mean the biggest increase in debt by any peacetime government, equivalent to £10,000 for every man, woman or child in the country or more than £40,000 for every family. (*Mail*, 14 October 2008)

And in another article in the *Mail* an even higher estimate was given which was then linked to arguments about the need to cut spending:

A £16,000 BILL FOR EVERY TAXPAYER IN THE LAND (Headline)
THE £500 billion bank bailout is equivalent to a £16,000 bill for every taxpayer and will mean inevitable tax hikes and cuts to public spending, experts warn. The jaw-dropping liability amounts to more than a third of the annual value of the British economy. It is approaching almost £600 billion of total government spending. (*Mail*, 9 October 2008)

These estimates in the *Mail* were questionable because they assumed that the taxpayer would lose their entire investment in bank shares as well as all the monies made available for liquidity support and loan guarantees. This was always extremely unlikely. An even higher estimate was provided in a headline in the *Telegraph*, but this was at least caveated as a possibility:

THE BAIL-OUT EXPLAINED: Bailout could cost every taxpayer £19,000 (*Telegraph*, 9 October 2009)

Another *Telegraph* article cited a cost of £37 billion though it qualified this by reporting that 'officials hope that the Government's new holdings will eventually make a profit for the state when the shares are sold back to private investors'. Despite this the article, headlined 'Bail-out cost equal to tax rise of 11p', then provided an estimate of the necessary tax increase based on the assumption that the bailout costs would be repaid in a single year entirely through an increase in the basic rate of tax. The article also included predictions from unnamed 'economists' about how the part-nationalisation of RBS could quadruple government debt without mentioning that the Government would also be taking control of RBS's assets which were larger than its liabilities:

> According to the Treasury's own figures for 2008–09, adding a penny to the basic rate of income tax raises £3.45 billion. If it had to be paid off in a single year, the £37 billion package would therefore be the equivalent of 10.7p on income tax. Economists have also warned that the Government's decision to take control of Royal Bank of Scotland could send Government debts to four times their current level. Economists say that the bank's £1.8 trillion of liabilities would technically leave the Government with debts worth roughly 160 per cent of gross domestic product. The last time public sector debt was so high was in the 1950s as Britain laboured under the burden of the borrowing that funded the Second World War effort. (*Telegraph*, 15 October 2008)

Both the *Mail* and the *Telegraph* then focused on highly improbable worst case scenarios and presented these as either what would happen—or what could happen. Sometimes these predictions were then linked to arguments about the necessity to cut public spending and raise regressive taxation. These arguments were buttressed by claims that the public sector was wasteful, staffed with 'non-jobs' and 'featherbedded' at the expense of those in the private sector. For instance, a *Telegraph* leader titled 'The public sector needs to share people's pain' argued that:

> Until now, Labour has refused to countenance any diminution in its client state. But, as the recession bites, voters will be less tolerant of the glossy leaflets being pushed through their letter boxes by local authorities. They will no longer grin resignedly at the armies of gender mainstreaming advisers and liaison units and disability awareness counselors and compliance officers producing their plans and strategies and consultation documents, breaking off occasionally to sue each other for discrimination. Nor will they be fobbed off by the claim that reducing these bureaucracies will mean 'cuts to vital services' or 'taking money from schools and hospitals'. People are starting to hurt. They want the pain to be shared by those whose salaries they are paying. (*Telegraph*, 13 October 2008)

The *Mail* juxtaposed the alleged largesse being given to groups such as asylum seekers or public sector workers with the suffering of 'hardworking taxpayers':

By the next election, we will be two distinct nations. One, a Britain of feath-erbedded bankers, public sector workers with lavish pensions and Afghan mothers-of-seven on £170,000 benefits. The other will be the nation of hardworking taxpayers, desperately worried about keeping their jobs, feed-ing their families and providing for their own old age, who will have to prop up the other lot. For this Britain, the rescue is the lousiest of deals. (*Mail*, 9 October 2008)

The burden on the taxpayer has become enormous overnight....All govern-ments, whether of the Left or Right, will have no choice but to hack back viciously at the public sector...It is true that employees in the state sector still have gold-plated and guaranteed pensions – collectively a liability to the taxpayer of more than £800 billion. But this is utterly unsustainable and any responsible government will have no choice but to end this costly privilege. (*Mail*, 9 October 2008)

When it came to discussion of the downsides of the bank rescue plan most attention was focused on the six issues highlighted in Fig. 2.4. The most frequent complaint directed against the bailout, which appeared particu-larly frequently in both the *Telegraph* and *Mail*, was that the suspension of dividends in banks who had participated in the bailouts, would damage shareholders. The *Mail* primarily focused on the impact on individual

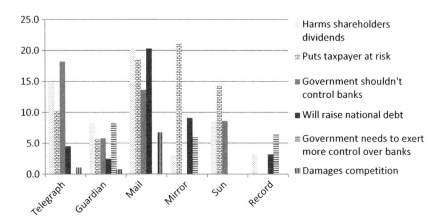

Fig. 2.4   Top six downsides of bailouts (percentage of newspaper articles featur-ing each downside)

shareholders and pensions whilst the *Telegraph* also suggested that the suspension on dividends would make it hard for bank share prices to recover and thus the government to recoup its investments. Part of the reason that this angle got so much coverage was that City institutions were reported to be 'piling pressure' on the Government behind the scenes to have the ban lifted (*Telegraph*, 16 October 2008). All newspapers except the *Record* also focused heavily on the potential impact on the taxpayer, both in terms of the immediate impact on the national debt and the concern that the investments might never be recovered. Perhaps the most striking difference between newspapers was how they approached the issue of state involvement in the banking sector. The two Labour supporting tabloids featured no criticism of this but in the *Guardian* various City figures such as Howard Davies and the HSBC chief, Michael Geoghegan, argued that the state shouldn't be involved in banking—but was faced with little choice on this occasion. The columnist Michael White also took this line in two articles (Table 2.4):

> Nationalising the banks was a necessary expedient, but a return to nationalisation is not the answer, however tempting to old lefties. If China and Russia have given up, it's no time for us to relaunch a People's Republic of our own. (*Guardian*, 10 October 2008)

Table 2.4 Additional downsides of bailouts (percentage of newspaper articles featuring each downside)

Daily Telegraph	2.3% Banks being unfairly bullied; 2.3% may harm other banks; 1.1% reduces competition in the sector; 1.1% won't restore capital ratios; 1.1% doesn't deal with debt write-downs
Guardian	2.5% doesn't deal with debt write-downs; 0.8% may harm other banks; 0.8% doesn't control bonuses; 0.8% costs will worsen recession in long term; 0.8% reduces competition in the sector
Daily Mail	3.4% doesn't control bonuses; 1.7% creates moral hazard
Daily Mirror	3.0% creates moral hazard
Sun	None
The Record	3.2% creates moral hazard; 3.2% could lead to a sterling crisis

Labour leftwingers have understandably rejoiced at the sight of nationalisations, their long discredited recipe for anything that moved. (*Guardian*, 8 October 2008)

In the *Sun* a leading article claimed the banks 'cannot power the economy back to life with the dead hand of Governmental red tape bogging them down' (*Sun*, 14 October 2008) whilst the columnist Bill Leckie argued that:

> See, it was my understanding that this country had long since decided nationalisation was a no-no. That's why we sold off coal, steel, phones, gas, electricity, water, trains, planes, buses, roads and anything else that wasn't nailed down. We did it because state ownership had made them all inefficient, debt-ridden and an unbearable burden on the taxpayer. But that was yesterday. (*Sun*, 14 October 2008)

However the most developed attacks on public ownership appeared in the *Telegraph* and *Mail*, both of which devoted a number of long comment pieces to the topic. One, penned by Simon Heffer, was titled 'We're all socialists now, comrade: A state-backed banking system will impoverish us all' and drew on a repertoire of New Right critiques of the 1970s:

> By the 1970s the inevitable endgame of socialism was being played out: unions battling with government over rates of pay, prices and incomes policies, food subsidies, the three-day week, the winter of discontent. The state had to create jobs because there was precious little incentive for the private sector to do so. Investment was scarce. The state was everywhere. The maxim of the American writer and philosopher Ayn Rand came close to fulfillment before the denouement of Old Labour on May 3 1979: that the difference between a welfare state and a totalitarian state is a matter of time. (*Telegraph*, 9 October 2008)

The linkage of the bank bailouts with totalitarianism was also made in a *Mail* headline titled 'Gone is Mr Bean, but don't turn into Stalin' which argued:

> But we must sound the clearest possible warning about his rescue package. Yes, these measures may have been necessary to avert a catastrophe. But make no mistake: the nationalisation of our tottering banks is fraught with terrible dangers for Britain's future. Until Margaret Thatcher came to the

rescue, we saw how the dead hand of Whitehall crushed everything it touched. It stifled enterprise and drained our resources dry to prop up inefficient companies that had no hope of competing in the real world. If we are not to go down that road to ruin again, it is imperative that ministers keep well out of the day-to-day running of the banks they now control. (*Mail*, 14 October 2008)

The writer in the *Mail* most frequently arguing against state ownership was Peter Oborne who produced three comment pieces (7, 9 and 14 October 2008). These contained a series of false and misleading statements such as the claim that the banks had been fully nationalised— 'there's no such thing as a 'partial' nationalization of the banks any more than a woman can be a little bit pregnant' (*Mail*, 9 October 2008), or that nationalization would mean that 'Britain would become a centrally planned economy' (*Mail*, 7 October 2008). In one piece Oborne made the standard comparison with the nationalised industries of the 1970s:

> Politicians will view the banks as a vast pot of public money to be ransacked at will. Ministers will be able to bully bank managements into placing depositors' money into giant vanity projects like the Olympics…The wretched [Fred] Goodwin may have wasted billions of shareholders' money at RBS. But the Labour government has squandered hundreds of billions of pounds in the National Health Service over the past 11 years, not to mention all those lame-duck nationalised industries in the Sixties and Seventies, such as British Steel. Those with long memories will also remember what a disaster public ownership of the motor industry was with British Leyland. However well intentioned Alistair Darling may be, public ownership of banking will be every bit as bad. (*Daily Mail*, 14 October 2008)

However, although there was a great deal of criticism of the bailouts the overwhelming consensus expressed across all newspapers that there was no alternative to the rescue plans:

> HSBC's chief executive, Michael Geoghegan, said the initiative 'sets a bad precedent but the Government had no alternative'. (*Telegraph*, 10 October 2008)

> That is not to say that the new state of affairs [bank rescues] is desirable; rather that the alternative – a total collapse of confidence in the banking system – would have been calamitous. (*Telegraph*, 10 October 2008)

The plan is bold, risky and carries no guarantee of success, but there is no alternative. (*Guardian*, 9 October 2008)

The semi-nationalisation of the banking system is not exactly Plan A in a market economy, but it turned out to be the only option powerful enough to stand a chance of stemming the flood of pessimism and fear that has engulfed the financial markets. (*Guardian*, 9 October 2008)

No alternative, perhaps, but it'll be us who foot the bill for this bonanza of socialist indulgence. (Headline – *Daily Mail*, 14 October 2008)

If we must stump up the money to save these banks – and there really does seem to be no choice – then it should be on terms that are acceptable to consumers. (*Mail*, 15 October 2008)

But there's little choice. If banks keep collapsing, businesses big and small will go bust, millions will lose work and we will be plunged into a deep recession. (*Mirror*, 8 October 2008)

Brown and Chancellor Alistair Darling had no option but to spend to save the banks. Collapsing city citadels would wreck the entire economy, with factories, shops and offices dragged under. (*Mirror*, 9 October 2008)

The £50 billion part-nationalisation of our High Street banks is an emergency measure that would never have been contemplated in normal times... But this is the only show in town. The alternatives are horrific. All we can do now is hold our breath – and hope it works. (*Sun*, 8 October 2008)

No one knows how this crisis will play out. As the facts stand, Brown and Darling had little choice. (*Sun*, 8 October 2008)

Gordon Brown and Alistair Darling are expected to announce a pounds £50 billion rescue package today. In these desperate times they have no choice. (*Record*, 8 October 2008)

In terms of presenting alternatives a single article in the Scottish *Mail* expressed the option that the banks should have been allowed to go bankrupt. Headlined 'Let the bad banks die naturally', John MacLeod argued that 'contrary to myth' the Great Depression had been turned from a 'recession to a catastrophe' by 'ongoing, frenzied interventionism' (*Mail*,

9 October 2008). Macleod argued this showed that 'the safest way out of a recession was through it, not around it'.

Despite frequent mention of the 1992 Swedish bank rescues which involved full nationalisation of two banks and the liquidation of bond and shareholders, not a single article in the sample argued for this approach. The other alternative for the state to permanently nationalise part of the banking system was mentioned in seven articles by John McDonnell (three times), and (once each) by Tony Benn, Ken Livingstone, the tax campaigner Richard Murphy and the *Guardian* journalist Seamus Milne. Most of these mentions were brief and lacked any substantial argumentation or justification. For instance, the only reference in the *Mirror* was the following three lines in one article:

> Labour Left-winger John McDonnell said it was taxpayers who were left with all the risks – and called for full nationalisation. He said: 'Without full nationalisation the government is effectively nationalising the banks' losses and privatising the profits.' (*Mirror*, 9 October 2009)

In the *Guardian*, McDonnell put his case in a letter (8 October 2008) and short comment piece (9 October 2008) whilst Milne argued:

> Better surely to guarantee deposits and take over such banks once they've effectively failed, as in the case of Northern Rock and Bradford & Bingley, securely recapitalising them as fully publicly owned enterprises. They could then become the core of a newly accountable and publicly controlled banking sector able to channel investment where it's needed, rather than into reckless speculation in debt and housing bubbles. (*Guardian*, 9 October 2008)

The *Telegraph* also featured a short comment piece from 'the most dangerous man in Britain...in the 80s' Tony Benn, who argued that 'a publicly owned and accountable banking system would be better for Britain' (10 October 2008). The *Telegraph* also featured comments backing state ownership from Ken Livingstone but in the context of a brief acerbic piece:

> Financially illiterate he may well be, but Ken Livingstone, the former mayor of London, still has some friendly (retrospective) advice for Gordon Brown about how to handle the credit crisis. 'I would have waited for the banks to fail and then nationalised them for nothing', Ken told an audience at the

Cheltenham Literature Festival. Strangely enough, Livingstone – a high spender during his days at City Hall – isn't a graduate of the London School of Economics. (*Telegraph*, 17 October 2008)

Although there were few articles advocating public ownership of the failed banks, there were ten articles in the *Guardian* as well as two each in the *Mirror* and *Record* which argued for the government to exert some control over the nationalised banks by securing representation on their boards or setting lending targets. So there were instances where commentators argued for greater invention in failing institutions even if these fell short of calls for full nationalisation.

How to Reform the Financial System? (Sample One: 6 October 2008–17 October 2008)

This section examines the various measures that were discussed for reforming the sector. As the data in Fig. 2.5 demonstrates, by far the most frequently cited response was the need to restrict bonuses—primarily in the banks that were being nationalised. Across the press it was argued that bankers should not be receiving bonuses when their banks were being kept afloat by the taxpayer. These arguments dominated the reporting of responses in the tabloids which meant that the majority of people who read newspapers will have encountered little beyond this proposal. The next most discussed response was the need for 'more regulation', though very few reports actually went into any detail and specified what this actually meant. Gordon Brown's calls for a new 'global financial architecture' was reported in all newspapers but again little detail was provided about what this would actually entail. Even in the broadsheets, very few articles explained what changes would be required to the structures and rules regulating global financial flows, leading one reader to write in to complain about the *Guardian*'s reporting:

> Larry Elliott (Get ahead of the game, October 7) says 'this weekend's meeting of the IMF and World Bank in Washington should be used to sketch out a new international financial architecture'. Unfortunately, except for Robert Zoellick's idea of expanding the G7 group to include a G7 group of rapidly developing nations, the column provides no ideas of what new financial architecture is required. Doubling the number of countries into a group that do not know what to do, however, does not make for a 'knowing' report on the needed international financial architectural changes. (Letter, *Guardian*, 9 October 2008)

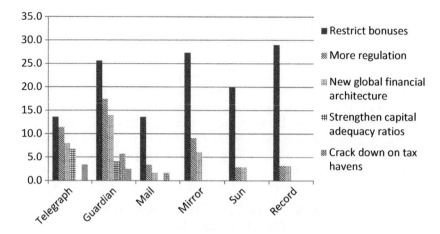

Fig. 2.5 Top six solutions (percentage of newspaper articles featuring each solution)

Other important proposals such as greater regulation of the shadow banking system (3.4 per cent of articles in *Telegraph*, 2.5 per cent of articles in the *Guardian*), splitting up the banks (1.1 per cent in *Telegraph*, 1.7 per cent in *Guardian*), the reform of credit agencies (1.1 per cent in *Telegraph*, 1.7 per cent in *Guardian*) or regulation of the derivatives market (1.1 per cent in *Telegraph*, 2.5 per cent in the *Guardian*) received the odd mention in the broadsheets but were absent from the mass circulation tabloids (see Table 2.5).

The crucial issue of who would oversee the re-regulation of the finance sector appeared once across our sample in a comment piece by Polly Toynbee:

> Brown himself can only regain lost trust if he realises quite what a monumental task that is, as well as for finance. That means far more than simply getting the City back on its feet, dusting down its worst excrescences and lopping off a few bank managers' heads (with their multimillion pensions intact). It will take more radical action and more resonant language. Alas, his committee of advisers consists of the City people who got us into this: the takers of the fattest pay, the sitters on each others' boards. Paul Myners, late of the *Guardian*, will be no radical steam cleaner as City minister, more

of a feather duster. Brown needs a severe committee of those economists who were right when he was wrong – people to frighten the City, not to soothe its frightened feathers. Appoint the Richard Murphys, Will Huttons and Larry Elliotts not as City tsars but as City Savonarolas to flush out tax avoidance and evasion, to close down tax havens, to appoint honest non-executives to company boardrooms and institute a regime built on public trust. (*Guardian*, 13 October 2009)

Overall, the tabloid press provided almost no meaningful information about the reforms that would be necessary to prevent a repeat of the crisis. What little information that was available concentrated almost entirely on the need to restrict bonuses to bankers in bailed out institutions. Whilst the broadsheets provided a wider range of debate, they too tended to concentrate primarily on bonuses as well as vague arguments on the need for more regulation or changes to the rules and structures of global finance. Whilst some major reforms were mentioned they tended to appear very infrequently which meant that readers would need to follow extremely

Table 2.5 Additional solutions (percentage of newspaper articles featuring each solution)

Telegraph	3.4% Put Bank of England back in charge of regulating banks; 2.3% 'Clearer' not more regulation; 2.3% Introduce more free market principles; 1.1% split up banks; 1.1% Have institutional shareholders vet executives; 1.1% Fund public financial education; 1.1% Make non-executive directors accountable for banks; 1.1% Reform credit agencies/rules; 1.1% Link inflation targets to House Price increases; 1.1% Regulate 'Over The Counter' derivatives market; 1.1% Restrict reliance on wholesale money markets; 1.1% Reduce leverage; 1.1% Have banks insured by IMF; 1.1% Have bank accounts audited by government or specialists
Guardian	3.3% Introduce variable capital ratios linked to business cycle; 2.5% Regulate 'Over The Counter' derivatives market; 1.7% Reform credit agencies/rules; 1.7% Have bank accounts audited by government or specialists; 1.7% Link inflation targets to House Price increases; 1.7% Split up banks; 0.8% Make non-executive directors accountable for banks; 0.8% Reduce leverage; 0.8% Have banks insured by IMF; 0.8% Introduce Tobin/Financial Transactions Tax; 0.8% Bring in non-City people as non-executive directors of banks; 0.8% Introduce Land Value Tax to reduce volatility in house prices; 0.8% Introduce criminal charges for over lending.
Mail	1.7% Link inflation targets to House Price increases

closely to pick up details on some of the key changes necessary to prevent a repeat of the crisis.

NEWSPAPER FINDINGS: SAMPLE 2 (6 JULY 2009–10 JULY 2009)

How to Reform the Financial System?

On 8 July 2009, Alistair Darling unveiled the Government's White Paper on banking regulation which drew heavily on the recommendations of Adair Turner's (2009) report on banking reform. The White Paper recommended keeping the Tripartite structure of banking regulation (Treasury, Bank of England and Financial Services Authority) intact though it added an extra layer of oversight with the creation of the Council for Financial Stability. Banks were to be subject to tougher—but not specified—capital requirements and would be forced to pay a fee to fund a programme of financial literacy for consumers. There would also be stricter penalties against misconduct and 'systemically' important hedge funds would now be monitored. However, the White Paper stopped short of the most serious reforms including breaking up the banks, introducing a new 'Glass-Steagall' provision to separate utility from casino banking, mandating curbs on bonuses and licensing derivatives.

It was clear from the analysis that the dry technical nitty gritty of reform proved to be of much less interest to the tabloids than the stories of fat cats and banker bonuses. The *Sun* featured one 137 word article which focused on the introduction of a 'traffic light' system to indicate the safeness of financial products and the requirement for banks paying 'big bonuses' to hold 'extra cash to cover future risks' (9 July 2009). The *Mirror* featured two articles. One was a brief 151 word editorial which said very little bar the claim that the reforms would 'check irresponsible bankers by strengthening the hand of regulators' so as to 'reduce the risk of another global financial meltdown' (*Mirror*, 9 July 2009). The other article was more critical of the White Paper. It argued that much of what was proposed such as the provisions for financial literacy education were 'worthy but hardly radical' and that many other aspects of the reforms were 'vague – drawing allegations of a whitewash' (*Mirror* 9 July 2009).

The *Mail* featured five articles, four of which were largely critical of the proposals. Although *Mail* journalists argued that curbs on bonuses were a worthy idea they doubted that the measures put forward would address the problem, pointing to the large bonuses still being paid to Steven

Hester at part-nationalised RBS. However the bulk of criticism in the *Daily Mail* was directed at the decision to maintain the Tripartite system of bank regulation with journalists backing Conservative party proposals to return bank regulation to the Bank of England.

The *Telegraph* was also highly critical of the decision to maintain the Tripartite authority and again argued that the Bank of England should return to being the key regulator. *Telegraph* writers also took a particularly distinctive line that we didn't find in other parts of the press. This was that tougher regulation was either pointless or potentially damaging. So, for instance, Jeremy Warner argued in a comment piece that the government should have broken up the banks and separated retail from investment banking because the crisis was caused by personal irresponsibility rather than poor regulation.

> Failure by regulators to see the risks was one thing, but by lulling everyone into a false sense of security, instructive regulation also had the perverse effect of making the financial system more irresponsible and therefore less safe. The origins of the banking crisis lie in the very human characteristic that if you take away from people all sense of responsibility for their own actions and instead make conduct enforceable through an externally imposed, all-seeing system of monitoring and rules, then you remove the element of choice that enables organisations and individuals to behave decently as a matter of conscience... The idea that all human ills can some-how be regulated away is one of the great public policy delusions of the modern age, for the effect is to diminish any proper sense of corporate and individual responsibility. (*Daily Telegraph*, 7 July 2009)

In another article, focused on City reaction to the proposals, a variety of lobby groups such as the British Bankers' Association and Association of British Insurers, although welcoming some aspects of the White Paper were critical of other for allegedly damaging corporate profitability and making the sector less internationally competitive (*Telegraph*, 9 July 2009). On a very different note, the *Telegraph* also featured a comment piece from the merchant banker Tony Shearer who offered a critical account of City deal making. Shearer took aim at the failures of accountants, financial advisers, lawyers and rating agencies and argued that the 'UK economy would have been better off without large parts of our financial services'. A key problem with the White Paper, Shearer argued, was the reform process was being driven by the same investment bankers who had crashed the system:

The current 'reforms' are dominated by the investment bankers who hold the senior positions in the FSA, controlling UK Financial Investments and advising the Treasury. They have little understanding of why they have destroyed our economy over the past 10 years, and every desire to get back to earning large sums as soon as possible. Even though investment bankers are at the heart of the causes of the banking crisis, press speculation is that the new chairman of Lloyds Bank needs to be an investment banker. Have we learned so little? (*Telegraph*, 6 July 2009)

The *Guardian*'s coverage was once again an outlier in comparison to other newspapers. Although it featured many of the same criticisms that appeared in other parts of the press—such as the failure to break up the banks and the inadequacy of the Tripartite system—the *Guardian* alone featured angles like the need to fully license financial products in regulated exchanges and the need to provide more detail on capital requirements. However, the most distinctive feature of the *Guardian*'s coverage was its willingness to step back and ask questions about what role the financial system should play within the broader economy. For instance, Will Hutton argued that the 'design of our financial system should be focused' on 'mobilising long-term equity and loan finance to build a balanced economy along with creating safe financial products for the saving and investing public' (9 July 2009). In a comment piece the former Labour MP Bryan Gould offered a critical account of Conservative and New Labour approaches to the City and the impacts that these had on the rest of the economy:

Macroeconomic policy was largely abandoned. Keynes was dismissed and forgotten. Interest rates were pressed into service to maintain the value of the currency and to underpin financial assets that might otherwise have been regarded as of dubious value. Little or no attention was paid to the competitiveness of the rest of the British economy, so that any thought of following an exchange rate policy that would stimulate exports, employment and investment simply never occurred to our policymakers; manufacturing in particular was allowed to continue its relentless decline. Most of our economic eggs were placed in the financial services basket and only City operators had access to the golden eggs among them. That is why the global crisis has hit the United Kingdom harder than anywhere else. (*Guardian*, 9 July 2009)

Ken Livingstone in another comment piece argued that the White Paper didn't 'remotely grasp the scale of the problem' and that 'the approach of bailing out bank shareholders with billions of pounds of taxpayers' money while leaving the same people and policies in charge has been a failure' (*Guardian*, 9 July 2009). Instead Livingstone argued, the government should have introduced 'more radical measures' including 'nationalisation and direct control by government of the core of the banking sector' to direct investment to the 'cutting edge of the emerging new economy around the creative industries, the internet and environmental and the most technologically advanced manufacturing sectors'.

Overall then most newspaper saw the government White Paper as distinctly underwhelming. The reforms although seen as creditable in part, were widely dismissed as too little, too late and there was broad scepticism as to whether any of them would ever be enacted in the face of the looming General Election.

BROADCAST FINDINGS: SAMPLE 1 (15 SEPTEMBER–31 OCTOBER 2008)

Patterns of Source Access

In examining who were the most significant sources in coverage this chapter examined two samples. The first sample covered the six-week period from 15 September 2008, the day Lehman Brothers went bankrupt, to 31 October 2008 a fortnight after the UK bank rescues. It found a total of 233 source appearances. The data in Fig. 2.6 presents the big picture analysis of the relative prominence of different source categories over this period.

Coding here was not always straightforward since many individuals could be categorised in different groups. For instance, Adair Turner has been an investment banker, Director General of the CBI, an academic economist who lecturers at the LSE and a regulator at the Financial Services Authority (FSA). In order to maintain consistency, sources were categorised by their most recent group affiliation. Since many of the individuals classified in Graph 2.8 as politicians, regulators, academics and business representatives also have close links with the financial services community, the prominence of 'City voices' is conservatively estimated. As can be seen representatives from the financial services community

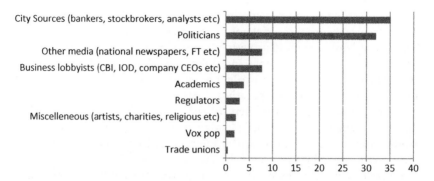

Fig. 2.6 All sources sample 1: Each source as a percentage of total sources (15/9/2008–31/10/2008)

were the largest group of sources accessed (35.1 per cent of all source appearances) followed by politicians (32 per cent). Since the main two British political parties were committed to free markets and relatively permissive regulation, there was a narrowness in the range of opinion available to listeners. This was magnified by the presence of other groups such as business lobbyists, and journalists from the national financial press who all tended to share a similar laissez-faire outlook.

Voices from civil society were almost completely absent from coverage. For instance, organised labour was represented by a single appearance from one union leader (0.4%).

BROADCAST FINDINGS: SAMPLE 2 (6 OCTOBER 2008–17 OCTOBER 2008)

Who and What Caused the Crisis

As can be seen in Fig. 2.7, the banks themselves were most likely to be cited as responsible for the crisis. However, in contrast to press reporting the criticism of the banks on the *Today programme* was relatively subdued. Out of the 19 references to the culpability of the banks, two came from City sources and these were relatively restrained. One from private equity partner John Moulton stated that the 'the banks have not exactly shown that they can look after themselves' (*Today programme*, 8 October 2008). The other came from George Cox, a director of Bradford of Bingley when

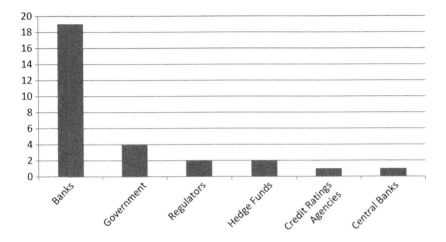

Fig. 2.7 Attribution of responsibility for the banking crisis (number of times each actor cited)

it went bust, who offered a rather muted account of the responsibility of Fred Godwin in the collapse of RBS:

Journalist: How will he [Fred Goodwin] be looked back on do you think?

George Cox: I hope with a measure of sympathy. We look around for villains in this. We look initially at Adam Applegarth at Northern Rock and I perhaps look at him rather differently. People like Adam and Sir Fred have been recognised in recent years as heros in banking you know people who've done great things but then walked into these circumstances and that's the end. (*Today programme*, 13 October 2008)

Most of the criticism of the banks came from journalists themselves, either in the form of brief statements from BBC journalists (four mentions) or more commonly from the reporting of stories which appeared in national newspapers as part of the review of the press segments (eight mentions). Potentially, this offered the opportunity to develop a critical journalism which explored the culpability of different actors within the City. However, since City sources were so prominent such criticisms tended to be immediately challenged by someone from the finance sector. For instance, on one occasion a journalist brought up the role of hedge fund managers which was immediately rebutted by an investor in hedge funds:

Journalist:	Can you explain why hedge funds are saying this, and why we should care when for some, hedge funds are the villains of the peace and it's through their speculative risky trading that we're in the mess that we're now in?
Ian Morley (Corazon Capital):	I would reject that analysis. I think we're in the mess we're in because of the problem of moral hazard with the banks. I don't think hedge funds are involved in the creation of sub-prime, they just take a view on it and I think the money that hedge funds manage increasingly is actually for institutions, a lot of pension fund money is being managed there. (*Today programme*, 16 October 2008)

Those working in the finance sector should have the opportunity to challenge accusations against them but the lack of critical voices from outside the sector meant the BBC's journalism lacked the bite found in some newspaper reporting.

In fact, the most serious criticism of the banks on the *Today programme* during this period came from reported newspaper accounts rather than journalists or interviewees. For example, on 10 October, a BBC journalist reported on a statement from Max Hastings in the *Daily Mail* that 'some of the fattest cats on Wall street and the City have screwed up our lives' and on another occasion:

The *Mail* is unforgiving in its attitudes to those bankers who are accused of driving the country's financial system to the brink of collapse and threatening untold hardships for millions of families. 'Britain has a right to be outraged' it says the banks are turning to same ordinary taxpayers for rescue from the consequences of their greed. (*Today programme*, 14 October 2008)

Government was also accused of being responsible for the crisis on four occasions, three times by politicians (two Conservative and one Plaid Cymru) and once (reported) by the *Economist* magazine, whilst regulators were cited twice (once by the *Telegraph* and once by the macroeconomist Patrick Minford).

In terms of what had actually caused the crisis the *Today programme* cited 14 separate factors (see Fig. 2.8). Its issue profile resembled that of the two broadsheets in the sample with a strong focus on greed/risk taking, overlending and inadequate regulation. However there were some issues such as the role of global trade imbalances, leverage, capital ratios and auditing failures, which appeared in both broadsheets but were not mentioned on the *Today programme*. It should also be noted that the explanations for the crisis were often brief and jargon heavy. For instance in one bulletin the hedge fund manager George Cooper pointed to the impact of central banks keeping interest rates too low:

> What's caused this crisis is not the private sector, it's been the policies of the central banks that have been forcing liquidity in the system over the last two decades. (*Today programme*, 7 October 2008)

The problem with this sort of account is that it assumes a level of contextual knowledge that much of the audience is unlikely to possess, a problem common to other areas of reporting such as international news (Philo and Berry 2004, 2011).

Figure 2.9 presents data on the range of interview-based sources who were consulted by the *Today programme* during the two-week period around the British banking bailout. These were the experts who were

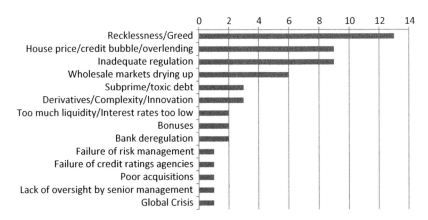

Fig. 2.8 Explanations for the banking crash (number of times each factor cited 6/10/2008–17/10/2008)

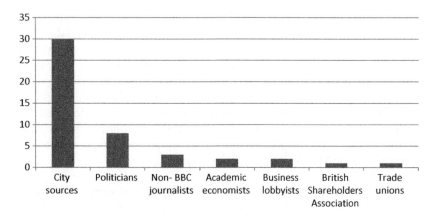

Fig. 2.9   Interview sources (Sample 2 6/10/2008–17/10/2008)

given extended periods to discuss the bailouts and what might be done to reform the sector. City voices dominated core coverage of the bank nationalisations, accounting for 30 of the 47 interviews. There were eight interviews involving politicians—five for Labour, two for the Liberal Democrats and one for the Conservatives. Representatives from the CBI and British Chamber of Commerce were also interviewed along with journalists from the *Financial Times*, *Economist* and the financial commentary service *Breaking Views*. Domination by City voices is even more pronounced during this period and there is little space for critical commentators from outside financial services.

Evaluations of the Bank Rescue Plans

This section examines the debate around the British bank rescue plan which was announced on 8 October 2008. In total 36 separate sources offered a verdict on the bank bailouts: 19 City sources, nine journalism sources, five politicians, and one source each from the CBI, trade unions and the academic economics profession. The overwhelming consensus (33 of 37) from commentators on the *Today programme* was that the bailouts were the correct response. A selection of some of the comments is reproduced below in Table 2.6. Of the other four evaluations, a reported statement from the *Guardian* offered a noncommittal perspective 'Is the Government's £500 billion bailout of the banks a welcome step forward

Table 2.6   A Selection of positive comments on the bank bailouts

Source	Source category	Comments
George Cox	City	'Good', 'decisive', 'bold move', 'they are taking a stake in businesses that are fundamentally good businesses and at a very good price…In the long term this could be quite a good move from the taxpayer's point of view in terms of getting a return'
Neil Mackinnon	City	'A very good package and a very timely package', 'the prime minister and the chancellor are to the applauded for putting together this package at very short notice and given the very severe crisis across all markets'
David Buik	City	'A fantastic package'
Nick Clegg	Politician	'Whole heartedly support this government package'
John Cridland	CBI	'We're encouraged by the package, an important first step' 'vital to keep the whole economy going, not just the banks'
Daily Mail	Media	'A triumph for bold and decisive thinking'
Sun	Media	'The deal should go a long way towards unfurring the arteries of the financial system'

or a reckless handout?' and there were three critical commentaries on the bailout. One consisted of a reported statement from the *Morning Star* that the bailouts were 'socialism for the rich' whilst the other two critical commentaries came from politicians and City voices. One, from the journalist and City economist Liam Halligan, argued that the bailouts wouldn't unthaw the interbank markets because they weren't addressing bank's bad debts—and the money created would be 'pure inflation injected into the system'. The other from the Conservative politician John Redwood argued that the bailouts were unaffordable, would weaken confidence in the sector and didn't put 'enough discipline on those banks to do what they needed to do for themselves'.

No source put forward an alternative plan or argued that the banks should be fully nationalised. Although nationalisation was mentioned by four interviewees during this period, it was quickly dismissed:

Howard Davies (Former Chairman of FSA and non-executive Director of Morgan Stanley):

I have to say that I don't think that full nationalisation should be necessary or indeed would be ideal because once you fully nationalise a bank, you take it out of the market, you take it out of its pressure to be competitive. I think you will then find it very hard to sell. But taking a 10% stake a 20% stake in a bank as a signal to the market that the Government stands behind it may well mean that you could get out of that stake when markets return to normal as we hope they must do one day. So I think that rather than full nationalisation is a better option. (*Today programme*, 7 October 2008)

Norman Lamont (Former Chancellor of the Exchequer and director of Hedge Fund RAB Capital):	I think we should have regulation but not over-regulation. What we don't want and I wouldn't have wanted would have been for the government to run the banks that would have been a terrible error. But I think there are a lot of things like remuneration structures that need to be looked at. (*Today programme*, 8 October 2008)
Journalist:	George Cox, do you think there would have been a case for going even further and just saying look banks failed you are dependent on huge amounts of liquidity support from the taxpayer you are dependent on huge amounts of implicit government guarantees and if those weren't lurking around in the background there would clearly be a run. We will withdraw all support unless you want to walk into our arms and we will take you over completely?
George Cox (Former non-executive director of Bradford and Bingley):	No that would have been the wrong move. That would have been a huge mouthful for the government to bite off. It's already bitten off a big mouthful as I said earlier and I think to have taken over the whole lot would have been unnecessary. I mean you are then taking full responsibility for recovery. Now as it is much of it lies with the banks themselves and I am sure that's right. (*Today programme*, 13 October 2008)

Peter Warburton (Economic Perspectives & Institute of Economic Affairs):	I think to really nationalise the industry and take away all its incentives to perform would be disastrous. (*Today programme*, 8 October 2008)

The only other time full nationalisation was commented on by news sources was during the section where journalists reviewed the newspapers. This meant the arguments against nationalisation from the right wing press were again reproduced:

Few will feel comfortable with the either the semi-nationalisation of the banking sector or the truly monumental scale of taxpayer exposure. (*Telegraph*, cited on *Today programme*, 9 October 2008)

The *Sun* is worried the banks won't be able to power the economy back to life with the dead hand of government red tape bogging them down and that's a view shared by the *Mail* which believes that the nationalisation of our tottering banks is fraught with terrible dangers for Britain's future. (*Today programme*, 14 October 2008)

The *Daily Mail* acknowledges that the PM has shown great stature and gravitas in recent days 'gone is Mr Bean' the paper says but 'he must never turn into Stalin with his mania for state control'. (*Today programme*, 14 October 2008)

However it was clear that journalists were aware that nationalisation was an alternative to the UK bank bailout as can be seen in the following exchange:

Journalist 1:	Do you think this was as good a deal as the taxpayer could have got?
Journalist 2:	Well as good a deal as the taxpayer could have got would have been to simply expropriate the assets and to have taken the whole thing you know for nothing and, *I guess*, there could have been an analysis done that these were basically businesses that weren't viable without huge government support and in particular these guarantees for interbank lending. You know, *I guess*, there would have been a route for them to do that. I think the government in the end just took the view that full scale nationalisation of that sort would have done such damage to confidence in the British

banking system that it was a step too far which is why they
decided to maintain them as going concerns. (*Today programme*, 13 October 2008, my italics)

The journalist indicated that that the government has concluded that it
would be a 'step too far' then the option isn't explored further. This can
also be seen in the way in which journalists addressed questions to
leading politicians. During an interview, Alastair Darling was robustly
questioned by a journalist who repeatedly raised the problem that under
the terms of the bailout the government couldn't compel the banks to
lend to each other or to the wider economy:

Journalist:	Yes but what the taxpayer is being told this morning is that these vast amounts of money are buying, we hope, confidence but not influence. We cannot force the banks to do anything.
Alastair Darling:	Well if we put money into the system then yes we can.
Journalist:	What buying these preference shares?
Alastair Darling:	Yes hold on.
Journalist:	But these are not even voting shares?
Alastair Darling:	Hold on. In return for doing this we want to ensure that we reach an agreement with those individual companies in relation to amongst other things a commitment to extend support to small businesses and homebuyers.
Journalist:	So you haven't got that undertaking yet?
Alastair Darling:	Well I've just announced the scheme today so the next stage is to enter into agreements with the banks.
Journalist:	So it's conditional upon that agreement is it? In other words you could come back here next week and say the scheme's off because they wouldn't give us these promises? (*Today programme*, 8 October 2008)

This inability to actually compel the bank to provide credit to the wider
economy without taking them under direct state control was one of the
key arguments for full nationalisation. During the credit crunch states
such as the UK and US, which had AAA credit scores from the rating
agencies, were unlike most banks, able to borrow large sums at very low
rates of interest. As Joseph Stigltz put it: 'The US government can borrow
at 1pc so why can't it lend directly to poor people for mortgages at 4pc?'
(*Daily Telegraph*, 2 February 2009). However, during interviews the

option of nationalisation was not put to the Chancellor. It was outside the terms of debate.

There were also occasions when journalists went further and directly endorsed free market views on the bailout and nationalisation. The tendency for financial journalists to endorse free market perspectives was noted by Doyle (2006) in her interviews with financial journalists, though it was clear that some reporters were uneasy with this approach. But during the reporting of the crisis there were occasions when this happened:

> Journalist: Old Labour veterans used to dream of nationalising the commanding heights of the economy but as Margaret Thatcher used to say you can't buck the market. (*Today programme*, 15 October 2008)

In another segment a journalist comments:

> What we are into now is *I'm afraid* state controlled banking of the sort we didn't think we'd see since Margaret Thatcher was elected in 1979. I mean I think one of the things that's been announced today that's not been given enough play is these banks are being forced to lend to homeowners and small businesses. I mean that is the sort of thing we saw you know in Eastern Europe [laughs]. We have not seen control of credit like that for decades. (*Today programme*, 13 October 2008)

In reaching for an analogy to state involvement in the banking sector the journalist chooses a comparison with the authoritarian Eastern Block rather than a mainstream social democratic European state such as Switzerland, Germany or the Netherlands. As a later report on the BBC website noted:

> Across Europe, governments routinely set performance targets and compensation packages – all without much of an outcry from anyone. There is no real acceptance of the very Anglo-Saxon idea that banking services are something that only the private sector does or should do. (BBC 2012)

On his official BBC blog one journalist commented on the 'paradox' of the bailouts in that the need for the banks to speedily pay back the vast sums of public money they have been lent means that they are limited in their ability to extend credit to the wider economy. However, the journalist argued:

> ... if we don't demand our money back, we'd be formalising that there's been a semi-permanent nationalisation of the entire banking system. And that would massively encroach on the ability of our banks to operate as independent commercial entities. There would be massive political pressure on them to become quasi-social utilities, providing loans at the behest of ministers and officials rather than on the basis of commercial criteria. So here's what may turn out to be the choice: less lending for years or public ownership of the banks for the foreseeable future. It's not an easy choice, is it? (Peston 2008)

In one segment during a discussion of the American bailouts a journalist commented:

> Henry Paulson has come out now and is telling them how to spend it [the bailout funds]. So he's come out and said you can't hoard this money you have to start lending immediately. So that's where this thing about government and politicians comes in. How much *meddling* are they [politicians] going to do? (*Today programme*, 15 October 2008, my italics)

The assumption built into some reporting and the position taken by all sources was that nationalisation would be bad for banking and bad for the wider economy. However, this position is contested. In terms of financial stability, the three banks rated as the world's safest in a 2011 study—KFW (Germany), Caisse des Depots et Consignations (France) and Bank NederlandseGemeenten (Netherlands)—were all either wholly or partially state owned (*Global Finance Magazine*, 2011). The notion that state-owned banks are detrimental to the wider economy is also contested. For instance, Andrianova et al.'s (2009) study of a large number of countries between 1995 and 2007 found that a large state presence in banking was associated with higher rates of economic growth:

> When it comes to banks that are in the public sector, democratic accountability of politicians is more likely to discourage them from engaging in speculation. In such banks, top managers are more likely to be compelled to focus on the more mundane job of financing real businesses and economic growth. (Andrianova et al. 2009: 5)

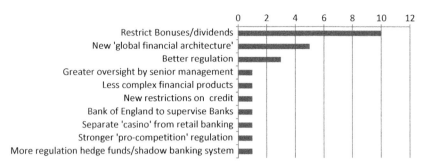

Fig. 2.10 Proposed reforms to the finance sector (number of times each reform was mentioned)

The purpose of this analysis was not to argue for one model of banking over another. There are arguments for and against state involvement in banking. However, BBC listeners were offered a very limited range of debate in which the case for either short- or long-term full nationalisation was missing.

Reforms to the Banking/Financial System

Overall, there was relatively little space given over to ideas for reform on the *Today programme* during this period. Figure 2.10 shows how often different ideas for reform were mentioned. This included assessments of proposed reforms as well as calls for the sector to change (or not change) in certain ways. In line with press reporting the great bulk of references concerned restrictions of bonuses/dividends in the part-nationalised banks and the need to create a new international Bretton Woods' style financial architecture. The analysis thus points again to the key agenda setting role of political elites and how their policy prescriptions tend to structure coverage. Less attention was paid to reforms such as separating 'casino' from retail banking or restrictions on credit creation, both of which were mentioned very briefly on a single occasion.

The heavy concentration of financial sector sources meant that sometimes when major reforms were mooted they were immediately downgraded. For instance, the one occasion when increased regulation of hedge funds was mentioned took place in the context of a debate between a journalist and two City sources who immediately questioned its appropriateness:

Journalist: It certainly seems to be the case that there are an increasing number of people, we're hearing reports of an email sent to Fuld of Lehmans from Hank Paulson that he wanted to regulate heavily the hedge funds. We hear Nicholas Sarkozy last night call for a clampdown on them.

Terry Smith (TulletPrebon): Everybody loves to find a scapegoat in these circumstances and they're certainly in the cross-hairs for the finding of that but it probably is unfair to call them the villains of the peace. I think if you're looking for villains of the piece there are plenty of other candidates you could include. Having said that, there's no doubt that some of the hedge funds were engaged in, in effect banking by taking in borrowed monies and then lending it to people and we basically had in some hedge funds a parallel and unregulated banking system which was pretty dangerous and that we probably had collusion in short selling in some cases which was injurious to some of our financial institutions. Having said that we're talking about some hedge funds and I'm sure you could find similar people to blame in plenty of other sectors.

Journalist: Ian Morely, do they need regulating as a result of all those things that Terry Smith said?

Ian Morley (Corazon Capital): Well again I think there's a fundamental misunderstanding. Hedge funds are heavily regulated. (*Today programme*, 16 October 2008)

In a similar vein, although greater regulation was mentioned on three occasions two of these were brief single sentence references from journalists whilst the third from a City source argued that although the government needed to design a 'better' regulatory system it should be wary of 'over-regulating' the sector:

Martin Taylor (Former Chief Executive of Barclays):	...I think the very worst thing we can do is slam on an huge amount of heavy handed regulation on the system now, and everyone will want to do that and everyone will want to kick the bankers till they're black and blue but that wouldn't be very helpful. We need to get credit flowing again. We do need to design a regulatory system better so that five or six years from now when things are better – let's hope – we don't go through the same old cycle again. (*Today programme*, 14 October 2008)

The reliance on a narrow selection of financial sources also excluded opinion from outside this sector advocating more far-reaching reforms. Journalists were clearly aware of some of these issues. For instance in one segment two journalists discuss 'counter party risk' in the CDS market following the collapse of Lehmans and how much of the '$62 trillion market' involved speculation which was akin to 'taking out insurance on a neighbour's house when you know the wiring is faulty':

Journalist one:	Is there anything governments can do?
Journalist two:	Well currently the market is completely unregulated and to many people the craziest thing is that you claim a credit default swap without even owning the bond. That massively amplifies the problem and obviously speculators would hate it if there were rules actually forcing them to own the bonds but there is now an enormous amount of public money at stake. (*Today programme*, 16 October 2008)

The point here is that this key issue appears as an isolated fragment which isn't then developed into a discussion on what could be done in this area, primarily because outside critics of the sector are almost completely absent from coverage.

What was also missing was the structural critique about the role of the finance sector in Britain's economy. As Will Hutton (1996) has argued the City has negative impacts on the wider economy by forcing up sterling which damages manufacturing. He also argues that the City spurns long-term productive investment in favour of short-term financial speculation and that this unbalances the economy and creates asset bubbles and instability[3]:

> The City of London is now too big and too risky for a country our size. It is not just that bailing it out has cost £850bn, as the National Audit Office reported, and that the recession it imposed has led to the biggest ever increase in peacetime public borrowing. For years it has crowded out exporters and manufacturers. Money has flowed into the City forcing the pound up to crazy levels, and making it hard for exporters to compete, while at the same time generating credit flows that have made property, construction and financial services the routes to quick profits ... It should be no surprise that half the growth between 1997 and 2007 came from finance, construction and property. Over the same period, manufacturing shrank from 20% to 12% of our national output. (*Observer*, 6 December 2009)

Whilst this perspective was absent, the opposite view—that the sector was a major benefit to the country that shouldn't be regulated more heavily—appeared repeatedly in coverage:

Digby Jones (Minister of State for Trade and Investment):	One thing I hope we really do not get is a backlash against bankers because Britain's financial services community is enormously important, it's about 9% of GDP and employs hundreds of thousands of people. I don't want to wake up in five years' time and found we have overregulated, we've dis-incentivised innovation and Shanghai, Dubai and Mumbai think it's Christmas Day. (*Today programme*, 6 October 2008)
Ian Morley (Corazon Capital):	... I think the UK economy has in recent years been significantly based on the growth of financial services. Hedge funds in the UK are the second largest location in the world after the United States and if they get driven offshore it'll be a significant loss certainly to the financial economy and as the financial economy is a significant part of the UK economy today the knock on effect to the general economy as well. (*Today programme*, 16 October 2008)

Broadcast Sample 3 (1 January–31 July 2009)

Over this seven month news sample there were 35 days when the *Today programme* featured discussion of further nationalisation options or long-term reforms to the sector. These were January 19, 21, 22, 28; February 3, 9, 10, 11, 13, 16, 20, 23, 24, 25, 27; March 2, 3, 27; April 2, 3, 9; May 1, 4, 21; June 17, 18, 24, 12; July 7, 8, 16, 24, 31, 27, 20. Six days of coverage—where summaries on the BBC indicated banking had been discussed could not be checked—and potentially coded—because the audio files were not available either from the BBC website or Box of Broadcasts. These were 1 January, 20 January, 26 February, 18 March, 7 May and 15 May.

Patterns of Source Access

The range of interviewees featured during this sample period (see Fig. 2.11) were similar to those encountered in the earlier samples. Even though this sample did not cover the 6:00–7:00am section of the programme which includes the daily 'view from the City/markets' segments the largest source category was again people from the finance sector such as bankers, stockbrokers or analysts. These were often the same City voices who had appeared repeatedly in earlier samples such as George Cox (Ex- Bradford and Bingley chairman), Terry Smith (TulletPrebon), John Moulton (Alchemy Partners) and the head of the British Bankers

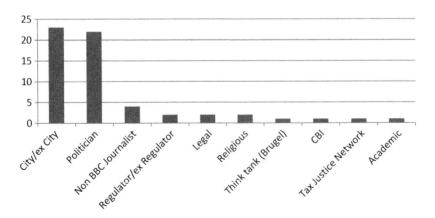

Fig. 2.11   Source appearances (Sample 3—1 January 2009–31 July 2009)

Association, Angela Knight. Politicians were the other dominant group in sourcing. Here two figures—Vince Cable (seven appearances) and John McFall (five appearances)—were particularly prominent accounting for more than half of all the political interviews. McFall was heavily featured because of his role as Chair of the Treasury Select Committee which was at the time examining banking and the role of 'bonus culture', whilst Cable was featured as the most high profile political critic of the finance sector. Aside from these groups two non-BBC journalists were interviewed—Gillian Tett (three appearances) and Fraser Nelson (one appearance)—as were two religious leaders: Tarek El Diwany (Founder of Islamic Finance) and the former Bishop of Worcester, Peter Selby. Aside from this, representation from civil society actors was again minimal. No trade union representatives were interviewed over the seven month period, and the sole representative of civil society was John Christensen of the Tax Justice Network whose appearance in one segment was balanced by the inclusion of a representative from a legal firm involved in setting up tax avoidance schemes.

The Debate Over Nationalisation

The need for further state bailouts in early 2009 once again opened up discussion about how to deal with the part-nationalised banks. However, during this period there was more space given over to arguments in favour of full temporary nationalisation. Four sources—John McFall, Vince Cable, George Magnus (UBS) and Peter Hahn of the Cass Business School argued in favour of full nationalisation, though all were clear that this should be a strictly time limited measure.

Ranged against these voices were four sources who argued against full nationalisation: Alistair Darling, Stephen Timms, Tim Congdon and Howard Davies. Congdon, an economist and subsequently failed UKIP parliamentary candidate, took a particularly strong line arguing that the part-nationalised banks were 'not bust' when they were bailed out and that the 'government has effectively been stealing from them' (*Today programme*, 21 January 2009).

The need for further bailouts and the emergence of a series of high profile sources suggesting full nationalisation should be considered, appeared to widen the range of discussion in interviews. Whilst in October 2008 the option of full nationalisation was not put to the chancellor, three months later it had become a live topic of debate:

Journalist:	[talks about the extra shareholding being taken on by taxpayer] Why not just nationalise it what's the difference?
Alistair Darling:	What we've announced today is an increase in shareholding and I think...
Journalist:	To 70%
Alistair Darling:	And I think that's essential but I said it on the 8th of October, on the 13th of October I said in the long term I don't believe governments ought to be running banks.
Journalist:	Why?
Alistair Darling:	Well because in the long term I think they're better in the private sector.
Journalist:	Really? What the private sector has made such a great job of it we can trust them you mean? (*Today programme*, 19 January 2009)

It is important not to overstate the significance of this shift. There was only one intervention in favour of permanent nationalisation and this was from a brief on the street conversation with Arthur Scargill—who is unlikely to be have been seen as a particularly credible source (*Today programme*, 2 April 2009). Furthermore, those arguing in favour of temporary nationalisation were clear that this was a last resort and that governments shouldn't normally have any role in banking. As Peter Hahn put it—'it's very undesirable I teach in a business school and I don't want government ownership' but unless they deal with their 'legacy loans' they won't be able to operate as 'viable institutions' (*Today programme*, 24 February 2009).

Reforms to the Sector?

In this sample period, debates over long-term reforms to the sector came much more to the fore. However as can be seen in Table 2.7 the issue of bank bonuses continued to be the most frequently discussed issue in coverage. The most important reasons for this were the *Today programme*'s focus on the Treasury Committee's investigation into remuneration and the fact that agenda setters such as politicians and newspapers continued to highlight the issue. What is also clear from Table 2.7 is that there was significant variation in the level of contestation around different reforms. For instance, issues such as restricting bonuses, increasing capital ratios and improving corporate governance were supported by all—or almost all

Table 2.7   Reform proposals (1 January –31 July 2009)

Reform	Number of segments	Interviewees in favour	Interviewees against
Restrict bonuses	18	9	0
Break up Banks	12	5	3
Separate Retail from Investment Banking	11	2	5
Increase capital ratios	7	5	0
Better corporate governance/ More executive oversight	7	4	0
More power to BOE/Reform tripartite system	6	4	0
Tougher regulation (unspecified)	5	5	0
Introduce macroprudential regulation	4	2	1
Bring OTC Derivative trading onto exchanges	4	2	2
Tighter liquidity controls between assets and liabilities	2	2	0
More shareholder activism/ oversight	2	1	0
More regulation of shadow banking sector	1	1	0
Reduce complexity	1	1	0
Abolish 'usury'	1	1	0
Reduce 'global imbalances'	1	1	0
Crackdown on tax havens	1	1	1
Introduce democratic control of money creation	1	2	0
Tighter regulation of hedge funds	1	0	1
Limit bank's proprietary trading	1	1	0
Controls on issuance of consumer credit	1	0	0
Better morality/values in banking	1	1	0
Reintroduce General Provisions	1	1	0

interviewees. In contrast, many of the proposals which were opposed by the City, such as cracking down on tax havens and hedge funds, regulating derivatives, or major structural reforms to the sector—such as separating investment from retail banking—were more likely to feature opposing speakers. This does not of course mean that arguments in favour of these reforms weren't covered. Proposals to break up the banks was supported on five occasions—mainly by Vince Cable who emerged as the major advocate of structural reform—and only opposed in three instances by Angela Knight and the head of HSBC Stephen Green.

Disquiet over government unwillingness to consider far-reaching structural changes to the sector was also at times channelled by journalists. For instance, when the Government White Paper on banking was released in July 2009 one journalist commented:

> Certainly there will be lots of critics of the previous regulatory regime who will say that the government simply isn't going far enough, that it is being far too timid and perhaps putting too much faith in the ability of a better generation of regulators to do their job rather than taking more radical action in a structural sense to make the banks safer again. (*Today programme*, 8 July 2009)

One proposal that was floated—and which has gained more traction in the intervening period through the creation of the Positive Money pressure group (Boait 2016) —was the argument that it should be the state rather than banks who are entrusted with the creation of credit:

> Peter Selby (Former Bishop of Worcester): We've really delegated to the banks the job of producing money so you have a situation where the government had to beg, beseech, bribe bankers to inject money into the economy rather than doing it itself as the democratically elected authority based on the people's values. (*Today programme*, 3 February 2009)

However such ideas remained peripheral in coverage and at the time lacked credible advocates. Another significant issue that remained relatively peripheral was the question of whether the City grandees who had put in charge of UKFI could be trusted to run the part-nationalised banks in the national interest. This issue was raised on a single occasion by the Labour MP Michael Meacher:

> What we shouldn't be doing when the state does own a majority of the equity is then outsourcing those assets to the very bankers who caused the problem in the first place. I mean that's exactly what we are doing with the UK Financial Investments at the present time where the original chair appointed was a US investment banker who had sat for years on a Lichtenstein trust that allegedly had extensive links to the tax haven

activity. We need a very different kind of model in banking and that requires strong regulation but holding to account those who've acted recklessly and with such disastrous consequences for the country. (*Today programme*, 27 March 2009)

With much sourcing drawn from City voices or politicians who had been amongst the strongest advocates of light touch regulation it is unsurprising that such perspectives were featured so rarely. The strong representation of sources supportive of City interests meant that other issues—such as the revolving door between politics and the world of finance which some argued led to 'regulatory capture' (Warwick Commission 2009; Miller and Dinan 2009)—were never mentioned. The preponderance of sources supportive of City interests also partly explains why the kinds of structural arguments put forward by Will Hutton—that having a large finance sector can damage other parts of the economy—were again absent, whilst the counter-argument that the City was a crucial economic asset was again repeatedly featured:

Angela Knight (British Banker's Association):	Some banks got into difficulties, some did not and the more we blanket right across the piece as if all our banks have made big mistakes, which they haven't, the more we jeopardise the UK's reputation as an international financial centre which is a big money earner for this country and a big employer. (*Today programme*, 1 May 2009)
Angela Knight (British Banker's Association):	I'd be very concerned if we started to break up some of the banks that are successful. We have got two banks in real problems obviously RBS and Northern Rock in particular and there's going to be some changes particularly we're starting to see them with RBS but if we say the big banks that are successful can't continue then not only will we jeopardise the ability of the UK to finance its own economy but we'll also particularly jeopardise what we've got here in London which is one of the largest financial centres in the world. It's been a huge money earner and still is a huge money earner for Britain and we need to manage them properly that's the key. (*Today programme*, 9 April 2009)

Richard Lambert (Director of CBI):	The financial services sector is really important to the UK's economy. It's an area of comparative advantage. It's not a popular place now and it's not a place that politicians are prepared to go to the mat to defend so it is an anxiety. (*Today programme*, 12 June 2009)
Fraser Nelson (Journalist):	What you shouldn't do is start to go back and tax bonuses years ago like Michael Meacher wants to do. That's the fastest way of getting these golden geese to fly away to Singapore or Tokyo. We need them to stay here and rebuild our economy...we've got one of the best banking systems in the world. There's very few industries where Britain has a larger comparative advantage than it does in banking. We attract the best talent from all the planet to come to London and we can't afford to sacrifice that...we need better regulation that can be done quite easily but if we come down too hard on these masters of the universe there are other parts of the universe they can go to. (*Today programme*, 27 March 2009)

At times journalists themselves endorsed such arguments:

Journalist: But Angela Knight is of course absolutely right. However, understandably angry people feel about the scale of the bailout from taxpayers for the banking system we do rely on the City of London for a big proportion of our economic output and it would be a bit of a problem for the UK if in a fit of pique we smashed that industry to smithereens so we do have to somehow have to get some kind of reconciliation with the people who caused this mess. We can't do without them. (*Today programme*, 1 May 2009)

At other points when 'radical' reforms were proposed journalists injected into debate the views of the City that these are problematic because they may harm 'innovation':

Vince Cable: President Obama came out with his own proposals for over hauling what is going on in the United States which are much more radical than what we are doing here. Obama for example explained that the Americans are now moving on these rather dangerous products these so called Credit Default Swaps these derivatives which at the moment don't have a proper market a proper clearing house where they can be regulated and the potential explosion that could arise from that could cause great damage to the system and that's not being addressed.

Journalist: If you took the sort of radical steps that by the sound of it you support the damage to the City could be very grave couldn't it? Its reputation as a financial centre, its ability to be innovative about investment? (*Today programme*, 17 June 2009)

City sources have every right to argue their corner and journalists are correct to note that financial services have become a significant part of the economy and the tax base. However, the counter-argument—that a very large financial sector can damage other parts of the economy—did not appear, raising once again questions about balance and impartiality.

The discussion of reform in the third banking sample was more extensive and had more of a cutting edge than that which appeared during October 2008. Some of the more radical ideas like breaking up the banks or introducing a British version of Glass-Steagall did get an airing. Vince Cable, in particular, emerged as the key voice arguing for structural reform. However, other significant issues such as the regulation of derivatives, the role of tax havens, and the problems of 'regulatory capture' received little or no attention in comparison to the extensive coverage given to the largely symbolic issue of Fred Godwin's pension pot. Furthermore, there were no journalists or sources asking difficult questions about a banking system where the overwhelming bulk of bank lending funds commercial and real estate purchases with only 3% going to companies involved in the production of goods and services (Kay 2015). In this sense reporting on the *Today programme* with its narrow range of largely insider voices mostly focused the debate on what could be done to shore up the current system, rather than ask questions about the role of the banks in Britain's increasingly financialised economy.

The Post-Crisis Politics of Regulatory Closure

The brief period during 2008 when the banking crash had put the activities of the finance sector under the media spotlight offered an opportunity to raise critical questions about regulation and the sector's impact on the rest of the economy. For the first time in many years financial actors were forced to step outside the closed elite-actor networks that characterised the secretive world of regulation and lobbying to argue their case in front of mass publics. However, as the analysis in this chapter has demonstrated, although individual bankers were held up to public scorn and ridicule, discussion of major systemic reform was relatively infrequent.

If the period from the end of 2008 through 2009 offered at least the possibility to harness public anger to a process of major reform the period since has seen debates over the re-regulation of the sector slip subsumed—as Polly Toynbee warned—within the closed world of elite political-financial networks. As Engelen et al. (2011: 168) note, although the crisis set off a series of turf wars between different elements of the tripartite regime it did not mean that financial elites lost their power to shape the regulatory framework:

> It [the crisis] did not democratize financial politics or disempower finan-cial elites. Individuals like Fuld and Goodwin may have been scapegoated, but the broader group of senior bankers and other financiers was not excluded from the process of reform. Because of the high specialised (and seemingly impenetrable) world of financial instruments and markets, some industry insiders were co-opted into the process of sorting out the mess and the rest could insert themselves into the process through lobby-ing. Thus the paradoxical outcome of the crisis has been bickering between different elite groups with different reform agendas overshad-owed by the successful regrouping by financial elites who lobbied to water down reform measures, and organised into distributional coalitions which told stories that encouraged a process of regulatory closure. (Engelen et al. 2011: 168)

The ability of financial elites to influence the regulatory response could be seen in two areas. One involved the production of key documents such as the Wigley and Bischoff reports and the 2009 White Paper (HM Treasury 2009; Engelen et al. 2011). The group which produced the Wigley and Bischoff reports was dominated by City grandees with almost no represen-tation from civil society, politicians or academic economists (Engelen et al. 2011: 181). The reports reproduced the same framing devices about the vital contribution that finance made to the economy that were heard on the *Today programme* and these arguments were then 'simply copied out and dropped into the text of the White Paper' which—like the 2010 Bank

Act—avoided far-reaching reforms such as the break-up of large banks (Engelen et al. 2011: 180).

The second way that financial elites shaped the regulatory response was through control of the newly part-nationalised banks. Public stakes in banks such as Northern Rock, RBS and Lloyds TSB offered the opportunity for elected politicians to influence lending decisions and executive remuneration. However, the Treasury, though the creation of the United Kingdom Financial Investments (UKFI), the holding company established to manage the government's stakes in the banks, succeeded in insulating the part-nationalised institutions from democratic control (Froud et al. 2010). The Treasury put UKFI under the control of a collection of leading City figures who re-instituted the arguments about the benefits of 'arms length control' and the centrality of 'shareholder value' in maximising returns to the taxpayer. The banks were to be returned to the private sector as soon as their share price allowed, in effect delimiting the role of UKFI to that of an 'active institutional investor' seeking to 'extract every last copper of value for the taxpayer as shareholder' (Froud et al. 2010: 34).

CONCLUSION: A MISSED OPPORTUNITY TO EXAMINE BRITAIN'S DYSFUNCTIONAL POLITICAL ECONOMY

Major crises potentially offer opportunities to see problems anew and formulate fresh responses. The collapse of the banking sector in 2008 revealed that deregulated financial markets were not stable, self-correcting and hyper-rational, nor that—in the words of the Nobel prize winning economist Robert Lucas—macroeconomics had solved 'the central problem of depression-prevention' (cited in Posner 2009). The crisis also revealed that New Labour's model of a service based economy centred on finance and debt fuelled growth had been at best unsustainable, and at worst no more than a 'fantasy' (Elliott and Atkinson 2007; Engelen et al. 2011). Yet a decade on from the crash the financial sector has largely escaped major systemic reform (e.g. Luyendijk 2015; Dolphin 2013) and remains vulnerable to a repeat of the crisis (Stone 2015; Spicer et al. 2016; Chu 2017). Furthermore, as a recent report from the IPPR (2017) found, key structural weaknesses in the economy that are intimately tied to financialisation—including weak productivity and manufacturing, a heavily indebted household sector, and a finance system more attuned to asset inflation and short-term extraction of shareholder value than long-term productive investment—have, if anything, got worse. This chapter has found during that the critical period in 2008 and 2009 when much of the banking system was taken into public ownership, the media rarely questioned the problematic relationship between financial services and Britain's broader political economy or advocated major democratic reforms to the banks. Instead many media accounts told a pared back story focused on 'greedy' bankers and the need to restrict their bonuses. The media thus functioned to channel the very real public anger than existed at the time into largely symbolic issues—like restricting Fred Goodwin's pension pot—whilst leaving the deep structural faults in the banking system and Britain financialised economy, largely unexamined.

NOTES

1. 'Zombie' banks are institutions which are weighed down by bad debts and therefore unable to provide credit to the wider economy. This sharp curtailment in the credit available to businesses and households can lead, as in the Japanese case, to a period of prolonged recession or stagnation.
2. Out of the seven months of coverage there were six days of coverage which could not be coded because the audio files were not available either from the BBC website or Box of Broadcasts. These were 1 January, 20 January, 26 February, 18 March, 7 May and 15 May.
3. See also Christensen et al. (2016).

REFERENCES

Andrianova, S., Demetriades, P., & Shortland, A. (2009). *Is Government Ownership of Banks Really Harmful to Growth?* (University of Leicester Discussion Paper in Economics 09/11). Available at: http://www.le.ac.uk/economics/research/RePEc/lec/leecon/dp09-11.pdf. Date Accessed 9 July 2018.

BBC. (2005, April 5). *BBC News Tops MPs Survey.* Available at: http://news.bbc.co.uk/newswatch/ukfs/hi/newsid_4440000/newsid_4444700/4444751.stm. Date Accessed 9 July 2018.

BBC. (2011). *RAJAR 2011 Quarter 2: Record Figures for Radio 4.* Available at: http://www.bbc.co.uk/pressoffice/pressreleases/stories/2011/08_august/04/rajar.shtml. Date Accessed 9 July 2018.

BBC. (2012). How Do Countries Run Their State Banks. Available at: http://www.bbc.co.uk/news/mobile/business-16789394. Accessed 9 July 2018.

Beattie, A. (2008, September 28). Washington's Waning Way: How Bail-Outs Poison a Free Market Recipe for the World. *Financial Times*.

Berry, M. (2013). The Today Programme and the Banking Crisis. *Journalism, 14*(2), 253–270.

Boait, F. (2016). Scrapping Cash: Don't Let the Banks Coin It. *Prospect*. Available at: http://www.prospectmagazine.co.uk/features/dont-let-the-banks-coin-it-cash-paper-currency-central-banks. Date Accessed 9 July 2018.

Brown, E. (2015). Why Public Banks Outperform Private Banks: Unfair Competition or a Better Mousetrap? *Huffington Post Blog*. Available at: https://www.huffingtonpost.com/ellen-brown/why-public-banks-outperfo_b_6654046.html

Buiter, W. (2009a, January 16). Time to Take the Banks into Full Public Ownership. *Financial Times Blog*. Available at: http://blogs.ft.com/maverecon/2009/01/time-to-take-the-banks-into-full-public-ownership/. Date Accessed 9 July 2018.

Buiter, W. (2009b). Too Big to Fail Is Too Big. *Financial Times Maverecon Blog*. Available at: http://blogs.ft.com/maverecon/2009/06/too-big-to-fail-is-too-big/#axzz4MJ7e5atZ. Date Accessed 9 July 2018.

Chang, H. J. (2008, October 22). Bretton Woods II with Caveats. *The Guardian*.

Christensen, J., Shaxson, N., & Wigan, D. (2016). The Finance Curse: Britain and the World Economy. *The British Journal of Politics and International Relations, 18*(1), 255–269.

Chu, B. (2017, November 28). Don't Be Fooled into Thinking That the UK Banking Sector Is Safe in the Face of Brexit. *Independent*. Available at: http://www.independent.co.uk/voices/uk-banks-brexit-stress-test-not-as-safe-as-they-make-out-a8080626.html. Date Accessed 9 July 2018.

Dolphin. (2013). *Don't Bank on It: The Financialisation of the UK Economy*. Available at: https://www.ippr.org/publications/dont-bank-on-it-the-financialisation-of-the-uk-economy. Date Accessed 9 July 2018.

Doyle, G. (2006). Financial News Journalism: A Post-Enron Analysis of Approaches Towards Economic and Financial News Production in the UK. *Journalism, 7*(4), 433–452.

Economist. (2009). *Efficiency and Beyond*. Available at: http://www.economist.com/node/14030296. Date Accessed 9 July 2018.

Eichengreen, B. (2008, October 23). New World Pragmatism. *The Guardian*.

Elliott, L., & Atkinson, D. (2007). *Fantasy Island*. London: Constable.

Elliott, L., Hines, C., Juniper, J., Leggett, A., Lucas, C., Murphy, R., Pettifor, A., Secrett, C., & Sims, A. (2008). *A Green New Deal* (The First Report of the Green New Deal Group). Available at: http://b.3cdn.net/nefoundation/8f737ea195fe56db2f_xbm6ihwb1.pdf

Engelen, E., Eturk, I., Froud, J., Johal, S., Leaver, A., Moran, M., Nilsson, A., & Williams, K. (2011). *After the Great Complacence*. Oxford: Oxford University Press.

Entman, R. B. (1993). Framing: Toward Clarification of a Fractured Paradigm. *Journal of Communication, 43*, 51–58.

Evans-Pritchard, A. (2009, February 2). Let Banks Fail, Says Nobel Economist Joseph Stiglitz. *Daily Telegraph*. Available at: http://www.telegraph.co.uk/finance/newsbysector/banksandfinance/4424418/Let-banks-fail-says-Nobel-economist-Joseph-Stiglitz.html. Accessed 9 July 2018.

Financial Services Authority. (2009, March). *A Regulatory Response to the Global Financial Crisis* (Discussion Paper 09/2). Available at: http://www.fsa.gov.uk/pubs/discussion/dp09_02.pdf. Accessed 9 July 2018.

Fishman, M. (1980). *Manufacturing the News*. Austin: University of Texas Press.

Foley, S. (2008, July 22). How Goldman Sachs Took Over the World. *Independent*.

Froud, J., Moran, M., Nilsson, A., & Williams, K. (2010). Wasting a Crisis? Democracy and Markets in Britain After 2007. *The Political Quarterly, 81*, 25–38.

Glasgow Media Group. (1976). *Bad News*. London: Routledge and Kegan Paul.

Glasgow Media Group. (1980). *More Bad News*. London: Routledge and Kegan Paul.

Glasgow Media Group. (1982). *Really Bad News*. London: Routledge and Kegan Paul.

Glyn, A. (2007). *Capitalism Unleashed*. Oxford: Oxford University Press.

Golding, P., & Middleton, S. (1983). *Images of Welfare: Press and Public Attitude to Poverty*. London: Blackwell.

Harvey, J. T. (2012, February 6). How Economists Contributed to the Financial Crisis. *Forbes*. Available at: https://www.forbes.com/sites/johntharvey/2012/02/06/economics-crisis/#418d22c23b30. Accessed 9 July 2018.

HM Treasury. (2009). *Reforming Financial Markets. CM7667*. London: The Stationary Office.

House of Commons Treasury Committee. (2009). *Banking Crisis: Dealing with the Failure of the UK Banks*. Available at: https://www.publications.parliament.uk/pa/cm200809/cmselect/cmtreasy/416/416.pdf. Accessed 9 July 2018.

Hunt, J. P. (2008). Credit Rating Agencies and the 'Worldwide Credit Crisis': The Limits of Reputation, the Insufficiency of Reform, and a Proposal for Improvement. *Columbia Business Law Review, 2009*(1). Available at: https://papers.ssrn.com/sol3/papers.cfm?abstract_id=1267625. Accessed 9 July 2018.

Hutton, W. (1996). *The State We're In: Why Britain Is in Crisis and How to Overcome It*. London: Vintage.

Institute for Public Policy. (2017). *Time for Change: A New Vision for the British Economy* (The Interim Report of the IPPR Commission on Economic Justice). Available at: https://www.ippr.org/files/2017-09/1505830437_cej-interim-report-170919.pdf. Accessed 9 July 2018.

Iyengar, S. (1991). *Is Anyone Responsible? How Television Frames Political Issues.* Chicago: University of Chicago Press.

Jones, C., & Masters, B. (2011, December 22). Research Suggests Ways to Avoid Financial Crises: FSA and Bank of England Surveyed Range of Global Strategies. *Financial Times.* Available at: https://www.ft.com/content/14349542-2b04-11e1-8a38-00144feabdc0. Accessed 9 July 2018.

Jones, S. (2009, January 19). RBS et mon droit: HM deficits. *Financial Times.* Available at http://ftalphaville.ft.com/2009/01/19/51341/rbs-et-mon-droit-hm-deficits/. Accessed 9 July 2018.

Kay, J. (2015). *Other People's Money: Masters of the Universe or Servants of the People.* London: Profile Books.

Keen, S. (2017). *Can We Avoid Another Financial Crisis?* London: Polity.

Koenig, P. (2008, September 27). Financial Crisis: Light Touch Regulation Failed to Control the Markets. *Daily Telegraph.* Available at: http://www.telegraph.co.uk/finance/financialcrisis/3093523/Financial-crisis-Light-touch-regulation-failed-to-control-the-markets.html. Accessed 9 July 2018.

Krugman, P. (2008, September 28). The Good, the Bad, and the Ugly. *New York Times.* Available at: http://krugman.blogs.nytimes.com/2008/09/28/the-good-the-bad-and-the-ugly/?_r=0. Accessed 9 July 2018.

Kumhof, M., & Rancière, R. (2010). *Inequality, Leverage and Crises* (IMF Working Paper WP/10/268). Available at: https://www.imf.org/external/pubs/ft/wp/2010/wp10268.pdf. Accessed 9 July 2018.

Lewis, J. M. W. (2004). Television, Public Opinion and the War in Iraq: The Case of Britain. *International Journal of Public Opinion Research, 16*(3), 295–310.

Lewis, J. M. W. (2008). The Role of the Media in Boosting Military Spending. *Media, War and Conflict, 1*(1), 108–117.

Lewis, J. M. W., & Hunt, J. R. (2011). Press Coverage of the UK Military Budget: 1987 to 2009. *Media, War and Conflict, 4*(2), 162–184.

Lilico, A (2009). *What Killed Capitalism? The Crisis: What Caused It and How to Respond.* Centre for Policy Studies. Available at: https://www.cps.org.uk/files/reports/original/111027112605-20090313EconomyWhatKilledCapitalism.pdf. Accessed 9 July 2018.

Luyendijk, J. (2015, September 30). How the Banks Ignored the Lessons of the Crash. *The Guardian.* Available from: https://www.theguardian.com/business/2015/sep/30/how-the-banks-ignored-lessons-of-crash. Accessed 16 Oct 2018.

McDonnell, J. (2008, October 13). Turning a Crisis into an Opportunity. *Guardian.* Available at: https://www.theguardian.com/commentisfree/2008/oct/13/economy-banking. Accessed 9 July 2018.

Miller, D., & Dinan, W. (2009, May 4–5). *Revolving Doors, Accountability and Transparency – Emerging Regulatory Concerns and Policy Solutions in the Financial Crisis, (GOV-PGC-ETH-2009-2).* Paper prepared for the OECD and the Dutch National Integrity Office organized Global Forum on Public

Governance 'Building a Cleaner World: Tools and Good Practices for Fostering a Culture of Integrity', Paris.

Miller, D., Kitzinger, J., & Berrell, H. (1998). *The Circuit of Mass Communication: Media Strategies, Representation and Audience Reception in the AIDS Crisis.* London: Sage.

Murphy, R. (2008, October 4). Light in the Dark Corners. *The Guardian.*

Neate, R. (2011, August 22). Ratings Agencies Suffer 'Conflict of Interest', Says Former Moody's Boss. *Guardian.* Available at: https://www.theguardian.com/business/2011/aug/22/ratings-agencies-conflict-of-interest. Accessed 9 July 2018.

Orrell, D. (2010). *Economyths: How the Science of Complex Systems Is Transforming Economic Thought.* London: Icon Books.

Peston, R. (2008). Paradox of Bank Bailout. Available at: http://www.bbc.co.uk/blogs/thereporters/robertpeston/2008/11/paradox_of_bank_bailout.htm. Accessed 16 Oct 2018.

Pettifor, A. (2006). *The Coming First World Debt Crisis.* London: Palgrave Macmillan.

Pettifor A (2016). *Brexit and Its Consequences.* Available at: http://www.primeeconomics.org/articles/brexit-and-its-consequences. Accessed 9 July 2018.

Philo, G. (1999). *Message Received.* London: Longman.

Philo, G., & Berry, M. (2004). *Bad News from Israel.* London: Pluto.

Philo, G., & Berry, M. (2011). *More Bad News from Israel.* London: Pluto.

Philo, G., Briant, E., & Donald, P. (2013). *Bad News for Refugees.* London: Pluto.

Posner, R. A. (2009, August 9). Economists on the Defensive – Robert Lucas. *The Atlantic.* Available at: https://www.theatlantic.com/business/archive/2009/08/economists-on-the-defensive-robert-lucas/22979/. Accessed 9 July 2018.

Pym, H. (2014). *Inside the Banking Crisis.* London: Bloomsbury Press.

Robinson, J. (2008, November 9). Shy, But the Mail's Powerful Editor Is Far from Retiring. *Observer.*

Roubani, N. (2008). The Shadow Banking System Is Unravelling. *Economonitor.* Available at: http://www.economonitor.com/nouriel/2008/09/21/the-shadow-banking-system-is-unravelling-roubini-column-in-the-financial-times-such-demise-confirmed-by-morgan-and-goldman-now-being-converted-into-banks/. Accessed 9 July 2018.

Sachs, J. (2008, October 21). Amid the Rubble of Global Finance, A Blueprint for Bretton Woods II. *Guardian.* Available at: https://www.theguardian.com/commentisfree/2008/oct/21/globaleconomy-g8. Accessed 9 July 2018.

Semetko, H. (1996). Political Balance on Television – Campaigns in the United States, Britain, and Germany. *The International Journal of Press/Politics, 1*(1), 51–71.

Sikka, P. (2009). Financial Crisis and the Silence of the Auditors. *Accounting, Organizations and Society, 34*(6–7), 868–873.

Skidelsky, R. (2014). *Post Crash Economics.* Available at: https://www.project-syndicate.org/commentary/robert-skidelsky-knocks-the-scientific-halo-off-mainstream-economists%2D%2Dteaching-and-research?barrier=accessreg. Accessed 10 July 2018.

Smaghi, L. B. (2010, April 15). *Has the Financial Sector Grown Too Big?* Speech at the Nomura Seminar, The Paradigm Shift After the Financial Crisis, Kyoto. Available at: https://www.ecb.europa.eu/press/key/date/2010/html/sp100415.en.html. Accessed 10 July 2018.

Smith, Y. (2010). *ECONned: How Unenlightened Self Interest Undermined Democracy and Corrupted Capitalism.* London: Griffin.

Spicer, A., Lindley, D., Gond, J., Mosonyi, S., Jaser, Z., Marti, E., Petersen, H., & Edwards A. (2016). *Cultural Change in the FCA, PRA & Bank of England: Practising What They Preach?* Available at: https://newcityagenda.co.uk/wp-content/uploads/2016/10/NCA-Cultural-change-in-regulators-report_embargoed.pdf. Accessed 10 July 2018.

Stephens, P. (2009, January 19). Shoot the Bankers, Nationalise the Banks. *Financial Times.* Available at: https://www.ft.com/content/a35c925c-e65f-11dd-8e4f-0000779fd2ac. Accessed 10 July 2018.

Stiglitz, J. (2006, October 3). How to Fix the Global Economy. *New York Times.* Available at: http://www.nytimes.com/2006/10/03/opinion/03stiglitz.html. Accessed 10 July 2018.

Stiglitz, J. (2008, October 22). A Crisis of Confidence. *Guardian.*

Stiglitz, J. (2010, January 3). 'Economists to Blame for GFC', Says Joseph Stiglitz. *Herald Sun.* Available at: http://www.heraldsun.com.au/finance/economists-to-blame-for-gfc-says-joseph-stiglitz/news-story/a35b84c2749dc00b-4be88b6069012c0c. Accessed 10 July 2018.

Stone, J. (2015, March 9). Government Doomed to Repeat the Mistakes That Caused the 2007 Banking Crisis, MPs Say. *Independent.* Available at: http://www.independent.co.uk/news/uk/politics/government-doomed-to-repeat-the-mistakes-that-caused-the-2007-banking-crisis-mps-say-10095376.html. Accessed 10 July 2018.

Tasch, B. (2015, July 15). The 17 Safest Banks in the World. *Business Insider UK.* Available at: http://uk.businessinsider.com/worlds-safest-banks-2015-7/#17-national-australia-bank-1. Accessed 10 July 2018.

Tuchman, G. (1972). Objectivity as Strategic Ritual: An Examination of Newsmen's Notions of Objectivity. *American Journal of Sociology, 77*(4), 660–679.

Turner, G. (2008). *The Credit Crunch: Housing Bubbles, Globalisation and the Worldwide Economic Crisis.* London: Pluto Press.

Turner, A. (2009, March). *The Turner Review: A Regulatory Response to the Global Banking Crisis.* Financial Services Authority. Available at: http://www.fsa.gov.uk/pubs/other/turner_review.pdf. Accessed 10 July 2018.

Turner, A. (2016). *Between Debt and the Devil: Money, Credit and Fixing Global Finance.* Princeton: Princeton University Press.

Utzig, S. (2010). *The Financial Crisis and the Regulation of Credit Rating Agencies: A European Banking Perspective* (ADBI Working Paper 188). Tokyo: Asian Development Bank Institute. Available at: https://www.adb.org/sites/default/files/publication/156043/adbi-wp188.pdf. Accessed 10 July 2018.

Wahl-Jorgensen, K., Sambrook, R., Berry, M., Moore, K., Bennett, L., Cable, J., Garcia-Blanco, I., Kidd, J., Dencik, L., & Hintz, A. (2013) *BBC Breadth of Opinion Review: Content Analysis*. Available at: http://downloads.bbc.co.uk/bbctrust/assets/files/pdf/our_work/breadth_opinion/content_analysis.pdf. Accessed 10 July 2018.

Warwick Commission. (2009). *The Warwick Commission on International Financial Reform: In Praise of Unlevel Playing Fields*. Warwick: University of Warwick. Available at: https://www2.warwick.ac.uk/research/warwickcommission/financialreform/report/uw_warcomm_intfinreform_09.pdf

Wilson, H., Aldrick, P., & Ahmed, K. (2011, May 6). Royal Bank of Scotland Investigation: The Full Story of How the 'World's Biggest Bank' Went Bust. *Telegraph*. Available at: http://www.telegraph.co.uk/finance/newsbysector/banksandfinance/8496654/Royal-Bank-of-Scotland-investigation-the-full-story-of-how-the-worlds-biggest-bank-went-bust.html. Accessed 10 July 2018.

Winnett, R. (2008, October 13). Financial Crisis: Gordon Brown Calls for 'New Bretton Woods'. *Daily Telegraph*. Available at: http://www.telegraph.co.uk/finance/financialcrisis/3189517/Financial-Crisis-Gordon-Brown-calls-for-new-Bretton-Woods.html. Accessed 10 July 2018.

CHAPTER 3

The Banking Crisis: Audience Studies

INTRODUCTION

This chapter explores what people believed and understood about the banking crisis and traces the source of audience beliefs. To do this the chapter draws on a series of focus group discussions conducted in Glasgow, Surrey and the Midlands over the summer of 2009. Since the workings of 'high finance' are quite remote from the lives of most people it was anticipated that the media would be important in establishing particular ways of making sense of the crisis (Ball-Rokeach and DeFleur 1976). However before discussing the audience data it is necessary to talk briefly about the vexed issue of media influence and how it can be assessed.

A BRIEF NOTE ON MEDIA INFLUENCE

The question of media influence remains a thorny and controversial issue because of the methodological difficulties in establishing impact. One way social scientists have attempted to gauge influence is by examining short-term direct effects on attitudes using experimental or survey methods. As McQuail (1977) notes, these kinds of studies have tended to find that media messages have little or no effect on what are often deep seated attitudes—though later research did point to attitudinal effects from some messages (e.g. Iyengar 1991). However, this methodological approach suffers from major weaknesses. One is the artificiality of the research situation and the fact that these studies only examine attitude change rather

© The Author(s) 2019   95
M. Berry, *The Media, the Public and the Great Financial Crisis*,
https://doi.org/10.1007/978-1-137-49973-8_3

than how media might establish patterns of knowledge or belief. Another is the short-term nature of exposure which bears little relationship to real life where people are subject to multiple overlapping information streams over many years.

The inherent difficulty in isolating the impact of individual messages has contributed to the development of a prominent strand of thinking in both academic and lay circles that the media have relatively little influence in comparison to other social, economic and political factors (e.g. Bennett and Iyengar 2008, 2010). Proponents of the 'minimalist influence thesis' (MIT) argue that media may reinforce but don't generally change opinions (Klapper 1968; Miller and Krosnick 2000; Newton 2006; Clarke 2012). People are seen to seek out news which fit their pre-existing views whilst filtering out information that contradicts cherished beliefs or opinions through processes of 'selective exposure' and 'confirmation bias'.

However, this begs the obvious question of where these pre-existing opinions came from in the first place—if not in part from prior media exposure, or other socialisation agents such as the family or education system—which are themselves constantly immersed in media flows. In a wide ranging review of the literature Gavin (2018) notes that the evidence for the claims of the MIT is thin. For instance, polling data shows that a large proportion of the population regularly consume newspapers that don't align with their own political views (Kellner 2015) and that many people could not even correctly identify the political leaning of their newspaper of choice (Ashcroft 2012). In addition, a significant body of both quantitative and qualitative research points to the existence of significant media effects.

One is agenda setting—the ability to influence what people think are the most important issues of the day (McCombs and Shaw 1972). This ability to put certain issues or policy options on the public agenda—whilst obscuring others—is widely recognised as a key 'face' of power (Bachrach and Baratz 1962; Lukes 1974). Longitudinal panel studies also find that consonant media messages—a feature of a number of reported issues in this book—can be effective at changing political opinions (De Vreese and Boomgarden 2006; Ladd and Lenz 2009; Feldman et al. 2012; Brandenburg and Van Egmond 2012).

However, the most significant impact of the media is not agenda setting or attitude change, but rather that it is part of a long-term process of cultural reproduction that provides audiences with the interpretative frameworks which allow them to understand social life and situate themselves within it. As McQuail notes:

> The media work most directly on consciousness by providing the constructed images of the world and of social life and the definitions of social reality. In effect, the audience member learns about his or her social world and about himself from the media presentation of society (given that most of the time this is not directly accessible). The media provide the materials for responding to experience and these accumulate over in a long-term process of socialisation. The effects of the media on the individual are not only indirect, they have happened long ago, certainly in the past (1977: 76 cited in Philo 1990: 5).

Such interpretative frameworks are created as part of a social and ideological struggle in which the mass media is a central site of contestation. For this reason it is important to analyse how particular debates and explanations are constructed in the media as well as how other social and political cultures—which themselves are interpenetrated and intersect with the media—may mediate them. As Philo notes such process are dynamic and in a contest state of flux:

> The cultures of any given moment are part of a social process in which beliefs are produced and contested in the conflict between groups and classes. The media are one site of this struggle to establish dominance of some ways of understanding. This is so whether the arguments relate to economic or political policy, such as on the role of strikes in the decline of the economy or whether they are about definitions of political action such as whether a 'terrorist' is to be called a 'guerilla' or a 'freedom fighter'. No one claims that exposure to a preferred media view will necessarily and instantly transform political allegiance. But it is crucial to study the manner in which such arguments are developed in media accounts and in audience beliefs to form strands of political cultures, and to analyse the processes by which they are overlaid by new information and different forms of experience (Philo 1990:7).

Qualitative research demonstrates that in some cases media influence can be so powerful it can overlay extensive personal experience. For instance, Philo's (1996) research on public attitudes towards mental illness found that a fifth of the participants in his focus groups—despite spending long periods in the company of mentally ill people who were never violent—

still felt afraid of them, citing media representations as the source of their fear. As one participant put it, 'it is not a very good attitude to have but it is the way things come across on TV, and films—you know, mental axe murderers and plays and things—the people I met weren't like that but that's what I associated them with them' (Philo 1996: 56). In a similar vein—but very different context—the pollster Deborah Mattinson (2010) found that in gauging whether New Labour's extra investment had improved the NHS, negative reporting caused people to discount their own experiences as 'an isolated lucky fluke':

> People were seeing the change with their own eyes as I had insisted they needed to. They were reporting them back to me as clear improvements. Yet they were not extrapolating this experience out to draw a wider conclusion about the improvements in the services they used. On the contrary, drawing on continuously negative news reports they believed their experiences to be not part of a bigger picture but an isolated lucky fluke…This was borne out by published polling too. Increasingly MORI were reporting a gap between perceptions of public services in a general sense and 'my' public services, so for the NHS satisfaction based on personal experience was 10 per cent ahead of satisfaction based on wider perceptions. Schools and transport produced similarly unhelpful gaps (Mattinson 2010: 120)

Reception processes are thus complex and mediated by a variety of both individual and social factors including knowledge, experience, logic, group membership and social values (Philo 1990, 1996; Philo and Berry 2004, 2011; Happer et al. 2012, Philo and Happer 2013). The challenge is to examine how these factors impact reception through close empirical research which seeks to establish what Lewis (2008) describes as the 'most plausible' explanations for relationships between media frames and patterns of audience belief, understanding and attitudes.

Audience Studies

Sample and Method

For the audience research both questionnaire and focus groups techniques were used. I moderated all 16 focus groups which involved between four and eight people. The groups were recruited on the basis on income, age and gender. So there were 14 groups of middle class or low income men and women (aged 20–65) plus two groups of senior citizens. This was a total of 75 people. A list of the groups is provided below. The focus groups were not intended to be a weighted representative sample from which precise probabilistic inferences about population characteristics could be drawn. Instead they provide qualitative data about patterns and structures of audience belief and understanding. Nevertheless where possible the findings from the focus groups have been linked to large scale polling data to put the results in a broader context. All of the groups were 'naturally occurring' in that they consisted of people who would regularly meet and speak with each other in the normal course of their lives. So, for instance, the groups were drawn from people who worked together as office workers, janitors, secretaries, or care assistants, whilst others were part of friendship groups or met for social activities such as pensioners who attended a forum.[1]

Participants in Focus Groups
1. Middle-class male and female residents, Coventry (four people)
2. Middle-class male and female residents, Coventry (four people)
3. Male and female senior citizens, Coventry (four people)
4. Middle-class male and female office workers, Warwickshire (five people)
5. Middle-class male and female office workers, Warwickshire (four people)
6. Low-income female care workers for disabled children, Surrey (four people)
7. Low-income female care workers for disabled children, Surrey (four people)
8. Low-income male janitors, Glasgow (five people)
9. Low-income male and female janitors and secretaries, Glasgow (five people)
10. Low-income males, residents, Glasgow (six people)
11. Low-income males, residents, Glasgow (five people)
12. Low-income males and females, residents, Glasgow (seven people)
13. Low-income males and females, residents, Glasgow (six people)
14. Low-income males and females, residents, Glasgow (five people)
15. Male and Female senior citizens, Glasgow (five people)
16. Male and Female senior citizens, Glasgow (six people)

Before commencing the focus group discussions participants completed brief questionnaires asking about how often they consumed different media products. The results indicated that television news was reported as a news source approximately twice as often as newspapers. Within television news the BBC mass audience bulletins (6 pm or 10 pm) were the most heavily accessed broadcasts closely followed by the ITV mass audience bulletins (6:30 pm or 10 pm). Both were also more significantly more likely to be reported as 'regular' as opposed to 'occasional' sources in comparison to other bulletins. The other key broadcast sources in descending order of popularity were Channel 4 News, Sky News, BBC News 24, Newsnight and Channel 5 News. Amongst newspaper outlets the most popular broadsheets in descending order were *The Times*, *Telegraph*, *Guardian*, *Independent* and *Financial Times*, whilst for the tabloids it was the *Daily Mail*, *Sun*, *Metro*, *Express*, *Star* and *Mirror*. Amongst the Scottish sample the *Daily Record* and to a lesser extent the *Glasgow Herald* were also key information sources. The readership of the sample thus broadly reflected the consumption habits of the UK population as a whole.

Who and What Caused the Banking Crisis?

The questionnaires also asked participants about their views about various aspects of the banking crisis. These included who they held responsible, whether they supported the bailout packages, if they had heard of the option of full nationalisation and whether they thought the problems in the finance sector had been resolved. These answers were then used as the starting point in discussions between the moderator and participants. In the written responses banks themselves were most commonly seen as being culpable for the crisis (44/56 respondents) followed by the government (18/56), the public (5/56), America (5/56), regulators (3/56), shareholders/investors (3/56) and Iceland (1/56).[2] The written responses therefore tend to match the range of culprits highlighted in media accounts whilst excluding those such as credit rating agencies, auditors, economists and central bankers who were largely absent from news reports. When the issue was discussed in the focus groups most participants saw three groups as being primarily responsible: the bankers (raised in all 16 groups), the government (cited in 14/16 groups) and the FSA (mentioned in nine/16 groups).

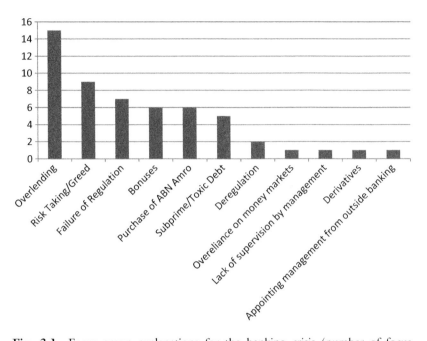

Fig. 3.1 Focus group explanations for the banking crisis (number of focus groups raising each explanation)

When it came to identifying what had caused the crisis responses again closely matched media accounts. Figure 3.1 provides data on the number of focus groups in which specific factors were cited. Issues that were mentioned regularly in the media such as greed/risk taking, lack of regulation and bonuses were the most commonly cited causes whilst issues which were more technical and had little media visibility—such as leverage or banks' over-reliance on the money markets—were mentioned rarely or not at all. Participants spoke of 'excessive greed' (Senior citizen group, Coventry) or 'super gambling on top of other gambling' (Low income group, Surrey). Such perceptions of banks were reinforced by participants' personal experiences. One spoke of how his bank had offered to amalgamate his debts but then found out that he was being charged 24 per cent. He commented that banks were just 'in it to cream you for the money' (Low income group, Surrey). It was also noticeable in that trying to make sense of the crisis participants drew on memories of previous financial scandals. Nick Leeson was spontaneously mentioned in five groups, whilst the case of Jérôme Kerviel was cited by one participant who commented that there 'should have been ringing bells because another guy in France did exactly the same thing three or four years ago' (Senior citizen group, Glasgow). On one occasion a participant cited the link, repeatedly made in some newspapers (see Chap. 2), that risk taking in the City had been ignored by Gordon Brown because his government had become reliant on the tax revenues it generated:

> The banks of course when they were making a lot of money we loved to call the banks greedy, but the consequence of that was that the Chancellor got a lot of taxes out of them and it was something like 23% of national income was coming from the financial sector, this is a big industry right and so the government in effect has allowed them to flourish because it allowed them to balance their books (Senior citizen group, Coventry)

However, by far the most regularly referenced issue was over-extension of credit which was raised in 15 out of the 16 focus groups. There appeared to be two key reasons for the dominance of this explanation. First, news coverage reflected strongly held social values about debt, thrift, responsibility and 'paying you way' (Stanley 2014, 2016). Second, media accounts resonated with people's own experiences or the experiences of friends and family. A number of participants mentioned Northern Rock's history of 'lending too much to people who were high risk' or offering 'dodgy mortgages', '125% mortgages' or 'self-certification mortgages'. As one person put it:

> It was Northern Rock this and Northern Rock that, they were just chucking it at people. That's what I think. They were giving it away like men with no arms without any kind of forward planning (Middle-class group, Warwickshire)

In another group a participant talked about her daughter who worked for a bank which gave people 'such big mortgages' that they were left with only '£10–£15' per week out of their housekeeping (Senior citizen group, Glasgow). Some participants argued that although the banks were mainly to blame 'society' was also partly to blame for agreeing to take on debts they couldn't afford:

[it was due to] irresponsible lending by Northern Rock and all the other banks and also our society. We welcomed all this so it can't just be seen as Northern Rock that did this…everyone knew they were taking debts beyond their means (Middle class group, Warwickshire)

Aside from mortgages a number of participants talked about the broader growth and visibility of unsecured lending. One spoke of the creation of a 'must have society' and commented:

Before all this happened how many applications for credit cards used to fall through your door? Credit, credit, credit, they tell you you're premium then you're gold and then you're this and you're that and before you know it you're up to here in it (Low income group, Glasgow)

In another group a senior citizen said that a 'plastic society' had been created with 'junk mail coming through the mail every day throwing money at you' (Glasgow low income). For this citizen who had grown up before the relaxation of lending regulations in the 1980s, there was concern that easy credit now meant that 'young people want everything now and they're not prepared to save for it'.

There was also evidence that knowledge of specific issues was clustered in certain geographical areas. Awareness of the problems created by the Royal Bank of Scotland's acquisition of ABN Amro was much more frequent in our Scottish focus groups (mentioned in five out of nine groups) as compared to the English groups (one out of seven) likely reflecting the higher visibility of this issue in the Scottish media and the fact that RBS is a major player in the Scottish economy.

However other core problems such as leverage or failures in auditing, risk management and credit rating were not mentioned by any participants whilst derivatives were mentioned briefly in a single group. The only individual to raise banks' overdependence on the wholesale money markets was an accountant with a specialist knowledge of finance, demonstrating that this issue did not form part of broader public understanding of the financial crisis:

For me it's a mismatch between their short term borrowing from the wholesale markets and their long term liabilities – lending out. So their offering of 100%, 125% mortgages exposed them to a lot of potential future bad debts but they are underwriting their loan book by short term borrowing and when the wholesale market dried up because of the liquidity situation then they couldn't underwrite their long term debts (Middle class group, Warwickshire)

In fact a number of participants spoke of their difficulties in understanding the crisis. In particular, participants struggled with the explanations and language used by journalists:

Respondent 1:   Sometimes when you are reading something in the media and you're not fully understanding it you kind of just gloss over it not gloss over it you kind of skim it but you're not fully understanding it and you are kind of getting a gist of what's going on but probably not understanding it.

Moderator: So you were very interested in watching it but sometimes you found that some of it went over your head.

Respondent 1:   Yeah.

Respondent 2:   Yes.

Respondent 3:   Yeah and maybe stuff that might be on now but at the time it all happened I was really I was listening to what they were saying but it did kind of go over your head.

Respondent 1:   Yeah.

Respondent 2:   It was quite technical and they would use all their jargon.
                 (Low income group, Glasgow)

And in another group:

Respondent 1:   Some of it was confusing but you got the gist of it but there were some things they were saying you would nae know unless you were really, really involved in it and you got the gist of what was happening right but some of the things that would come up on Sky news and that and they'd say something and you'd be like aye the banks are in trouble but anything they'd say did nae matter to you'd just hear the banks were in trouble what else they'd say for the past three minutes made absolutely nae sense.

Moderator: Ok so you'd understand they were in trouble but after that the explanations just made no sense. Is that right?

Respondent 1:   Yeah.

Respondent 2:   All you need to do is look at the three of those phrases [derivative, quantitative easing, credit default swaps].
                 (Low income group, Glasgow)

A participant in one group argued that a key problem was that the journalists assumed a level of background knowledge many people didn't possess and that what would really help would be if journalists provided more context and explanation:

> I have a bit of difficulty with the media and how they portray a lot of what's happening because they expect you to understand it and they don't actually get down to a level when you can actually understand what they are talking about. Because all you know is this banks in trouble it's got big debts and the governments going to bail it out end of story. They never go into the background – it's got big debts because this is what happened this is what they did and these are the decisions they made or anything like that. (Low income group, Glasgow)

One participant asked, 'Why don't the newspapers have a bit where they write definitions?' (Low income group, Surrey) whilst others had sought out other sources of information to help them understand the crisis. One said that she had read the novel 'City Boy' but found it 'very complicated' with much of it going 'over my head' (Low income group, Glasgow). Another highlighted the role of opinion leaders who could help them interpret the news. This individual said that a work colleague, who read the *Financial Times*, helped him understand television news. 'If that didn't happen it would go right over my head', he commented, but 'through discussion I got to understand the words on the television' (Low income group, Glasgow).

There was also a perception amongst some participants that the media, because of its reliance on financial sector sources, lacked a critical edge and this contributed to a broader sense that there was no real accountability for those who had caused the crisis:

> Respondent 1:   I mean the thing is the people in power, the likes of you have just said get their mates, the other experts in to start to try and rosy it all up whereas at the end of the day we're sitting there going 'wait a minute if that was me and I'd done my job like you'd done yours I'd be out the door'.
>
> Respondent 2:   Uh huh.
>
> Respondent 1:   Without a golden handshake, without anything I am out the door whereas you're sitting there getting all your wee pals in there just to rosy it all up – 'don't worry about it we'll get it all back' but whose paying it all back it's everybody. (Low income group, Glasgow)

Perceptions of the Bank Bailouts and Part-Nationalisations

Our participants' views on the bank bailouts were complex. On one level it appeared that people were split on whether they agreed with the rescue plans with 37 indicating support (in individual written responses) against 16 expressing opposition and three expressing no opinion. However when we discussed this issue in the focus groups most of those who had said they didn't like the bailouts thought that the government had 'no choice'. In our focus groups the great majority of participants made the argument, common across the media, that the government had no other option:

Moderator:	Did the government do the right thing in propping up these institutions when they got into financial difficulties?
Respondent 1:	I don't think they had any choice basically.
Respondent 2:	Yeah I'd agree with that.
Respondent 3:	I don't think they had any choice. They couldn't just walk away and let it all fold.
Respondent 1:	No, much as we might not like it. (Middle class group, Warwickshire)

This acceptance that there was no other option was held even when it was believed that the rescue plans had created a situation of moral hazard that made a repeat of the crisis likely:

Moderator:	Did the govt do the right thing in giving all these banks all this public money?
Respondent 1:	Yes.
Respondent 2:	Yeah probably.
Respondent 3:	There is no other way really was there?
Respondent 4:	They didn't have much choice I think but now they've done that the banks say in two or three years' time it's going to be forgotten you know and it'll just happen again.
Respondent 3:	Yeah.
Respondent 4:	I think they'll know now the government's always there to bail them out so what have they got to lose you know. I think that's the kind of culture they'll get into. Cos they know they've got that net to fall back on. (Low income group, Glasgow)

After ascertaining that most respondents saw the part-nationalisations as being the 'only option' the moderator then pointed out that the government could have fully nationalised the banks, without spending any money on shares whilst liquidating the shareholders. This provoked a surprised response amongst some groups who appeared unaware that other choices existed. Although there was a spectrum of views on the desirability of full nationalisation, reflecting large scale polling (Yougov 2008), there was a consensus that the media should have discussed alternative options. This was despite the fact that some participants expressed concern over losing money through their pension funds:

Respondent 1:   You see that was never really explained at the time. That they had that option [of full nationalisation].
Respondent 2:   Hmmm.
Respondent 1:   That they could have just waited a couple of weeks and got them for nothing?
Moderator: That's what they could have done.
Respondent 1:   Yeah.
Moderator: Should they [the media] have talked about that option?
Respondent 1:   Yes I think they should have possibly talked about that. If that option had been there to just take over the banks that would have cost us a lot less money.
Respondent 2:   But then the people would have lost all the money the shareholders, it wasn't just rich people who had shares in all the banks it was people like you, me and your pensions all the rest of it. It wasn't just rich people.
Respondent 1:   But then its cost us all that billions and billions of pounds anyway that's going to affect our share prices and pensions...That [option] was never explained at the time, if it had I'd have been all for it. (Low income group, Glasgow)

And in another group:

Moderator: What about the idea that they actually paid money for these bank shares but these banks were effectively.
Respondent 1:   Bust.
Moderator: They could just have taken them over and just taken them into public ownership.
Respondent 1:   Excellent idea.

Moderator:	Do you think that would have been a better idea rather than just saying we will pay this money for your shares?
Respondent 2:	You see the point is if you are a shareholder.
Moderator:	You would have got wiped out.
Respondent 1:	You'd have got wiped out but that's the risk you take. You see the problem with the banks and the bonuses it's great when the times are going good and you make the big bonuses its wonderful but you're not supposed to lose anything lose your job and pay your money back the point about shareholders if you invest in a share and it goes bust you've lost your money that's the way it's supposed to be.
Moderator:	Did you hear the option of just taking them into public ownership discussed in the media?
Respondent 1:	I think I did once or twice mentioned but very slightly.
Moderator:	Do you think it should have been discussed as an option?
Respondent 1:	Absolutely.
Respondent 2:	That was never one of the main options. It was always we've got no choice but to bail them out or people will be out of work and people are going to lose their money. (Middle class group, Warwickshire)

As stated previously there were a variety of views on fully nationalising the banks ranging from support to outright opposition. These appeared in part to be influenced by the overwhelmingly negative reporting of the option in the press and on television news. As one participant put it nationalisation was now a 'dirty word' (Middle class group, Coventry). Participants also picked up concerns in the media that nationalisation would create a 'stigma' which would make the banks more difficult to sell later or would weaken other banks who would see an outflow of deposits to nationalised institutions. However in most cases media influence was not straightforward. It wasn't simply a case that news accounts were accepted uncritically by audiences. Instead news reports on the desirability of full nationalisation were mediated by five factors.

First, there had been a collapse in public trust in politicians and government and this coloured participants' views of whether the government would run the banks well. The focus groups took place a few months after the MPs expenses scandal and this had had a highly negative impact on how participants viewed the political class. Our participants spoke of politicians as being 'rogues' who were 'more interested in filling their own back pockets than the country's back pockets' (Low income group,

Glasgow). Politicians were also seen as being in league with the super-rich and bankers. One participant stated that 'bankers and executives are all their mates' (Low income group, Glasgow). Another spoke of politicians 'being in the pockets of all these bankers' and argued:

> Who funds the parties? Businessmen fund the parties and who gives them huge consultancy fees, it was all these MPs expenses - thing came out, it was all the big firms paying huge amounts of money to these people for consultancy. And that is being in the pocket of and if these big organisations who are funding the parties they want to keep them sweet don't they? (Middle class group, Warwickshire)

Second, views of nationalisation were informed by negative perceptions of the competence and efficiency of the state sector and the history of previously nationalised industries. This appeared to be the result of both personal experience and information gleaned from the media. For instance one participant doubted nationalisation would be an improvement because government employees think 'they have a job for life' and 'don't have the same incentive to pull their finger out' (Senior citizens, Coventry). In another group participant spoke of previously nationalised industries as being 'poorly run' (Low income group, Glasgow). Some of these criticisms drew on 'anti-statist' narratives common in the press which focused on topics such as quangos (Deacon and Monk 2001):

Moderator:	So you think the govt would have done a worse job [in running the banks] than the private sector?
Respondent 1:	Definitely.
Respondent 2:	Oh yes they make a mess of everything else.
Respondent 3:	All these consultants they fleece them right, left and centre.
Respondent 1:	Quangos.
Respondent 2:	What did they ever achieve?
Respondent 1:	There are more people sitting on quangos in this country than there are in the armed forces. Yeah great. (Middle class group, Coventry)

Third, views on nationalisation were connected to the perceived failures of the private sector. This was true in relation to the banks themselves who had seen a catastrophic haemorrhaging of trust (Curtice and Park 2010). Anger about the behaviour of the banks was widespread in our focus groups over issues such as mis-selling, interest rates, account charges, greed and recklessness leading one participant to ask 'could the government do a worse job?' (Low income group, Glasgow). Concern over the private sector was also expressed in relation to the privatisation programmes of the 1980s which were not seen as being successful—particularly in areas such as rail and the utilities. This could sometimes lead participants to favour state ownership with one participant commenting that nationalisation 'makes people more responsible for it – look at the transport' (Low income group, Glasgow).

Fourth, for a few older participants attitudes towards public ownership were influenced by social democratic beliefs about the benefits of the mixed economy. One liked the idea of nationalisation because it 'spreads it amongst the people' (Low income group, Glasgow) whilst another spoke of the benefits of banks operating as quasi-utilities designed to meet the needs of industry:

> I believe in private industry and they should get all the help possible. I don't believe in, I believe in capitalism to a certain degree and I believe if there's a company down the road and he wants to go to the stock market fair enough. What I don't believe is it should be a bank or a water company. They should be there for the benefit of the people. The banks should be there for the benefit of the small company and for the company that is on the stock market. (Middle class group, Coventry)

Finally, for some participants arguments in favour of public ownership were simply unfamiliar. In one of our groups a participant commented that 'I did hear some talk of nationalisation but it's almost an unspoken word these days isn't it?' leading another participant to comment that 'I wonder if young people today would know what nationalisation was' (Middle class group, Warwickshire). There was a certain irony that in focus groups in both the Midlands and Glasgow participants spontaneously raised the issue of the decline of British manufacturing but didn't make the link to the banking sector and the absence of strategic funding. In one group a participant argued that Coventry used to be orientated to manufacturing and exports but now its biggest employers were the council and the NHS. This meant, he argued, that Coventry has 'hardly got a [manufacturing] base now and if you replicate that across the country and we are in a very bad position' (Senior citizen group, Coventry). In another group a participant said he was 'disturbed' that Britain was 'losing our expertise in manufacturing' and that being too reliant on the service sector made the country 'vulnerable'. The moderator then asked:

Moderator: So you don't think we can survive purely on services alone?
Respondent 1: No I don't think we can.
Respondent 2: Totally ludicrous.
Respondent 1: You have to diversify.
Respondent 2: Think of Germany and how well they do regardless.
                        (Middle class group, Warwickshire)

But in none of these groups did participants make the link that Will Hutton highlighted (see Chap. 2) between the dominance of the City and the decline in Britain's industrial base. When the moderator raised this issue with participants who had expressed deep concerns about the decline of manufacturing the link wasn't seen:

Moderator: But do you think as well though that because the City of
                        London has been allowed to flourish – do you see a rela-
                        tionship between that and manufacturing – does that dam-
                        age manufacturing if the City gets big?
Respondent 1: I don't see that.
Respondent 2: Not necessarily.
Respondent 1: When the financial sector gets into difficulties it hasn't got
                        capacity to loan out for manufacturing as a consequence
                        but when things are going well they've got money to lend.
                        (Senior citizen group, Coventry)

If, as we have seen, the press and broadcasting—which remain key information sources for most people—do not discuss how the dominance of the City can harm manufacturing through an inflated exchange rate or spurns productive investment in favour of real estate speculation, then it is not surprising that most people are unaware of such links. Media in this sense have the potential to play a powerful role in allowing people to make connections between the lived experience of deindustrialisation and regional polarisation, public policy and the operation of the banking system. However, as the content analysis demonstrates, apart from the occasional article in the *Guardian* such links were not made. Instead both the press and broadcasting predominately featured accounts that downgraded the potential role of public investment, and the *Today programme* in particular, with its heavy reliance on City voices, featured a number of sources who argued a large financial sector was a boon to Britain's economy. In this way, they sidelined alternative perspectives on how the banking sector could contribute towards a more diversified and productive economy. There is a certain irony in the fact that commentators now regularly talk of the need to 'rebalance the economy'—a view that accepts the over-reliance on the finance sector and its impacts on the broader economy—without ever really explaining how a very large financial services sector can damage the rest of the economy.

It was also the case that respondents didn't appear to be aware that running banks as public utilities is common in parts of Western Europe. It was noticeable that the only person to raise this issue in the focus groups was a German national whose discussion of how the state in her country offered low cost loans to poor families drew a surprised response from another member of her group:

Respondent 1:   Why doesn't this government straight away give people the loan for 0.5% so that the individual can profit by it? Why does it have to have the bank? Because in Germany we have this kind of thing when people don't have much money the country or the county lets them have the money at a very low interest rate so my friend who has three children and not very high income they could borrow I think about 100,000 euros at an interest rate of 0.5%.

Respondent 2:   Wow. (Low income group, Surrey)

The only area in which participants consistently saw public control as having a positive impact was in relation to restricting bonuses, an issue which, as we saw, had sustained media coverage. The disappearance of arguments in favour of an interventionist state were in large part the consequences of two processes. First, the decline in power and media visibility of civil society organisations, such as trade unions, who traditionally made the case for public ownership and control (Manning 1999; Wahl-Jorgensen et al. 2013). This has allowed even greater space for sources from business and particularly the finance sector who, as this chapter—and other research—demonstrate, now dominate discussion of economic and financial issues (Philo 1995; Duval 2005; Berry 2013, 2015, 2016; Rafter 2014). Second, the decision by Labour to embrace the free market. Crucially this removed the key voice who had argued in favour of state intervention in the post-war era.

Knowledge and Attitudes Towards Reform of the Banking Sector

In our focus groups participants were asked which policies they had heard of for reforming the banking sector in order to prevent a repeat of the crisis. In general knowledge of potential reforms to the banking system (Fig. 3.2) was low reflecting the paucity of debate in the media. Restricting bonuses, mentioned in 12 of 16 groups, were by far the most recognised policy and in seven out of 16 groups participants were unable to point to any policy aside from changing remuneration structures.

Unspecified calls for more regulation were mentioned in four groups with participants talking about the need for banks to be 'collared' although few could name any specific regulations that needed to be put in place. In general most participants struggled to name any policies to reform the system and the most informed account came once again from the accountant with a specialist knowledge of finance:

> You are looking at global coordination of strategy. A stronger financial regulator but how do you set that up? As I discussed before any good staff working for the regulator is going to be poached by the City so the regulator will always be playing catch up so in terms of regulating what the financial sector is doing. (Middle class group, Warwickshire)

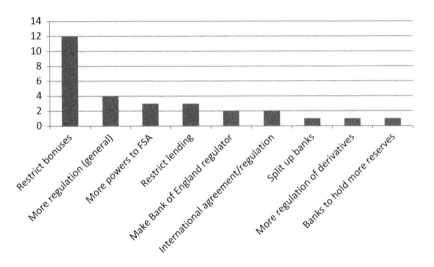

Fig. 3.2 Focus group reforms to the banking sector (number of focus groups mentioning each explanation)

Amongst almost all our participants there was a widespread perception that the crisis would happen again and little confidence that any of the main political parties would bring in the necessary reforms to prevent this happening:

Moderator: Has anybody heard of measures designed to prevent the crisis happening again?

Respondent 1:   No I haven't actually come to think of it.

Respondent 2:   Well no and that's why we all said in unison, didn't we? That it will happen again cos we don't really as though.

Respondent 3:   Anything has been done to alter.

Respondent 2:   learnt their lesson.

Moderator: You don't think they've learnt their lesson. Is that a widespread thing.

Respondent 1:   I think so.

Respondent 3:   Yeah. I mean we haven't heard anything to the contrary of that. (Senior citizens group, Coventry)

In another group a participant made the argument that rather than seeking to change the sector the government merely attempted to shore up the system without any meaningful reform:

You could say the government performed in a way to keep the markets as they are, working as they are and they have not changed. It has not changed anything fundamentally. They just went into the crisis they intervened and it has helped them now they [the banks] still owe the same, it could still happen the same again like that. They could do the same again. (Low income group, Surrey)

Although some participants said they weren't interested in news of the crisis this group was in the minority. More often people stated that they found news reports too difficult to understand or turned away from coverage because they felt they had no ability to influence what was happening. However a number of participants wanted more 'transparency' and discussion of how banks operate in order to prevent a reoccurrence of the crisis:

I think people now understand a lot more than they did about how banks behave because you just took them for granted. They did this and you put your money in and you could get a loan but what this disaster that has come upon us the fallout has meant that most people are more knowledgeable about how big business and banks work and I think we should and it should be more generally discussed so that people have a clearer understanding of what things are happening and then perhaps that would help to stop it if people are more knowledgeable about how they work. (Senior citizens group, Glasgow)

The audience findings reported here have been supported by the results of large scale polling conducted in 2011 and 2015 (Yougov 2015; Schifferes 2012). This found that audience interest in economic and business news reached 'unprecedented levels' following the crisis but that 'half the public feels it is not being well-informed by the media' (Schifferes 2012: 58). A key reason for this was the use of terminology with 'one in three people saying the news has too much economics jargon that they can't understand' (Schifferes 2012: 59). However the polling found that the 'biggest problem' concerned issues of public trust. Many felt that journalists were 'out of touch with how most people are affected by the crisis' whilst 'half the public' believed 'that business journalists are too close to their sources' and 'are not independent enough of the businesses they cover' (Schifferes 2012: 59).

CONCLUSION: MEDIA AND PUBLIC UNDERSTANDING OF THE BANKING CRISIS

The results of the focus group discussion reveal that when it came to understanding the crisis participants drew on knowledge of previous financial crises, personal experience, books, conversations with friends and family and—very occasionally—specialist occupational knowledge. However, it was also apparent that the working of the finance industry was to most people quite distant and esoteric. This meant—as was clear from people's discursive repertoires—that the mass media was a crucial information source. This could be seen, for instance, in the range of actors that participants saw as responsible and the factors they identified as being behind the crisis. Similarly the explanations for the crisis most frequently highlighted in news accounts were the same ones cited by members of our focus groups. This was especially so if media accounts coincided with their own personal experience or the experiences of family of friends. So by far the most cited explanation in our focus groups discussions was over lending by the banks—an account which was easily grasped but also chimed very strongly with their own experiences of being offered credit. Conversely explanations which appeared infrequently in press accounts—such as losses on derivatives or over-reliance on the money markets—were rarely mentioned by participants. In this sense, the media were effective in influencing the parameters of audience understanding.

The same patterns were also visible when participants were asked about their opinions on the banks bailouts. Almost all participants argued that the government had been left with 'no alternative' mirroring very closely the arguments in newspapers and broadcast news. When alternatives such as full nationalisation were raised, many people were unaware that this had been an option and felt that it should have been discussed in the media. When we drilled down deeper, it was clear that for most participants there was little awareness of arguments in favour of public banking—again reflecting the disappearance of such arguments from the media and wider public debate. Whilst numerous groups raised concerns about the decline of manufacturing none drew connections to the structure of the finance industry and its priorities. In this way, the press and broadcasting hindered the development of a broad public debate on how to address some of Britain's long-standing economic weaknesses.

In our discussion on possible long-term reforms to the sector the importance of the media was again clear. By far the most recalled reform was the issue which had dominated media coverage—restrictions on bonuses in the part-nationalised banks. Nearly half the focus groups couldn't name a single reform beyond this and the few additional responses reflected the issues which had been covered in press and broadcast news.

NOTES

1. For discussion on the advantages of using relatively homogenous focus groups who contain members who are already acquainted see Kitzinger (1994), Morgan (1997) or Krueger and Casey (2000).
2. The data from 19 of the questionnaires was lost in transit which means the discussion of written responses is based on 56 participants rather than the full 75 who took part in the focus group discussion.

REFERENCES

Ashcroft, M. (2012). *Which Party Does The Sun Support? Do Sun Readers Know?* Available at: http://lordashcroftpolls.com/2012/07/which-party-does-the-sun-support-do-sun-readers-know/. Accessed 9 July 2018.

Bachrach, P., & Baratz, M. (1962). Two Faces of Power. *American Political Science Review, 56*(4), 947–952.

Ball-Rokeach, S., & DeFleur, M. L. (1976). A Dependency Model of Mass-Media Effects. *Communication Research, 3*(1), 3–21.

Bennett, W. L., & Iyengar, S. (2008). A New Era of Minimal Effects? The Changing Foundations of Political Communication. *Journal of Communication, 58*(4), 707–731.

Bennett, W. L., & Iyengar, S. (2010). The Shifting Foundations of Political Communication: Responding to a Defence of the Media Effects Paradigm. *Journal of Communication, 60*(1), 35–39.

Berry, M. (2013). The Today Programme and the Banking Crisis. *Journalism, 14*(2), 253–270.

Berry, M. (2015). The UK Press and the Deficit Debate. *Sociology, 50*(3), 542–559.

Berry, M. (2016). No Alternative to Austerity: How BBC Broadcast News Reported the Deficit Debate. *Media, Culture and Society, 38*(6), 844–863.

Brandenburg, H., & Van Egmond, M. (2012). Pressed into Party Support: Media Influence on Partisan Attitudes During the 2005 UK General Election Campaign. *British Journal of Political Science, 42*(2), 441–463.

Clarke, A. (2012). *Political Parties in the UK*. London: Palgrave.

Curtice, J., & Park, A. (2010). A Tale of Two Crises: Banks, MPs' Expenses and Public Opinion. In A. Park, J. Curtice, E. Clery, & C. Bryson (Eds.), *British Social Attitudes: The 27th Report – Exploring Labour's Legacy* (pp. 131–154). London: Sage.

De Vreese, C. H., & Boomgarden, H. G. (2006). Media Message Flow and Interpersonal Communication: The Conditional Nature of Effects on Public Opinion. *Communication Research, 33*(1), 19–37.

Deacon, D., & Monk, W. (2001). New Managerialism' in the News: Media Coverage of Quangos in Britain. *Journal of Public Affairs, 1*(2), 153–166.

Duval, J. (2005). Economic Journalism in France. In R. Benson & E. Neveu (Eds.), *Bourdieu and the Journalistic Field* (pp. 135–156). Cambridge, MA: Polity Press.

Feldman, L., Maibach, E. W., Roser-Renouf, C., & Leiserowitz, A. (2012). Climate on Cable: The Nature and Impact of Global Warming Coverage on Fox News, CNN, and MSNBC. *International Journal of Press/Politics, 17*(1), 3–31.

Gavin, N. T. (2018). Media Definitely Matter: Brexit, Immigration, Climate Change and Beyond. *The British Journal of Politics and International Relations, 20*(4), 827–845.

Happer, C., Philo, G., & Froggatt, A. (2012). *Climate Change and Energy Security: Assessing the Impact of Information and Its Delivery on Attitudes and Behaviour*. UKERC Project Final Report. Available from: http://www.ukerc.ac.uk/publications/climate-change-and-energy-security-assessing-the-impact-of-information-and-its-delivery-on-attitudesand-behaviour.html. Accessed 9 July 2018.

Iyengar, S. (1991). *Is Anyone Responsible? How Television Frames Political Issues.* Chicago: University of Chicago Press.

Kellner P. (2015). *General Election 2015: How Britain Really Voted.* Available at: https://yougov.co.uk/news/2015/06/08/general-election-2015-how-britain-really-voted/.

Kitzinger, J. (1994). The Methodology of Focus Groups: The Importance of Interaction Between Research Participants. *Sociology of Health and Illness, 16*(1), 103–121.

Klapper, J. T. (1968). Mass Communication: Effects. In D. L. Sills (Ed.), *International Encyclopedia of the Social Sciences 3* (pp. 81–90). New York: Macmillan/The Free Press.

Krueger, R. A., & Casey, M. A. (2000). *Focus Groups: A Practical Guide for Applied Research.* London: Sage.

Ladd, J. M., & Lenz, G. S. (2009). Exploiting a Rare Communication Shift to Document the Persuasive Power of the News Media. *American Journal of Political Science, 53*(2), 394–410.

Lewis, J. M. W. (2008). Thinking by Numbers: Cultural Analysis and the Use of Data. In T. Bennett & J. Frow (Eds.), *The SAGE Handbook of Cultural Analysis* (pp. 654–673). London: Sage.

Lukes, S. (1974). *Power: A Radical View.* London: Macmillan Press.

Manning, P. (1999). Categories of Knowledge and Information Flows: Reasons for the Decline of the British Labour and Industrial Correspondents' Group. *Media, Culture and Society, 21,* 313–336.

Mattinson, D. (2010). *Talking to a Brick Wall.* London: Biteback.

McCombs, M. E., & Shaw, D. L. (1972). The Agenda-Setting Function of Mass Media. *Public Opinion Quarterly, 36*(2), 176–187.

McQuail, D. (1977). The Influence and Effects of Mass Media. In J. Curran et al. (Eds.), *Mass Communication and Society.* London: Edward Arnold.

Miller, J. M., & Krosnick, J. A. (2000). News Media Impact on the Ingredients of Presidential Evaluations: Politically Knowledgeable Citizens are Guided by a Trusted Source. *American Journal of Political Science, 44*(2), 301–315.

Morgan, D. L. (1997). *Focus Groups as Qualitative Research.* London: SAGE.

Newton, K. (2006). May the Weak Force Be with you: The Power of the Mass Media in Modern Politics. *European Journal of Political Research, 45*(2), 209–234.

Philo, G. (1990). *Seeing and Believing: The Influence of Television.* London: Routledge.

Philo, G. (1995). Political Advertising and Public Belief. *Media, Culture and Society, 15,* 407–418.

Philo, G. (1996). *Media and Mental Distress.* London: Pearson/Longman.

Philo, G., & Berry, M. (2004). *Bad News from Israel.* London: Pluto.

Philo, G., & Berry, M. (2011). *More Bad News from Israel.* London: Pluto.

Philo, G., & Happer, C. (2013). *Communicating Climate Change and Energy Security: New Methods in Understanding Audiences.* New York: Routledge.

Rafter, K. (2014). Voices in the Crisis: The Role of Media Elites in Interpreting Ireland's Banking Collapse. *European Journal of Communication, 29*(5), 598–607.

Schifferes, S. (2012). Trust-Meltdown for Business Journalism. *British Journalism Review, 2*(1), 3–7.

Stanley, L. (2014). We're Reaping What We Sowed': Everyday Crisis Narratives and Acquiescence to the Age of Austerity. *New Political Economy, 19*(6), 895–917.

Stanley, L. (2016). Legitimacy Gaps, Taxpayer Conflict, and the Politics of Austerity in the UK. *The British Journal of Politics and International Relations, 18*(2), 389–406.

Wahl-Jorgensen, K., Sambrook, R., Berry, M., Moore, K., Bennett, L., Cable, J., Garcia-Blanco, I., Kidd, J., Dencik, L., & Hintz, A. (2013). *BBC Breadth of Opinion Review: Content Analysis.* Available at: http://downloads.bbc.co.uk/bbctrust/assets/files/pdf/our_work/breadth_opinion/content_analysis.pdf. Accessed 10 July 2018.

Yougov. (2008). *Survey 9–10 October.* Available at: http://d25d2506sfb94s.cloudfront.net/today_uk_import/YG-Archives-pol-stimes-vi-081013.pdf. Accessed 11 July 2018.

YouGov. (2015). *YouGov/Post Crash Economics Society Survey.* Available at: https://d25d2506sfb94s.cloudfront.net/cumulus_uploads/document/1h0dojy3oj/PostCrashEconomicsSocietyResults_150128_economics_W.pdf. Accessed 10 July 2018.

CHAPTER 4

The Deficit Debate: Content Studies

INTRODUCTION

The 2008 banking crisis precipitated the most serious global recession since the Great Depression. It also triggered a worldwide surge in sovereign debt as governments attempted to maintain domestic demand and employment. This surge in public debts and deficits generated a series of debates over the appropriate macroeconomic response. Some of the key questions included: How serious a threat to economic stability did large deficits represent? Should states apply monetary or fiscal stimulus measures to maintain demand during recessions, or were austerity policies a more credible response? Should deficits be reduced via tax rises or cuts in public spending? Should tax rises be focused on labour or capital? Direct or indirect taxes? Levied on the average earner or targeted at those on higher incomes or with greater wealth? In Britain such debates proved to be particularly significant, with research suggesting concerns over the public finances were a key factor in both the 2010 and 2015 Conservative General Election victories (Ashcroft 2010; Hunter 2015).

This chapter examines how these debates were presented in the press and broadcast media. However, before presenting the findings of the content analyses this chapter will first unpack the factors behind the sharp rise in the deficit in early 2009. Then, the scale of the UK public debt and deficit will be examined in both historical and international contexts. This is necessary because many of the key debates over the public finances focused

© The Author(s) 2019
M. Berry, *The Media, the Public and the Great Financial Crisis,*
https://doi.org/10.1007/978-1-137-49973-8_4

on the size and impact of Britain's debt and deficit. This section will conclude by examining the range of debate on how to respond to the rise in government debt.

What Caused the Rise in the UK Public Deficit?

In assessing the factors behind the rise in the UK debt and deficit it is important to isolate the impact of increased public spending after 1997 from the effects of the 2008 recession. This is because these distinct effects were conflated both in media accounts and audience beliefs.

Following their election victory in 1997, the Labour government began a major programme of public investment in areas such as health and education (IFS 2010). Public spending as a proportion of GDP rose from 40.6 per cent in 1997 to 44.1 per cent in 2007, a level just below its European neighbours such as France and Germany (IFS 2010). Labour initially ran budget surpluses between 1997 and 2001 but after 2002 it began to run deficits. These hit a high of over 3 per cent of GDP in 2004 before falling back to just over 2 per cent in 2006–8 (Wren-Lewis 2013b). Summing up the 1997–2007 period, the macroeconomist Simon Wren-Lewis argues 'policy was too tight in the early years, overcompensated in the middle of this period, and failed to correct sufficiently in the final years' primarily because of 'forecast errors' (Wren-Lewis 2013b: 44). Despite this, public debt as a proportion of GDP actually fell from 40.5 per cent to 36.7 per cent between 1997 and 2007 (Wren-Lewis 2013b).

As Table 4.1 shows, the key reason for the rise in the deficit was the sharp contraction in tax revenues in 2008 and 2009 as Britain entered a recession.

Table 4.1   UK public revenue and expenditure 2003–2010 (In £ Billions)

Year	Government revenue	% Change year/ year	Government expenditure	% Change year/ year
2003	423.4	6.9	467.1	8.4
2004	453.2	7.0	509.4	9.1
2005	487.8	7.6	541.6	6.3
2006	518.9	6.4	568.3	4.9
2007	549.2	5.8	602.9	6.1
2008	536.3	−2.3	653.6	8.4
2009	516.1	−3.8	686.3	5.0
2010	555.3	7.6	706.5	2.9

Source: IFS (2012)

VAT receipts fell sharply (13.1 per cent), in part, because Labour cut the tax from 17.5 per cent to 15 per cent in November 2008 in an attempt to boost demand as the recession took hold. However, the steepest falls in tax revenues were concentrated in the sectors most responsible for the period of uninterrupted growth between 1992 and 2007 – financial services and the residential and commercial property markets. This was reflected in the sharp contraction in revenue from Corporation tax, which fell 22.7 per cent, and stamp duty which declined by 44 per cent (IFS 2012).

The banking crisis and the fall in the residential property market also led to a sharp fall in credit issuance which depressed demand, employment and government revenue. As noted in Chap. 1, an important factor driving growth after 1979 had been the sharp rise in mortgage equity release (MER) as home owners cashed in the increase in the value of their homes through re-mortgaging. There are varying estimates of what proportion of MER flows back into aggregate demand. An OECD study estimated that 89 per cent of UK MER went directly into consumption (Catte 2004). However other research has produced lower estimates for consumption with a greater proportion of MER estimated to go into paying down debts, saving and the giving of gifts to relatives (Benito and Power 2004). Figure 4.1 presents the data on MER from 1997 to 2011.[1]

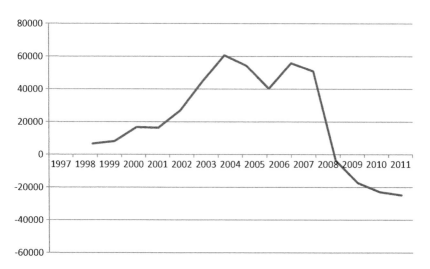

Fig. 4.1   Seasonally adjusted changes in mortgage equity release 1997–2011 (In Millions). (Source: Bank of England 2018)

The data shows that MER rose sharply in the early 2000s peaking in 2003. The fall in house prices which began in late 2007 reduced the equity available for extraction and led banks to sharply restrict lending. As Pawson and Wilcox (2013: 47) note, the impact of the aggregate switch from withdrawing equity to paying down mortgages amounted to 'a huge retraction of economic stimulus'.

Demand was also hit by the fall in unsecured credit. Whilst credit issuance dried up in the recession consumers continued to pay down historic debt with the consequence that the quantity of money in circulation contracted. As can be seen in Fig. 4.2. unsecured debt rose from 23.2 per cent of average income in 2000 to 30.3 per cent in 2008 before falling back to 25.1 per cent in 2012. At the peak, the average household held £11,215 in unsecured debt up from £6,462 in 2000 (TUC 2016).

However, it wasn't just the drying up of credit which worsened the deficit it was also the impact of debt accumulated during the credit boom, which as the Bank of England noted deepened and prolonged the recession:

Britain's recession was the deepest and longest in post-war history because households were so heavily indebted going into the crisis, new research from the Bank of England today suggests. Bank researchers said that an analysis of 'microdata' on UK households' finances shows that those with

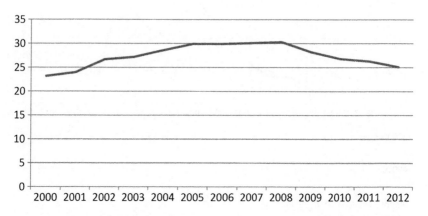

Fig. 4.2 Household debt (3rd quarter data) as a percentage of income. (Source: ONS data cited in TUC 2016)

high levels of debt in 2008 cut their spending by more, relative to their incomes, than others. And because gross household debt reached a historic high of around 160 per cent of combined incomes in 2007, these spending cutbacks had a profoundly negative impact on demand when the downturn came. This debt overhang increased the depth of the recession and made it much longer than previous ones. (Chu 2014)

The relationship between household debt levels and reductions in consumer spending post-2008 was also supported in research from both the USA (Dynan 2012; Mian et al. 2013) and Denmark (Andersen et al. 2014).

There is also evidence from the USA that the corporate debt overhang had a significant impact on employment with heavily leveraged firms being much more likely to shed staff during the downturn than those with lower debt levels (Giroud and Mueller 2015). Although comparative studies have not been conducted in the UK, the far higher level of non-financial corporate debt in the UK suggests that this may also have been a problem in Britain (McKinsey Global Institute 2010).

To summarise, the reason why the public deficit rose sharply after 2008 was the recession triggered by the banking crisis and the fall in the housing market. This had a dramatic impact on the government finances because Britain's growth and tax revenues had become very dependent on the financial services sector and the housing market. Furthermore, the banking crisis and housing fall led to a sharp contraction in the issuance of consumer credit which had underpinned a significant part of the UK's growth in the decade leading up to 2008. In fact, the fall in new credit issuance meant that, in aggregate, consumers were deleveraging rather than taking on more credit. This sucked demand out of the economy—two thirds of which was based on consumer spending—and led businesses to cut back investment (World Bank 2017). These developments left Britain facing what Koo (2011) described as a 'balance sheet recession' which threatened to become a slump.

THE SCALE OF BRITAIN'S DEBT AND DEFICIT IN HISTORICAL AND INTERNATIONAL CONTEXTS

A key element of the post-2008 debates over the public finances concerned the size and sustainability of public debt. There was particular controversy over the economic risks associated with high debts and deficits.

This section will examine four key indicators of debt sustainability in both a historical and international context. These are (a) the size of Britain's public debt, (b) the size of its deficit, (c) the costs of servicing the debt and (d) the maturity profile of government debt. The maturity profile refers to the average length of government bonds and is a significant element in how organisations such as the IMF (2000) and ECB (2017) estimate debt sustainability. Debt maturity is important because countries with long maturity profiles have to roll over their debt less frequently making them less vulnerable to gilt strikes and potential interest rate rises (Alloway 2011).

Prior to the start of the recession in 2007 Britain's public debt stood at 35.5 per cent of GDP.[2] It rose the following year to 50.4 per cent and then to 64.8 per cent in 2009 (Keep 2017a). As Fig. 4.3 below illustrates this represented a relatively modest debt burden in a long historical context. The first 11 years of Labour's administration from 1997 to the onset of the GFC had seen the net public debt average 32.5 per cent of GDP, which was above the level of the previous Conservative government of John Major (30.4 per cent) but below that of Margaret Thatcher's government (35.4 per cent) (Keep 2017a). When the period of the GFC is added in the average debt for the 1997–2010 Labour administration rises to 38.9 per cent of GDP.[3]

Figure 4.4 provides an international comparison of the UK's net public debt. Net public debt is equal to gross public debt minus government

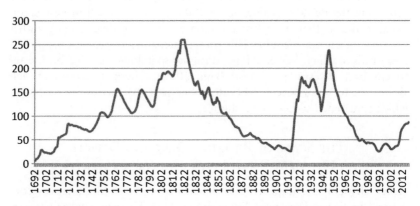

Fig. 4.3 UK public debt as a percentage of GDP 1692–2012. (Source: UK Public Spending 2018)

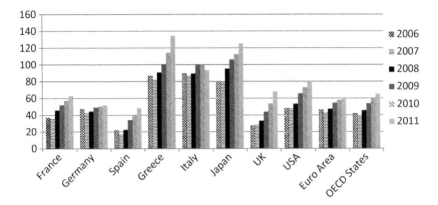

Fig. 4.4 Net public debt levels 2007–2011 as a percentage of GDP. (Source: OECD data cited in Webb and Bardens 2012)

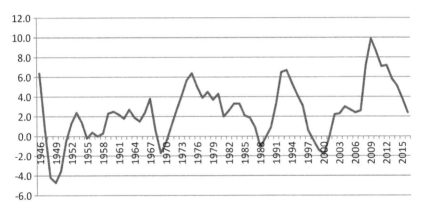

Fig. 4.5 PSNBR as a percentage of GDP 1946–2015. (Source: ONS & OBR cited in Keep 2017a)

holdings of financial assets. In 2007 prior to the onset of the recession the UK's debt burden was 11.8 per cent below the OECD average and 14.4 per cent below the Eurozone average. However this rose above the OECD and Eurozone averages in 2011.

Figure 4.5 shows the UK's budget deficit since the end of the Second World War. Up until 2008 the Labour government had run deficits that were on average lower than those of its Conservative predecessors.

Between 1997 and 2008 the Public Sector Net Borrowing Requirement (PSNBR) averaged 1.1 per cent of GDP whilst under the Major government it averaged 4.3 per cent and under Mrs. Thatcher 2.1 per cent. When the data for 2008–2010 is added the average deficit for 1997–2010 rises to 2.7 per cent. The year 2009 saw a record post-1945 deficit (9.9 per cent), though by 2011 this had dropped to 7.1 per cent a level close to that seen in consecutive years (6.5 per cent in 1992 and 6.7 per cent in 1993) during the Major administration:

Figure 4.6 compares the UK's deficit data with some of its international competitors. During the period between 2009 and 2011 the UK had one of the largest deficits of any of the G7 or European economies. However, the sharp rise that the UK experienced also occurred in almost every other economy, albeit at a lower rate. The three major economies which saw the largest deficits (Spain, USA and the UK) either experienced especially large credit/real estate booms before the crash and/or hosted very large finance sectors.

Figure 4.7 shows the changes in the debt servicing burden from 1955. The peak of debt servicing costs was during the Thatcher government in the 1980s when they reached 3.9 per cent of GDP. Despite the rise in the government debt from 2008 debt servicing costs fell to 1.7 per cent in 2009 and after a small rise to 2.5 per cent in 2010 and 2011 they have

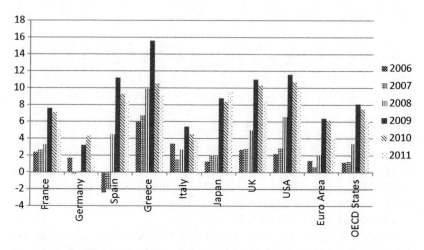

Fig. 4.6 An international comparison of budget deficits as percentage of GDP. (Source: OECD data cited in Bardens and Webb 2012)

Fig. 4.7   UK debt interest payment as percentage of GDP. (ONS and OBR data cited in Keep 2017a)

since fallen back close to historic lows. Part of the reason that the UK debt servicing costs have remained so low is that the quarter of the national debt is now owned by the state via the asset purchase facility (APF) is effectively interest free. This is because as Keep (2017a: 3) notes 'when the government makes debt interest payments for the bonds held in the APF it is making them directly to another public sector body – this is a transfer within the public sector and the net effect is £0'.

Figure 4.8 provides an international comparison of debt servicing expenditure which illustrates that since 2008 the UK has seen its costs rise above those of close competitors such as France and Germany as well as the OECD average.

In terms of debt maturity the UK in 2009 had on average the longest dated government bonds in the developed world at 14 years as compared to 4.7 years for the USA, 6.4 years for Germany and seven years for France (*Telegraph*, 26 April 2009). An international comparison of the maturity profile of UK debt can be seen in Fig. 4.9. It shows that Britain was in a less vulnerable position than other states because it had less debt to refinance in the short to medium term and was therefore less exposed to interest rate rises and concerns over the country's credit worthiness. A majority of Britain's debt was also domestically held which meant that much of the interest amounted to domestic transfer payments which, if necessary, could be eliminated via offsetting taxes (Coppola 2013).

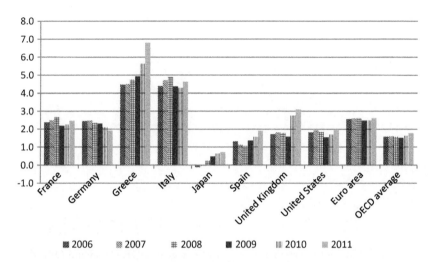

Fig. 4.8 International debt servicing levels as a percentage of GDP. (Source: OECD 2012)

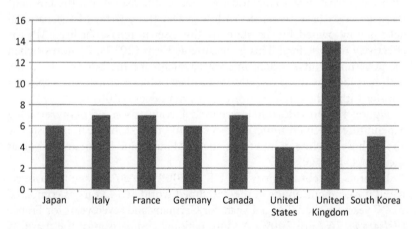

Fig. 4.9 Maturity profile (in years) of sovereign debt. (Source: McKinsey Global Institute 2010)

How to Respond to the Deficit: Timing and Policy

The deterioration in the public finances led to a debate on both the pace and the means by which to reduce the deficit. Some on the right argued that the size of the deficit posed such a threat to the economy that the pace of deficit reduction should be accelerated (Lilico et al. 2009; Taylor et al. 2009). Without accelerated deficit reduction, it was argued, Britain faced interest rate rises, currency devaluations and a possible bailout from the IMF:

> Failure to bring borrowing under control risks being disastrous for the UK economy and for the stability of public spending. The UK's credit outlook has already been downgraded by Standard & Poor's to 'negative', and unless fiscal tightening efforts are sufficiently credible, interest rates on government debt could increase to unsustainable levels and Sterling could undergo a further dramatic fall, risking a trip to the IMF mirroring the one in 1976. (Taylor et al. 2009: 6)

However, this was contested by those who argued that the recovery was fragile and that it was necessary to run large deficits until the recovery was well established (Krugman 2009a; Irwin et al. 2009; Dolphin 2009; Chang 2010b; Reich 2009; Hutton 2009; Brittan 2009; Neild 2010; Koo 2009, 2011). Pointing to evidence from the Great Depression, it was argued that premature attempts at fiscal consolidation whilst the private sector was deleveraging threatened to create a debt deflationary spiral which could create a depression and make it even harder to reduce the deficit. It was also argued that it was unlikely that demand for government bonds would fall or interest rates would rise because in a low growth environment companies and fund managers were hoarding funds that would create a strong demand for low risk government debt:

> Except for certain countries in the Eurozone which will be discussed below, there is no reason why a government should face financing problems during a balance sheet recession. The amount of money it must borrow and spend to avert a deflationary spiral is exactly equal to the un-borrowed and un-invested savings in the private sector ... that is sitting somewhere in the financial system. With very few viable borrowers left in the private sector, fund managers who must invest in fixed income assets without foreign exchange risk have no choice but to lend to the government, which is the last borrower standing. Although deficit hawks pushing for fiscal consolidation often talk about 'bond market vigilantes', the fact that 10-year bond yields in the U.S. and U.K. today are only around 2 per cent unthinkably low given fiscal deficits of nearly ten percent of GDP — indicates that bond market participants are aware of the nature and dynamics of balance sheet recessions. (Koo 2011: 27–28)

Even if there was a sudden market panic, some argued that Britain because it retained its own currency and central bank could always cover any shortfall in demand for its debt by printing money and that in a low inflation environment and with a credible long term plan to bring down debt this posed few risks (Wren-Lewis 2013a; Clark and Reed 2013).

In terms of how to reduce the deficit again there was a broad spectrum of opinion. Some argued that the best strategy to reduce the deficit should involve attempts to revive growth via state investment in infrastructure and 'sunrise' industries as part of a broader industrial activism (e.g. Rosewell 2009; Pettifor 2009; Irwin et al. 2009; Chang 2010a, b; Mazzucato 2010, 2011). Since the deficit was largely the result of the collapse in tax revenues in finance and housing the objective, it was argued, should be to diversify the economy so as to generate growth that was more balanced, sustainable and regionally dispersed:

> In the medium to long run, the most effective way to reduce the deficit is to revive growth, which will increase tax revenue and reduce welfare payments, rather than cutting welfare entitlements ... In the British case, discussion of longer-term growth strategy has a particular urgency, as its engine of growth in the past few decades – the City – is going to slow down, with the forthcoming global tightening of financial regulation. Especially for the parts of the UK that have relied on government jobs funded by City taxes – Scotland, Wales, Northern Ireland and certain northern English regions – alternative sources of growth and jobs are even more urgently needed, as many of those jobs are going to disappear soon. (Chang 2010a)

A second school of thought argued that the best way to bring down the deficit would be via sharp cuts to public spending. Some argued that public spending had grown too high under Labour and needed to be curtailed. The argument was also made that higher public spending would actually reduce growth by 'crowding out' private investment, which would also be deterred by the prospect of future tax increases. Instead, government should undertake a course of 'expansionary austerity':

> A wealth of academic evidence, from the OECD, European Central Bank and others, reveals that higher taxes slow economic growth, while lower government consumption spending increases growth. Both the IMF and the EU Commission have concluded that fiscal consolidations that are largely comprised of lower spending, with credible fiscal rules, are more durable than those largely comprised of higher taxes. (Taylor et al. 2009: 6)

Some argued for real terms across the board cuts to public spending. Others advocated cuts in specific areas such as public sector pay and pensions or abolishing programmes which aid disadvantaged children such as Sure Start (Taylor et al. 2009). Another approach put forward by the Labour party pressure group Compass was to reduce spending on foreign wars, nuclear weapons, PFI projects and ID cards (Irwin et al. 2009).

A third option involved closing the deficit via increasing the tax take. This could be achieved via regressive taxation targeted at low and middle income earners via raising VAT and/or the standard rate of tax (e.g. Taylor et al. 2009). Other proposals focused on raising revenue from high earners, the wealthy or corporations. These included a clampdown on tax evasion/avoidance, increasing the top rate of income tax or removing the ceiling on national insurance contributions (Dolphin 2009; Irwin et al. 2009; PCS 2010; Sikka 2008). Another strand of opinion argued for the introduction of land, property or wealth taxes (Irwin et al. 2009; Dolphin 2009; Philo 2010). Revenue could also have been raised via the elimination of tax relief on company borrowing, which it is argued, contributed to the financial crisis by providing an incentive for companies to become over-leveraged (Sikka 2009). There were also calls at the time for the introduction of a financial transactions tax (Irwin et al. 2009; PCS 2010) and a tax on derivative trades (Sikka 2008).

NEWSPAPER: SAMPLE AND METHODS

The sample for this study was drawn from the same six newspapers examined in Chap. 2: the *Guardian, Telegraph, Mail, Sun, Mirror* and *Daily Record* plus the *Express*. These newspapers were chosen on the basis that they represented all three segments of the UK national newspaper market (broadsheet, mid-market and tabloid), were high circulation and thus likely to have a broad impact on public knowledge and attitudes. The sample period was January to August 2009. This timeframe was chosen because it was the period when the deficit became a major political issue which was covered extensively in the media. In order to generate a representative yet manageable selection of press accounts two sampling techniques were used. For the three mass market tabloids (*Sun, Mirror* and *Record*), which featured far less news about the public finances, all articles captured by the Nexis search string: 'public debt OR national debt OR government debt OR deficit OR public finances' were included. For the other newspapers in the sample the same search string in Nexis was run for each day for the first seven months of 2009 in order to identify the peak days for coverage. The two peak days for each month were selected for the sample with the proviso that they had to come from separate weeks. If the two peak days occurred in the same week then the peak day would be sampled together with the next highest newsday from another week within that month. This reduced the possibility that a single newsworthy event, such as the Budget, would capture all the coverage for a particular month and skew the representativeness of the sample. The 14 days sampled for the broadsheets and mid-market tabloids were 5 and 26 January, 2 and 20 February, 20 and 26 March, 9 and 23 April, 7 and 22 May, 19 and 25 June, 6 and 22 July. In total the Nexis search captured 227 articles: 50 from the *Telegraph*, 37 from the *Guardian*, 41 from the *Mail*, 20 from the *Express*, 36 from the *Sun*, 28 from the *Mirror* and 15 from the *Record*.

The sample was then analysed to identify:

(1) The range of sources featured in coverage.
(2) Explanations for the rise in the deficit.
(3) Evaluations of the deficit – in particular discussion of its scale and consequences.
(4) Policy responses to address the deficit.

BROADCAST NEWS: SAMPLE AND METHODS

The broadcast sample for this part of the research consisted of BBC News at Ten coverage of the deficit debate drawn from the same period as the newspaper sample. BBC News at Ten was selected because it remains a mass audience bulletin with between 4 and 5 million viewers and is thus a key site in the formation of public knowledge and attitudes. I viewed all episodes of News at Ten between 1 January and 31 July 2009 and then selected out any stories which mentioned the public finances. This identified a total of 25 relevant stories occurring on: 12, 21, 28 January; 19 February; 19, 23, 24, 25 March; 2, 6, 20, 21, 22, 23, 24 April; 6, 21 May; 10, 16, 17, 24, 29 June; 1, 21, 22 July. Each of these stories from BBC News at Ten was transcribed generating a total of 1124 lines of news text—which were then analyzed, examining the same themes addressed in the print news sample.

NEWSPAPER FINDINGS

What Caused the Rise in the Deficit?

As can be seen in Table 4.2 the press provided a range of explanations for the rise in the deficit and there were clear differences in the accounts offered by newspapers. The most immediate factor in the rise in the deficit—the contraction in tax revenues—was mentioned in all newspapers but received proportionally more attention in the *Mail, Guardian* and *Express.* Some newspaper accounts featured detailed explanations as to which parts of government revenues were being affected. For instance:

> Tax revenues are being decimated by sharply contracting economic activity, declining corporate profitability, surging unemployment, markedly reduced bonus payments, the VAT cut and substantially weakened housing market activity and prices. Sharply rising unemployment is also resulting in higher benefit claims, pushing up government expenditure. (*Guardian*, 20 March 2009)

> Details of the ballooning public debt came as new figures revealed a massive drop in government income. The recession led to a near £7 billion fall in tax in January. This reflected lower company profits, the VAT cut and the falling income from stamp duty. Ironically, it also reflects a big drop in tax receipts as a result of lower City bonuses. (*Mirror*, 20 February 2009)

Table 4.2 Explanations for the rise in the deficit (percentage of articles featuring each explanation)

	Telegraph (%)	Guardian (%)	Mail (%)	Express (%)	Sun (%)	Mirror (%)	Record (%)
Fall in tax revenues	12	27	42	25	14	15	7
Benefit bill rising in recession	8	11	17	5	0	7	0
Bank bailouts	10	14	24	15	3	15	20
Maintaining demand in recession	2	5	0	5	3	15	13
Labour overspending/ profligacy	14	3	17	50	14	0	7
Global financial/ economic crisis	4	3	5	0	3	15	0

There was also significant space given over to highlighting the costs involved in bailing out the banks across the newspaper sample. However, the prominence given to this explanation meant that coverage tended to overstate the impact of the bank bailouts as later research suggests that they only contributed 5–6 per cent of the increase in the deficit (Keep 2017b). Some accounts also presented alarmist and misleading accounts of how the bank bailouts had impacted on the public finances. For instance, in February 2009 it was reported that the Office for National Statistics had decided to add the £1.5 trillion of liabilities from the nationalised and part-nationalised banks to the Government's balance sheet. However, because of international accounting rules the banks' assets—which were £139 million larger than its liabilities—could not be placed on the government's balance sheet (ONS 2011). As a *Mail* article briefly noted:

> The figures are actually quite misleading. Because of the way the ONS does its figures, it tallies up the banks' liabilities but has to largely ignore the fact that the banks still have assets. The result is the national debt looks far more worrying than it actually is. (*Mail*, 20 February 2009)

However whilst all the reporting in the *Guardian* and three out of the four *Telegraph* articles included this caveat only one out of the five *Mail* stories and none of the reports in the *Sun*, *Mirror* or *Express* featured it. This meant that they presented a misleading picture of the public finances:

> The Office for National Statistics revealed that our national debt has soared towards a dizzying £2 trillion … Even though this is equivalent to 147 per cent of GDP, the worst since 1954 and one of the highest in the western world, Labour's borrowing frenzy shows no sign of abating. (*Mail*, 20 February 2009)

> BAILING out the banks and soaring borrowing by Gordon Brown has sent Government debt spiralling to more than £2 trillion, shocking public finance figures revealed last night. (*Express*, 20 February 2009)

> The Office for National Statistics said yesterday it had added Lloyds and RBS banks' 'toxic' debt to Britain's books for the first time – saddling the nation with £1.5trillion more debt. (*Sun*, 20 February 2009)

> BAILING out the banks will send national debt rocketing to £2.1TRILLION – equivalent to £35,000 for every man, woman and child

in Britain. We already owe more than £700 billion, the highest amount since records began in 1993. (*Mirror*, 20 February 2009)

The positive case for deficit spending, that it prevented a depression, appeared relatively infrequently in coverage except in the *Mirror* and *Record*. This article which sourced from Labour and union representatives provided one of the most developed accounts:

> Treasury minister Angela Eagle said Tory calls for the Government to rein in spending in a bid to balance the books were 'a recipe for complete disaster'. She said: 'We are unashamedly sustaining public expenditure at a time when there is a global economic downturn to support the economy. We will return the public finances to a sustainable pathway after the recession is over and we'll do that in a fair way.' TUC general secretary Brendan Barber defended the Government's handling of the economy. He said: 'It is absolutely right to let the deficit grow. When companies and consumers stop spending, the public sector must fill the gap'. (*Record*, 20 February 2009)

The false argument that the deficit was caused by Labour overspending prior to the recession was featured in the right-wing press but was almost completely absent from accounts in the left leaning titles:

> Until Gordon Brown accepts he must bring the public finances back under control ending the profligacy of recent times the Labour Government is going to face a far harder task in selling its bonds. (*Mail*, 26 March 2009)

> The extent of Gordon Brown's mishandling of the economy is now plain for all to see. He borrowed like a man possessed in the boom years when he should have been paying off debt. (*Express*, 22 July 2009)

> Our plight is worse than most because we have spent and borrowed the money that might have helped us through [the recession]. Now Gordon insists the only way to avoid hellfire and damnation is to throw more taxpayers' cash on the flames. (*Sun*, 12 January 2009)

> ...We ALL will have to foot the bill for Labour's years of showering the state with our money. (*Sun*, 23 April 2009)

> As the latest figures showed yesterday the state has borrowed and spent too much. (*Telegraph*, 22 May 2009)

Press accounts then provided a variety of explanations for the rise in the deficit which correlated with newspapers' political orientation. Right leaning newspapers tended to provide more dramatic and alarmist accounts of the deficit and also falsely attributed the growth of the deficit to alleged historical overspending whereas left leaning papers tended to present more accurate accounts. Finally, it should be noted that there was little mention of how the disappearance of consumer credit had harmed growth or the negative impact of the household and corporate debt overhang on demand.

Size and Consequences of the UK Deficit

As noted in the introduction, the UK had entered the 2008 recession with an internationally and historically low public debt burden (Neild 2010; Bardens and Webb 2012). Furthermore, most of its debt was long dated and domestically held. Writing in the newsletter of the Royal Economic Society, Neild (2010, 12) commented:

> Today's ratio of debt to GDP does not look abnormal, let alone alarming ... Our deficit – the one figure picked out by the Chancellor – is high, but our debt to GDP is average and our tax ratio is low. Our good corruption score indicates that we are capable of raising tax or cutting expenditure. And, it might be added, our history is outstandingly good. Few if any other countries have managed their national debt for 300 years without default. One would conclude that some action was needed, but not that there were any grounds for alarm.

A very different picture was visible in the British press. Here discussion of Britain's deficit was infused with fear appeals and apocalyptic language, some examples of which are reproduced in Table 4.3.

Details of international and historical comparisons featured in newspaper accounts can be seen in Table 4.4. The first thing to note is significant difference between the three mass market tabloids (*Sun, Mirror* and *Record*) and the rest of the sample. This divergence—and the divergence noted in Table 4.5—is primarily due to differential sampling strategies. The broadsheets plus the *Mail* and the *Express* were selected on peak coverage days which were more likely to involve dramatic news about the public finances such as when the deficit had spiked or when Mervyn King, the governor of the Bank of England warned against further stimulus.

Table 4.3   Descriptions of the public finances in the press

Newspaper	Descriptors of the public finances
Telegraph	Debt disaster' (19 June 2009) 'horrendous fiscal burden' (23 April 2009), 'gargantuan' (23 April 2009), 'monstrous burden' (23 April 2009), 'a crisis ...almost unprecedented outside wartime (23 April 2009), 'catastrophic' (23 April 2009)
Guardian	'Horrifying' (23 April 2009), 'colossal black hole' (23 April 2009), 'public finances are in meltdown' (19 June 2009) 'plunging into the abyss' (April 23 2009) 'staggering levels of public debt' (20 February 2009)
Mail	'Borrowing needs are escalating exponentially' (26 March 2009), 'terrifying' (20 February 2009), the most poisonous inheritance imaginable' (23 April 2009), 'catastrophe' (23 April 2009), 'public finance bloodbath' (23 April 2009), "titanic' (5 January 2009) 'extremely scary' (23 April 2009)
Express	'A full blown economic emergency' (22 July 2009) 'off the Richter scale' (20 February 2009), 'nightmarish' (23 April 2009), 'epic scale of Labour's debt crisis' (23 April 2009), 'horrific' (23 April 2009), 'the brink of meltdown' (26 January 2009)
Sun	'Ruinous' (26 March 2009)'perilous' (7 May 2009), 'frightening' (7 May 2009), 'off the Richter scale' (20 February 2009), 'truly astronomical' (20 February 2009)
Mirror	'extraordinary level of public debt' (25 June 2009) 'the highest amount since records began in 1993' (20 May 2009),
Record	'mammoth ... colossal debts' (15 July 2009), 'the fiscal damage ... is breathtaking' (24 April 2009)

Table 4.4   International and historic comparisons of the public finances (percentage of coverage featuring each comparison)

Assessment	Telegraph (%)	Guardian (%)	Mail (%)	Express (%)	Sun (%)	Mirror (%)	Record (%)
Unfavourable historical/ International comparisons	70	59	87	95	28	11	20
Favourable historical/ International comparisons	4	14	10	0	0	4	0

However, the mass market tabloid sample included all articles which mentioned the debt or deficit, however briefly, during the sampling period. It should also be noted that the figures only captured positive/negative comparisons in a historical or international context. So although only 10

Table 4.5 Deficit dangers (percentage of articles featuring arguments and counter-arguments)

Assessment	Telegraph (%)	Guardian (%)	Mail (%)	Express (%)	Sun (%)	Mirror (%)	Record (%)
Deficit dangers-Bankruptcy – Not able to sell debt-IMF coming-Internet rates will rise	70	51	73	70	19	4	0
Counter-arguments to deficit dangers – Not going bust now, can sell debt at moment, IMF not coming etc.	10	27	10	5	0	4	0

of the 36 *Sun* articles involved a negative historical or international comparison, almost all their coverage reported on the deficit/debt in a negative light by using words like 'ruinous', 'rocketing' or 'sky-high'.

Some coverage offered misleading or false accounts of Britain's public debt. At the close of 2008 the national debt was 57.1 per cent of GDP (Webb and Bardens 2013). In 1970 it had been 70 per cent, for the whole of the inter-war years it was well over 100 per cent and in 1945 it was 225 per cent (Neild 2010). However, the *Mail* reported that: 'The shortfall sent the national debt soaring to £799bn – a record 56.6 per cent of national output' (22 July 2009). Incorrect international comparisons were also employed. In 2009 the UK's debt burden stood at 68.7 per cent of GDP which was lower than the USA's 84.8 per cent, Italy's 115.8 per cent or Japan's 218.6 per cent and was projected to remain below those countries in the foreseeable future (BBC 2009). But the *Express* reported that:

> BRITAIN will soon have the biggest national debt in the industrialised world, finance experts said last night. The International Monetary Fund warned that Treasury borrowing is on course to hit £165 billion next year. That would make the country's public debt 11 per cent of Gross Domestic Product – the highest in the G20 group of industrialised nations. (Express, 20 March 2009)

The same incorrect claim also appeared in the *Sun*: 'The International Monetary Fund forecast that by next year Britain will have the highest level of Government debt of any of the top 20 economies in the WORLD' (20 March 2009). An even more erroneous international comparison was offered in the *Mail*:

These latest official figures show that Britain's financial state is now far, far worse than countries such as Greece or Italy, which we have traditionally looked down upon and sneered at for their profligacy. Italy's indebtedness, though frightening, stands at little more than 100 per cent of GNP. Ours stands at twice that percentage and may well not be sustainable in the long term. (Mail, 20 February 2009)

Other reports drew direct analogies with struggling Eurozone economies such as Ireland, ignoring the fact that the UK retained its own central bank and currency and its debts were largely domestically held. Another dubious comparison, initially made by David Cameron but repeated uncritically in all newspapers (23 April 2009) except the *Guardian* and the *Mirror* was the claim that Britain would borrow more between 2009 and 2011 than all previous governments had borrowed. This claim was based on borrowing in nominal rather than real terms.

The analysis also examined what newspaper accounts claimed could be the economic impact from the rise in the deficit. Here six dangers were identified which were used to justify calls for either accelerated deficit reduction or opposition to a further fiscal stimulus. The six dangers were:

- Britain might lose its AAA credit rating
- Foreign creditors may stop buying UK gilts
- Sterling could fall sharply
- Interest rates may rise making debt servicing very expensive
- The IMF might be required to bail out Britain
- The UK could go bankrupt.

These arguments were made primarily by City economists, right-wing think tanks and Conservative politicians. As can be seen in Table 4.5, these arguments were prominent in all newspapers except the *Mirror* and the *Record* both of which barely discussed these warnings. Such warnings tended to be particularly prominent in the right-wing newspapers, whilst the *Guardian* was more likely to feature balanced articles with counter-arguments. However, even in the *Guardian* these warnings were common and directly endorsed by reporters. For instance:

The International Monetary Fund thinks the downturn will plunge the UK into the deepest deficit among the G20 countries next year, at 11% of gross domestic product ... At this level, Britain's deficit starts to become unsustainable because financial markets would lose confidence and refuse to buy any more government debt except at very high rates of interest. This in turn would drive up the government's debt-service costs and add even more to the deficit. There could also be a further run on sterling if the country looks at risk of losing its AAA rating as a sovereign debtor. (*Guardian*, 26 March 2009)

In the *Sun* these warnings often appeared in strongly worded comment pieces. One cited comments from an unnamed 'city analyst' that 'there is a 25-per-cent chance of a run on the Pound in the next six months' (*Sun*, 6 April 2009) whilst another argued:

If only one or two things go wrong, as they almost certainly will – slower growth, a slide in our credit rating, higher interest rates – our worst night-mares become reality … This year's budget was the moment to act – not in two years' time when we may be bust, begging for IMF money and watching a once proud nation turn into a banana republic. (*Sun*, 27 April 2009)

It was also the case that newspapers—particularly on the right—tended to frame ambiguous events in the most threatening manner possible. For instance on 26 March 2009, all newspapers reported on a bond auction that had not been fully 'covered', with only £1.63 billion out of £1.75 billion of Government debt being bought by investors. There were a number of explanations for the failure to sell all the debt including the fact that the 40 year bonds were ineligible to be sold back to the Government under the quantitative easing programme, and miscommunication between the Bank of England and the bond markets. The *Telegraph* reported:

Although some blamed the failure on the fact that the particular bond for sale was a 40-year gilt which is ineligible to be sold back to the Bank of England through the QE programme, experts said Mr King's comments [about not buying the full quantity of government bonds through quantitative easing] were largely to blame. Graham Turner, of GFC Economics, said: 'Mr King has shown his colours, and the market now realises that the commitment to QE is hollow. It is not working because yields have barely fallen. The injection of monetary base is irrelevant, QE only works through lower bond yields. Mr King may not understand this point. Hence, perhaps, the significance of the Governor's intervention on the likely success of QE may have been lost on him. He will perhaps be a little wiser this lunch-time.' (*Telegraph*, 2 March 2009)

However most reports attributed the failure of the bond auction to investors not being willing to fund the UK's rising deficits because of fears over the build up of public debt with some claiming the Government could no longer sell its debt. For instance:

BRITAIN'S ability to borrow tens of billions of pounds to fight the economic crisis was called into question last night after the Treasury failed to sell Government gilts for the first time in more than a decade. Fears are growing on the financial markets that Britain may not be able to repay the billions of pounds in debt it is amassing to rescue banks and revive the economy. (*Telegraph*, 26 March 2009)

Back in London, investors sent shockwaves through financial markets by shunning a £1.75bn auction of government IOUs – gilts – amid mounting fears about the Treasury's ability to pay for its bank bailouts and fill the hole left by collapsing tax revenues. 'This is a bit of a shot across the government's bows,' said Jonathan Loynes, of Capital Economics. (*Guardian*, 26 March 2009)

NO BUYERS FOR GOVERNMENT BONDS AS DEBT FEARS GROW. (Headline – *Mail*, 26 March 2009)

BROWN SPOOKED BY THE MARKETS (Headline) City experts blamed doubts over Mr. Brown's economic policy for the Treasury's failure to find buyers for £120 million worth of debt, or 'gilts'. It was the first time since 2002 that the Government has been unable to sell its debt, and this will be seized on by those who have warned that there is insufficient demand for the volume of debt being sold by the Treasury. Officials played down the significance of the shortfall, but economists said investors were beginning to doubt the Government's credit rating. (*Mail*, 26 March 2009)

Now international investors won't buy Government debt. This is a very dangerous moment for Britain and its PM. Our debt repayments will go through the roof if the world's moneymen decide the pound can no longer be trusted. (*Sun*, 26 March 2009)

The most serious warning that Britain could go bankrupt, which had been raised by Conservative politicians, appeared in 16 articles: five in the *Telegraph* and the *Mail*, three in the *Express*, two in the *Sun* and one in the *Mirror*. Of these only one each in the *Mail*, the *Mirror* and the *Telegraph* featured balanced articles which challenged the notion that Britain could go bankrupt. The rest directly endorsed the idea that bankruptcy was a real possibility:

> Mr. Brown recklessly overspent during golden economic years when he should have been reducing the national debt. Now recession has struck there is no money in the kitty and the nation is hurtling towards bankruptcy at breakneck pace. (*Express* 23 April 2009)

> Whoever is in power must find urgent spending cuts of £50 BILLION ... Without such drastic surgery, Britain is going bust. (*Sun*, 6 July 2009)

> This is a time when Britain stands on the brink of bankruptcy, with the Government's debts expected to reach an unprecedented £1.5trillion. (*Mail*, 5 January 2009)

> Should the Government's economic credibility deteriorate much further, it faces not the odd one or two but a series of failed gilt auctions. And only then as a prelude to a possible slide into insolvency. (*Telegraph*, 19 June 2009)

But Britain as a sovereign with a central bank and currency issuing powers cannot be forced into bankruptcy because it can always print money to buy its own debt in the event of a gilt strike (Coppola 2013; Wren-Lewis 2013a; Clark and Reed 2013). This might generate inflation but that was unlikely due to the depth of the post-2008 recession. However, even newspapers which featured the most apocalyptic assessments of the public finances occasionally featured dissenting voices. For instance, Professor Ray Barrell of the National Institute of Economic and Social Research argued in the *Mail* that the national debt was relatively modest in historical and international terms and that the UK had entered the recession 'in a better position than most large countries' (26 January 2009). The upshot, argued Barrell, was that the debt 'would be dealt with' and that those who warned of a possible default 'can be safely ignored'. However, arguments warning of the dangers the deficit posed were much more heavily featured and directly endorsed by almost all newspapers.

Policy Options for Dealing with the Debt/Deficit?

As noted in the introduction, there was a range of debate over how quickly the deficit should be reduced and whether it should be achieved via tax

Table 4.6 Solutions to the budget deficit (percentage of articles featuring each solution)

	Telegraph (%)	Guardian (%)	Mail (%)	Express (%)	Sun (%)	Mirror (%)	Record (%)
Austerity measures – cuts to public spending and/or regressive tax increases	56	38	63	70	67	61	47
Improve efficiency	4	5	2	15	3	11	20
Scrap NHS computer, Quangos, ID cards, Trident	6	5	10	5	6	11	0
Increase in top rate of income tax to 50p	12	15	7	30	11	15	20
Increase tax on 'super-rich'	0	0	0	0	3	0	0
Increase tax on non-doms	2	0	0	0	0	0	0
Introduce land/ property/wealth/ financial transaction taxes	0	3	0	0	0	0	0
Crack down on tax evasion/avoidance	2	8	0	0	0	0	0
Invest for growth – house building, etc.	0	8	0	0	0	0	0

rises or spending cuts. As can be seen in Table 4.6, by far the most referenced solution was to cut public spending or raise regressive forms of taxation. Part of the reason why this option was so dominant was that it was clear that both parties were planning to undertake major reductions to public spending, and so much reporting concentrated on debates over what might be cut. However, there was relatively little discussion of the dangers of austerity measures. Across almost all newspapers—whether left or right—the view that austerity was inevitable was dominant:

> The deterioration in the public finances means the winner of the next general election – which has to take place by next summer – will have no choice but to slash public spending and hike taxes. (*Mail*, 22 July 2009)

> It is increasingly obvious that it will not be sufficient for the nation to make a grim choice between public spending cuts or tax rises. Both will be

required to get us out of the financial disaster visited upon us by Labour. (*Express*, 22 July 2009)

Cuts and tax rises: there is no other way. (Headline – *Telegraph*, 25 June 2009)

We must freeze or even cut the cost of keeping six million state workers on the public payroll– or be abandoned by international creditors. There can be no sacred cows. The NHS budget has trebled in ten years. It must accept real cuts. So must every other Whitehall and town hall budget. (*Sun*, 6 July 2009)

Labour is portraying the Tories as the old enemy of the public sector but it too will have to slash spending if by some miracle it hangs onto power. (*Guardian*, 19 June 2009)

WE are heading for a new age of austerity. Whether Labour or the Tories win the next election, the country will be faced with making massive spending cuts. The reason is starkly simple. This year the Government will borrow £175billion – around £2868 for everyone in the UK. (*Mirror*, 3 July 2009)

The *Mirror*'s coverage—although accepting the inevitability of cuts at some point in the future—argued that during the recession the government had to keep spending:

ALISTAIR Darling should hold his nerve and dare to spend, not cut, in Wednesday's Budget. We recognise collapsed banks and the global financial crisis leave money tight for the Chancellor of the Exchequer, with Government borrowing poised to soar. Yet Mr. Darling must ignore siren voices urging him to repeat disastrous Tory cost-cutting of the 1980s and 1990s. This international crisis is a golden opportunity to prove the value of Labour policies. (*Mirror*, 20 April 2009)

It's core argument—as a Labour supporting newspaper—was that only Labour could be trusted to carry out the inevitable cuts in a fair or 'compassionate' way that didn't damage vital public services. As one headline put it 'THE REAL CHOICE: WHO DO YOU TRUST WITH A SCAPEL?' (*Mirror*, 16 June 2009).

The only newspaper where journalists didn't directly endorse austerity policies was the *Record*, although even in this newspaper, there were high status sources who argued in favour of austerity. For instance:

IFS director Robert Chote said the Treasury had taken 'a permanent hit' of £90 billion a year as a result of the recession. And he warned taxpayers would be feeling the effects for years to come .... 'It is important to look beyond debates about whether the economy will recover quite as quickly and quite as strongly as the Chancellor claimed, to the scale of the underlying problem that the Treasury's detailed forecasts identify. It is this that will require two full parliaments of mounting austerity to repair'. (*Record*, 24 April 2009)

Calls to cut specific areas of spending such as public sector staff, pay and pensions were prominently featured across the right-wing press. These accounts suggested that such cuts were economically unavoidable and argued that public sector workers should face similar pay and jobs cuts to those in the private sector:

While unemployment in the private sector has been rising steeply, so that almost 2.4 million people are out of work, the state is still recruiting, still paying wage increases and still supporting early retirement for public sector workers on inflation-proof pensions. Yet the Prime Minister insists that his government will avoid public spending cuts if the British electorate returns him to Downing Street next year. (*Mail*, 22 July 2009)

Public sector pay must be on the table. So, in due course, must public sector pensions and staff numbers. Talking about these issues is as politically uncomfortable as it is economically unavoidable. (*Telegraph*, 6 July 2009)

A fortune goes on fattening the State cow, with six million people – one in four workers – now paid by the taxpayer. Civil servants are lucky souls who can bank on a job for life – or at least until they retire at 60 on an inflation-proof pension. The rest must slog on until they drop – if they still have a job – because they can't afford a pension. This is an issue the Tories, if they are honest, cannot afford to ignore. We need fewer civil servants and more wealth creators. (*Sun*, 12 January 2009)

The *Sun* also justified cuts by linking public spending to groups such as asylum seekers and public sector employees:

Meanwhile, the Treasury will throw caution to the wind and borrow a trillion pounds for the biggest spending spree in human history. Yet nobody seriously suggests saving a cent or laying off a single £35,000-a-year street football coordinator. (*Sun*, 12 January 2009)

PEN-PUSHERS ON £2K 'DIVERSITY' JUNKETS (Headline) Shadow Cabinet Office minister Nick Hurd said last night: 'At a time when millions face losing their jobs and government debt is at record levels, do ministers really think sending civil servants on five-day diversity courses at a luxury hotel, costing £2,000 a pop, is prudent and the right thing to do?' (*Sun*, 6 January 2009)

Failed asylum seekers who judges have ordered out of the country are now costing £73 million a year as they use every trick in the book to avoid being sent home – up from £4 million just four years ago ... There will be some difficult choices when public spending has to be cut to pay for the huge state debts. But some will be dead easy. (*Sun*, 22 June 2009)

Whilst the press contained many accounts arguing for the necessity of austerity measures, the opposing argument that sharp cuts to spending would prolong the recession and make it more difficult to pay down the deficit were much more rarely featured, especially outside of the *Mirror* and *Guardian*. The scattered accounts that stressed the necessity to keep spending during the recession consisted primarily of brief reported statements from Labour politicians or union leaders stating that you couldn't cut your way out of a recession but needed to keep investing. In right-wing papers these brief statements were sometimes directly challenged or placed in the midst of articles strongly advocating austerity. They were also undermined by reporting that revealed that Labour had abandoned plans for a further fiscal stimulus and were planning on making similar cuts to the Conservatives had they won the 2010 election. One of the more developed arguments highlighting the negative impact that cuts would have on growth and the deficit was voiced by a union leader in the *Sun*, though this was an outlier in their coverage:

TUC boss Brendan Barber said: 'A mania has gripped commentators who are calling for deep cuts in public spending to reduce the budget deficit. They talk as if cuts would have no effect on the private sector, but the net result would be to plunge the economy into a further downturn, making the deficit worse as the tax take falls and jobless benefit rises.' Public spending had soared by £174 billion in the past decade. Mr. Barber claimed cuts now would 'choke off' any hope of recovery. He added: 'The best way to close the deficit is to go for growth and increase the tax take from the super-rich'. (*Sun*, 14 July 2009)

Brendan Barber was also cited in the *Mirror* arguing strongly against cuts to public spending during the recession:

> TUC general secretary Brendan Barber said ministers should resist calls for public spending cuts. He added: 'Big spending cuts are the last thing we need. They could tip the economy into an ever deeper downturn and make the deficit worse when the tax take falls and spending on unemployment rises. As consumers and companies fail to spend, the public sector must fill the gap'. (*Mirror*, 25 July 2009)

As can be seen in Table 4.6, arguments in favour of reducing the deficit via tax cuts directed at the better off were almost entirely accounted for by discussion of the introduction of the 50 per cent tax rate on high earners in the April 2009 budget. Although broadly welcomed in the left leaning titles—some *Guardian* articles even suggested it didn't go far enough —it was subject to uniformly negative coverage in the right-wing press. These newspapers argued that the decision to raise the top rate of tax would raise minimal revenue, deter entrepreneurialism and lead to a 'brain drain' of 'wealth creators' overseas:

> It [increasing the top rate of income tax] will simply encourage tax avoidance and lead wealth-creators to reduce their effort and working hours. In the end it will raise no money, reduce economic activity and initiate a 'brain drain' of talent abroad, leaving the whole country worse off. (*Express*, 23 April, 2009)

> The Chancellor drove a stake through the heart of New Labour yesterday by stinging top earners with a new 50p tax rate. Experts said the move resisted for a decade by Tony Blair was largely symbolic and could even lose the Treasury money by prompting an exodus of the rich. (*Mail*, 23 April 2009)

> High earners will pay a 50 per cent rate – which threatens an exodus of entrepreneurs and making foreign businessmen think twice about coming here. (*Sun*, 23 April 2009)

Other arguments for reducing the deficit by making the tax system more progressive appeared very rarely in coverage. The only exception in the right of centre press was the article in the *Sun* cited above where a Brendan Barber argued for taxing the 'super-rich' and an article in the *Telegraph* (23 April 2009) by the Dragon's Den entrepreneur Duncan Bannatyne which advocated that non-doms, tax exiles and CEOs' tax free pensions should be taxed more heavily. The *Guardian* did feature three articles which argued that the deficit could be closed via a crackdown on tax evasion and avoidance. There was also a single line mentioning property taxes in a *Guardian* article which noted the 'perverse' concentration on cuts when the deficit was caused by a 'collapse in tax revenues':

> It seems perverse that the current debate is all about which bits of spending should be cut rather than which taxes should be raised. There are plenty of ways to raise revenues. Darling could delay the introduction of the 50% tax rate but lower the threshold; he could prevent corporate tax avoidance by taxing companies on their turnover rather than their profits; he could deter speculative holdings of property through a land value tax. (22 July 2009)

Overall then there was a high level of consensus across the British press that austerity measures were unavoidable, little discussion of the potential downsides and relatively little space given over to alternatives.

Patterns of Source Access

The data on the range of voices in coverage finds that both main political parties were prominently featured across the sample. In the right-wing press the Conservatives appeared more often than Labour, particularly in the *Telegraph* and *Sun* where they were featured more than twice as often. In two of the left leaning papers (*Guardian* and *Record*) representation was approximately equal whilst at the *Mirror*, Labour voices were slightly more prominent (Fig. 4.10 and Table 4.7).

The other key source whose opinions routinely structured coverage was City experts. Their primarily role was to explain how the markets viewed the public finances and offer policy prescriptions. These usually involved claims that deficit reduction needed to be prioritised and austerity measures were the appropriate policy tool. In this way the economy tended to be seen in large part through the prism of the financial markets. The view of City experts were often endorsed by journalists, particularly in the right-wing press, and their very negative perspectives on the deficit and its consequences tended to dominate coverage. In contrast academic economists most of whom believed that austerity policies were not the

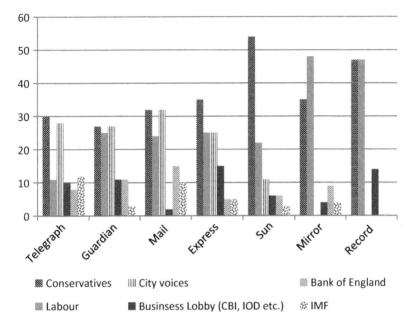

Fig. 4.10   Top six sources in newspaper coverage (percentage of newspaper articles featuring each source)

Table 4.7   Additional sources cited (percentage of newspaper articles featuring each source)

Telegraph	12% ONS; 6% Ratings Agencies; 4% Liberal Democrats; 4% IFS; 4% NIESR; 4% Audit Commission; 4% Trade Unions; 2% Policy Exchange; 2% OECD; Adam Smith Institute; 2% Debt Management Office; 2% Duncan Bannatyne
Guardian	14% Liberal Democrats; 11% IFS; 8% ONS; 5% Trade Unions; 3% Audit Commission; 3% Debt Management Office; 3% Ratings Agencies; 3% David Blanchflower
Mail	7% ONS; 5% Ratings Agencies; 2% US politicians; 2% European politicians; 2% Audit Commission; 2% IFS; 2% Trade Unions; 2% IPPR; 2% OECD
Express	15% Taxpayer's Alliance; 5% Liberal Democrats; 5% ONS; 5% Trade Unions;
Sun	6% OECD; 3% Inland Revenue; 3% European Council; 3% IFS; 3% Taxpayer's Alliance; 3% Trade Unions; 3% Unnamed 'economist'
Mirror	11% Public (letters); 11% Trade Unions; 7% IFS; 7% Liberal Democrats 4% Unnamed 'economist'; 4% OECD;
Record	20% Liberal Democrats; 20% Public (letters); 13% SNP; 7% IFS; 7% Trade Unions

appropriate response in a weak economic environment were much more rarely featured (Chu 2015). A notable exception was David Blanchflower in the *Guardian* who was one of the most consistent critics of austerity amongst the economics profession.

Below City voices there were another tier of experts and lobbyists who were supportive of accelerated deficit reduction and/or austerity measures. These included the CBI, IOD, BCC, the Bank of England, the IMF and the IFS. Statements or reports from these sources often had the ability to drive coverage and set news agendas across the press. For instance, the report released by the IMF in March 2009 on how much the UK government was likely to borrow was featured in all newspapers.

At a level beneath this group of experts were the Liberal Democrats who as the third party in British politics struggled to gain sustained attention. Trade unions who represented one of the most consistent voices against austerity and early deficit reduction were featured in all newspapers but at a low level. Think tanks and pressure groups, aside from the IFS, were also not featured prominently particularly in the left of centre press. Right-wing newspapers tended to feature think tanks in line with their editorial line such as the Taxpayers' Alliance, Policy Exchange and Adam Smith Institute.

Broadcast Findings

What Caused the Rise in the Deficit?

Unlike much reporting in the press, the BBC News at Ten accounts provided an accurate picture of the immediate factors behind the rise in the deficit. As can be seen in Fig. 4.11, most explanations focused on the impact of the recession, falling tax receipts and the bank bailouts.

These explanations provided in BBC coverage tended to be concise and clear:

> The recession means company profits have fallen so corporation tax revenues are much lower than last year. And with fewer people in work, income tax revenues are down, too. Houses aren't selling, so stamp duty receipts are also down. All while spending on things like Jobseeker's Allowance has gone up. The result is even more borrowing than the government feared. (News at Ten, 19 February 2009)

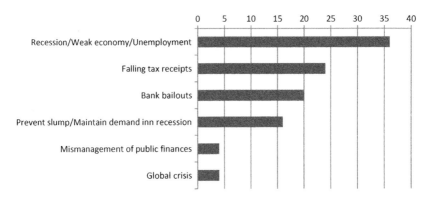

Fig. 4.11 Explanation for the rise in the deficit (percentage of bulletins featuring each explanation)

Whilst journalists didn't raise the role of debt and the impact of deleveraging, reporters did on occasion discuss how public spending prior to the crash had been dependent on a boom in financial services that was unlikely to return:

> There is an even deeper problem with public finances which the credit crunch has simply brought to the surface. During the boom years the government had got used to tens of billions of pounds of revenue from the world of finance. And a lot of that money is probably never coming back. (News at Ten, 21 April 2009)

There were four references, primarily from Labour politicians that the rise in the deficit was helping to maintain demand and employment during the recession. For instance:

Journalist: The lessons from the past he [Alistair Darling] said is that
                   Government should continue spending more now to help
                   the victims of the recession ... The alternative was a return
                   to the 80s when he claimed a whole generation were
                   abandoned to a future on the scrapheap. (News at Ten, 23
                   April 2009)
Angela Eagle: It's important we do not do what the Conservatives are
                   calling for, to slash £5 billion in the next two months
                   from public expenditure. That would make more people
                   unemployed just at the time when we need to support the
                   economy. (News at Ten, 19 February 2009)

However these references were very brief and not always explicit in making a direct connection between the rise in borrowing and the necessity to maintain demand in the downturn. They also tended to be overwhelmed by the wide range of political and financial sector sources who were arguing for accelerated deficit reduction. Despite the accuracy of most explanations some bulletins featured confused accounts as to the origins of the deficit. In a segment on the rise in the top rate of tax in the April 2009 budget, a BBC correspondent commented:

> Back in the 90s, these two ambitious young chaps would bound around the City of London, declaring that Labour had changed. Gone were the days of taxing high earners until the pips squeak, they would say. And never again would a Labour government court financial disaster by borrowing too much. Crusty old bankers and crotchety old business leaders listen politely and didn't believe a word, although in the early years of the Labour government, such scepticism seemed well a bit unfair. But today as the Chancellor pushes up the top rate of tax and forecasts an eye-watering increase in public sector debt, the noise you can hear from the city is of older bankers saying 'I told you so'. (News at Ten, 22 April 2009)

There are three points that can be made about this report. First, it appears to turn on its head the factors responsible for the deficit. These were a banking crisis caused by speculation, leverage and the over-extension of credit. Yet in the account above, the culpability of the City disappears from the analysis, and the 'eye watering increase in public sector debt' is only attributed to Labour 'borrowing too much'. Second, the journalist says 'never again would a Labour government court financial disaster by borrowing too much'. However over the last 70 years Conservative administrations have on average borrowed more than Labour governments (Murphy 2016). Third, many economists argued that cutting rather maintaining deficit spending during a severe recession would be more likely to 'court financial disaster' especially when monetary policy options were limited with interest rates close to the zero low bound (ZLB).[4] In another account, a journalist reported on comments from the Bank of England that Britain could not afford another fiscal stimulus:

> But just as Gordon Brown was arriving in France, news arrived that the Governor of the Bank of England had issued an extraordinary public warning that, for Britain at least, the days of spend, spend, spend were now over. (News at Ten, 24 March 2009)

The use of the term 'spend, spend, spend' will be familiar to older viewers as a reference to Viv Nicholson, the Yorkshire housewife who won £152,319 on the football pools in 1961. Nicholson famously spent the fortune within a few years, so the phrase has become a byword for profligacy. Yet although Labour had substantially increased public spending after 1997, the national debt to GDP ratio had actually fallen before the recession hit, which is difficult to square with the recklessness implied by the use of the phrase 'spend, spend, spend' (Wren-Lewis 2013b).

Size and Consequences of the UK Deficit

BBC reporting of the scale and consequences of the deficit showed both similarities and divergencies from accounts that appeared in the press. One significant area of difference was the BBC didn't provide false or misleading international comparisons. News accounts noted that Britain had a high deficit in relation to its international competitors, but also that its position was not uniquely bad:

> Our national debt, what we own as a nation, will be more than £790 billion by the end of this year or £13,000 for everyone in the UK. That is not as high as some, but it's rising fast. (BBC, 21 May 2009)

However, like press accounts BBC reporting focused heavily on the 'record' size of the deficit and debt. Nearly half (48 per cent) of all stories mentioned the 'record' or 'unprecedented' size of the deficit and/or debt, but only one (4 per cent of stories) mentioned information about the level of UK debt coming into the recession, and none discussed who owned it or its maturity profile. Reporting also at times discussed Britain's debt in nominal terms, rather as a proportion of GDP:

> The national debt has hit a new record of just under £800 billion. (News at Ten, 21 July 2009)

> Now with unprecedented levels of borrowing and debt. (News at Ten, 22 April 2009)

This approach, as some of the BBC's own journalists have argued, is misleading. For instance, Michael Blastland (2008) in an article titled *The Myth of Record Debt* argued that presenting debt in nominal terms is 'fatuous' and 'treats the public like fools'. 'Context', Blastland argues 'takes only a moment' and 'good and simple start would be to present figures as a percentage of GDP, whether for spending, taxation or borrowing'. The picture of a dangerous deficit was magnified by the high level of access given to Conservative politicians, Bank of England representatives and City/institutional sources, who were highly critical of the deficit:

Mervyn King: We are confronted with a situation in which the scale of the deficit is *truly extraordinary*. (News at Ten, 24 June 2009)

David Cameron: The scale of our deficit is *truly horrific* and we need to act on that and act on that now. (News at Ten, 2 April 2009)

Such language was then picked up and used by journalists:

Stephanie it is obvious that no governing party will be able to escape the *full horror* of these finances? (News at Ten, 10 June 2009)

What really changed today Huw I think is this: no longer do politicians decide what they will do with the fruits of the economy. They wait and see the *horror* the economy has to deliver to them and wonder how to live with it. (News at Ten, 22 April 2009)

Journalists also on occasion endorsed the Conservative argument that the UK government had 'run out' of money, despite the fact that currency issuing sovereigns cannot 'run out' of money. In one segment a journalist visited a soon to be closed building site which is used as an analogy for the economy:

This is just one example of what can happen *when the money runs out*, a project half complete, the builders soon to be sent home. It is a glimpse of the future in the new age of austerity. (News at Ten, 23 April 2009)

There was also controversy over the timing of any deficit reduction. Did the deficit pose such a threat to the economy that it needed to be reduced immediately or could it wait until the economy was growing strongly so that it would not face the constraint of the ZLB? Here, the patterns in coverage were clear. Coverage was split with 24 per cent (6/24) of articles featuring arguments, exclusively from Labour politicians, that spending in a recession was necessary to prevent a slump, while 28 per cent (7/24) of articles featured the Conservatives, the Bank of England, the OECD and a select committee of Members of Parliament (MPs) advocating a faster rate of deficit reduction. Despite their appearing to be a parity in coverage the arguments for accelerated deficit reduction were more developed, given more space and at times directly endorsed by journalists. For instance:

Journalist 1:   Let's stay on the economic theme because the pressure on the government to be more explicit about its plans to reduce the deficit have increased today. The Organisation for Economic co-operation and Development has echoed the recent appeal by Mervyn King, the Bank of England governor. The OECD say the plans for rebalancing the budget should be more ambitious. Well to talk about this our economics editor Stephanie Flanders is with me. It is really Stephanie becoming the real battleground?

Journalist 2:   Yeah and for good reason because whoever wins the next election is going to inherit a massive budget deficit and a very urgent challenge to get that deficit back down. And in fact we've already heard from the government quite a lot about the tightening that it thinks would have to happen in the budget over the next few years. In fact the Institute for Fiscal Studies reckons that all the measures that they've announced so far added together would amount to a squeeze in the budget of around £90 billion in today's money a year by 2017. So that's pretty significant. But as you suggested, the OECD thinks they should be more ambitious and they should be more explicit about where particularly the spending cuts are going to fall. (News at Ten, 29 June 2009)

Nowhere in coverage was the argument made that deficit reduction should not conform to the artificial timetables set out by the two main parties, but instead should wait until the recovery was established so as to avoid the constraint of the ZLB. The only reference in coverage (minus the macroeconomic justification) to this perspective was a brief comment by the Scottish National Party (SNP) MP Stewart Hosie:

This whole budget was predicated on coming out of recession this year which no one else seem to believe and predicated on massive cuts in the teeth of a recession. It was the wrong thing to do. (News at Ten, 22 April 2009)

The case that deficit reduction was urgent was tied to a series of arguments (see Fig. 4.12) about the consequences of a rise in public debt that were also highlighted in press coverage. The primary threat in BBC news accounts was future debt refinancing. In this account a reporter states that the UK could face a gilt strike and then access is given to a City voice to support this point:

Journalist: Borrowing this much means the government needs a lot of investors to buy its debt. Now there are plenty of takers but that may not last.
Ruth Lea: It is a risk the Chancellor should keep in mind that in fact investors could go on strike and say they are not going to buy British debt.
Journalist: To prevent that the Conservatives think we should be counting the pennies now. (News at Ten, 19 February 2009)

And in another news broadcast the danger of a gilt strike was linked to the argument that more stimulus was unaffordable:

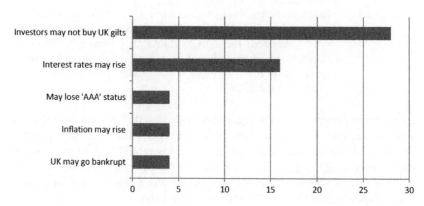

Fig. 4.12 Deficit dangers (percentage of articles featuring each danger)

Ken Wattret: (Chief European Economist BNP Paribus) Well potentially what it tells us is that there is a limited appetite in the investment community to continue to buy government bonds and the background to that is a genuine problem with the size of the Budget deficit in the UK.

Journalist: And this the day after the Governor of the Bank of England warned that another big fiscal boost to the economy would not be affordable because borrowing was so high. (News at Ten, 25 March 2009)

As noted in the introduction the perspective that there were 'bond vigilantes' poised to abandon UK gilts was a contested view (e.g. Krugman 2009b). However whilst it was regularly made by sources from the City, Bank of England and Conservative party the opposite view was barely mentioned. This perspective was also regularly endorsed by journalists. For instance:

Journalist: The trouble is Britain is very dependent on foreign investors buying up all this debt and there is so much debt, that is a real vulnerability. Investors have to believe that this [government growth forecasts] is going to be true now. They can't just take it as a leap of faith. That's the worry if they do lose faith if they don't think now that he is going to succeed, even his very difficult arithmetic does not add up. So it is a gamble and for very large stakes. (News at Ten, 22 April 2009)

The closest that journalists come to challenging these warnings was the argument that we aren't at a crisis point yet. For instance in discussing the potential loss of the UK's AAA credit rating a journalist commented:

Our national debt, what we own as a nation, will be more than £790 billion by the end of this year or £13,000 for everyone in the UK. That is not as high as some, but it's rising fast. As things stand Standard and Poor's thinks it will reach 100% of national income in less than five years. You can't stay at that level and keep your triple A. But that's all in the future. Britain has not been downgraded yet because whoever is in power in the next few years could take radical steps to bring borrowing back down before the debt gets so high. The trouble is, investors cannot know what is going to happen until they know the results of the next general election….A downgrade would push up the cost of government borrowing, though investors do not only look at ratings when deciding how much Britain's debt is worth. (News at Ten, 21 May 2009)

Although this account lacks some of the apocalyptic rhetoric seen in the right-wing press it endorsed the same core messages—that the deficit threatened Britain's AAA credit rating, that a downgrade would automatically raise interest rates and that 'radical' steps to bring down borrowing would help prevent this. Yet there was clearly an opposing view, rooted in mainstream macroeconomic theory that prioritising deficit reduction in a weak growth environment would damage the productive capacity (hysteresis effects) and tax base of the economy thereby threatening the UK's credit rating and its ability to close the deficit. As it was, that is what actually happened with Moody's downgrading government debt in February 2013 citing amongst other factors the Coalition Government's 'significant policy commitment to austerity'(Rodrigues and Foley 2013). Furthermore the downgrade did not drive up interest rates which continued to fall reaching a historic low of under 1 per cent in 2016 (Moore 2016).

The most serious warning—that the UK could go bankrupt —which was featured prominently in the right-wing press was not directly endorsed by any BBC journalist in our sample. However it was reported as a warning in one bulletin:

Journalist: Now is the Prime Minister listening to those siren voices in Europe who are so concerned? Is he listening to the Governor of the Bank of England? Is it the markets he's worried about? The answer is probably all of the above. He is very fond of history, Gordon Brown, he said here again the world should not repeat the mistakes of the London summit held many years ago in 1933, when there was no agreement and the Great Depression followed. At that time, the great British economist John Maynard Keynes said the answer was to spend, spend, spend your way out of depression. Mr. Brown recalled to the meeting he addressed this morning that a Treasury official had written on Keynes' work: inflation, extravagance, bankruptcy. The same warnings are being heard today and whether he likes it or not, the Prime Minister is having to listen. (News at Ten, 25 March 2009)

Once again the economy is primarily evaluated through the views of City analysts, the Bank of England and the financial markets. These are echoed by reporters and frame the contours of debate within which policy was discussed. However, what was missing is the opposing perspective, high-lighted earlier, of macroeconomists who questioned whether deficits would lead to interest rate rises and sterling depreciation, let alone inflation or bankruptcy. Whilst the accounts offered lack the strident editorialising seen in the national press which at times predicted national bankruptcy, BBC reports still operated with a framework which stressed the necessity of pre-emptive austerity to placate the financial markets.

How to Address the Deficit?

The range of perspectives featured in BBC reports can be seen in Fig. 4.13. The great majority (73.4 per cent) of news text concerned with solutions was devoted to arguments discussing cuts to public spending and/or regressive tax increases. The debate over public spending cuts alone accounted for 58.3 per cent of all news text. Arguments in favour of cuts were made by opposition politicians, Bank of England representatives as well as institutions such as the OECD. On some occasions, journalists directly endorsed the need for spending cuts:

> What will be cut, by how much and when? As the Government's coffers grow ever more empty, those are questions that can no longer be avoided. (News at Ten, 10 June 2009)

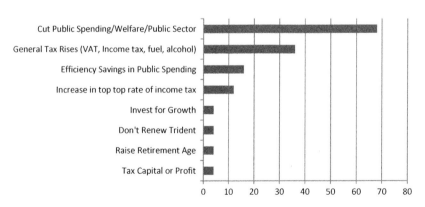

Fig. 4.13 Policy responses to the deficit (percentage of bulletins featuring each response)

The Chancellor refusing to spell out explicitly what cuts in spending he'll make. The opposition parties too, reluctant to do that but in the next 12 months they will have to do it. (News at Ten, 22 April 2009)

More typically, journalists worked within a consensus, shared by most of their sources, that cuts to public spending were the inevitable solution to the rise in the deficit. This view can also be seen in the way questions were put to politicians. During our sample period, there were three interviews where Gordon Brown, Andy Burnham and Alistair Darling were asked how the Government would address the deficit. These are the questions posed by the BBC's political editor:

> So what gets squeezed?
> Does that mean cuts?
> In plain English that's cuts?
> You know there will be spending cuts, why don't you say so? (News at Ten, 23 April 2009)

> What precisely will the government cut?
> What precisely will you cut?
> What are they? What will you cut?
> On your list what will you cut? Police, army will you cut those? (News at Ten, 10 June 2009)

> Are you being straight about hard this [reducing the deficit] could be?
> Forgive me Prime minister they are not asking questions about figures they are asking about you. They are saying, is my Prime Minister telling me the truth or hiding the truth about how bad the public finances are?
> What people will note that you will not say is that there will have to be cuts in certain programmes to pay to protect other programmes?
> What about the word cuts? What's wrong with the word cuts? Is it not right? (News at Ten, 1 July 2009)

It was perfectly legitimate for journalists to scrutinise the government's spending plans, especially when Labour were not being transparent about the cuts they were planning. It was also obvious cuts would be a dominant theme since they would be the key battlefield in the coming election. However, what was missing was any questioning of the wisdom of sharp cuts when the economy was so fragile and monetary policy was constrained by the ZLB. Journalists also did not put it to government ministers that there were alternatives to public spending cuts and question why these were not being considered. On occasions, journalists claimed they would explore the 'options', but these consisted of minor variations of cuts to public spending and/or increases in regressive taxation. For instance:

> British workers might have to put off their age of retirement to help repay the country's massive debt. That is one option proposed by independent think-tank .... Their report lays out three stark alternatives for bringing their debt level down. Government could cut all public spending by 10% in real terms or it could raise the basic rate of tax by 15p or it could raise the state retirement age to 70 by 2023. (News at Ten, 6 May 2009)

> Well If the Government did squeeze another £39 billion out of the budget, what would it mean for us? Well raising all of it through higher taxes would mean a tax rise of about £1250 per family. But of course not every family would pay the same amount. Or the Government could freeze all public spending in real terms for five years which would mean for most public services real cuts. Most likely is a mixture of both. (News at Ten, 6 April 2009)

In a bulletin on 28 January a journalist commented:

> The Treasury has already warned of a public spending clampdown. Education, health and other departments could well see a spending freeze over the next few years as attempts are made to stop the escalation of government debt. But the IFS warns that more tax increases may be needed. It suggests that VAT may have to be imposed on children's clothes and other items where there is currently no VAT payable.

A political decision to impose a regressive change to the tax system was presented as an economic necessity. There were no reports which said the deficit was so large that there would need to action against tax evasion/avoidance, or taxes would need to be raised on the wealthy or businesses via property, wealth or transactions taxes even though these are more popular and would raise larger sums than placing VAT on children's clothes (e.g. Yougov 2012; Ashcroft 2010). Such choices were invisible as public policy options. In another bulletin a journalist again cites comments from the IFS:

Journalist: Well some economists have already warned there will
                    have to be what they call two parliaments of pain before
                    the public finances enter a healthier phase. (News at Ten,
                    10 June 2009)

Views that challenge this perspective were very rarely featured. For example, there was only one instance where a direct link was made between
increasing growth and reducing the deficit:

Gordon Brown: It's growth that going to reduce the debt and the defi-
                   cits. It's growth that's also going to create the jobs of
                   the future. It's growth that's going to encourage young
                   people that when they leave school that there are oppor-
                   tunities for them and I'm determined to see it through
                   the next stage, having got through the financial crisis by
                   stabilising the banks. We've now got to get the growth
                   of jobs in the economy. The key to the reduction of
                   debt, the key to better public services. (News at Ten, 1
                   July 2009)

Another bulletin featured a suggestion from Nick Clegg that a reduction
to public spending could be made by looking at alternatives to the replace-
ment of the Trident missile, though this was balanced by a comment from
a source from the International Institute of Strategic Studies that it would
be 'impossible' to find a comparable weapons system 'at cheaper cost'
(News at Ten, 16 June 2009).

Discussion of raising taxes on the high earners appeared in 11.8 per
cent of the news text devoted to solutions and was accounted for entirely
by reporting of the rise in the top rate of income tax in the budget. A third
of this coverage consisted of commentary from business people and City
sources who argued the tax would be largely avoided and thus raise little
extra revenue. In addition, free-market narratives that such individuals
represented the 'wealth creators' in the economy were endorsed by
journalists[5]:

Journalist: So what is the view from Dragons' Den, from a wealth
                   creator?
Theo Paphatis: I don't think raising to 50% over 150 is going to cause
                   a mass exodus of people. I also don't believe he's going
                   to get a lot of money out of it. I think he will get

some headline from it and that's about the level of it. Because once you start encouraging people to find tax avoidance schemes, you actually don't benefit. (News at Ten, 22 April 2009)

Within the same bulletin a representative from one of the four big accountancy firms reiterated the same message that relatively little tax can be sourced from high earners and that regressive forms of taxation were the only realistic way to 'close the gap':

John Whiting (Tax partner PriceWaterhouseCooper):

The 50% tax rate, the phasing out of personal allowances, it will raise useful money but it is not going to paper over the holes in the bucket. What you need to do if you really want close the gaps you need to raise the basic rate of income tax, VAT, national insurance those are the big raisers. (News at Ten, 22 April 2009)

The notion that there are alternative tax raising options appeared as a single tiny fragment in coverage:

Will Hutton (Work Foundation):

You can make decisions about whether you are going to tax capital and profits, whether you are going to tax the rich or whether you are going to distribute the pain more across the entire population. (News at Ten, 23 March 2009)

The crucial point is journalists did not then explore these options and present them routinely as policy choices in coverage. Instead, BBC journalism operated as a closed circle excluding those who offered alternatives to cuts to public spending or regressive taxation.

Patterns of Source Access

Figure 4.14 shows the range of sources in the BBC sample. The most striking finding is the dominance of Conservative and Labour politicians who were featured far more frequently than any other sources and alone

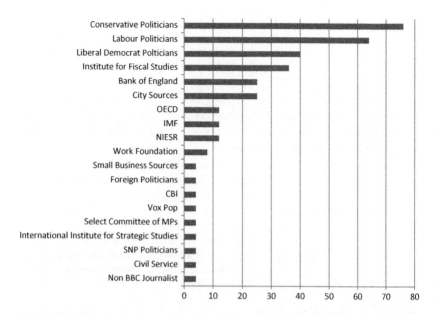

Fig. 4.14   Source appearances (percentage of bulletins featuring each source)

account for 45.9 per cent of news text. This is very much in line with previous research and reflects the BBC's place within Britain's unwritten constitution where it has a key role mediating the views of elected representatives in Parliament (Negrine 1994). Somewhat surprisingly, Conservative politicians were featured more often than Labour MPs bucking the trend which sees incumbents secure more representation (Semetko 1996).

The next most heavily accessed source was the Institute for Fiscal Studies. It was treated as both the authoritative voice on fiscal analysis and a key definer of solutions for reducing the deficit. The IFS occupies a unique space in BBC economic coverage. The former BBC economics editor Robert Peston has remarked that the think tank is 'regarded as the ultimate authority … basically, when the IFS has pronounced, there's no other argument. It is the word of God.' (Akam 2016). However to have a single organisation exercising such control over the framing of economic news raises questions about plurality in broadcasting. This is especially so when the IFS's accuracy and impartiality—particularly in its macroeconomic analyses—have been questioned. A number of economists have argued that because the IFS doesn't build in macroeconomic modelling into its spending and revenue predictions its analyses don't take into account how changes in public spending affect government revenues via the multiplier—especially when interest rates are at the ZLB (Pettifor 2017; Weeks 2017; Wren-Lewis 2015b, 2017). Weeks (2017) argues that this 'flaw' means that much of the IFS's work has an 'ideological commitment to the balanced budget dogma' in contravention of IMF advice not to 'cap deficits' and instead use 'flexible expenditure rules'. Other commentators have argued that the IFS in supporting regressive taxes like VAT whilst opposing wealth taxes favours the interests of the wealthy and capital over those in employment (Murphy 2015). In a *Times* article the head of the IFS, Paul Johnson, argued that the state can't raise significant revenue from a crackdown on tax avoidance and that concentrating primarily on taxing the better off through increasing income, transaction and wealth taxes will mean 'chasing away wealth creation and increasing poverty' (Johnson 2015). The IFS may be correct in these views—or they may be wrong—but the crucial point is that these views are disputed. This means that relying so heavily on fiscal analysis and policy prescriptions from the IFS inevitably raises questions around balance and impartiality.

Other sources were primarily drawn from economic institutions who were strongly supportive of accelerated deficit reduction and austerity. These include City analysts, the Bank of England, IMF, OECD and CBI. Reports or statements from such sources sometimes operated as news hooks that structured coverage. For instance, a report on 24 June 2009 was built around a statement from the Governor of the Bank of England that the 'Government should be doing more to reduce borrowing'. In this way such sources both drive news agendas but also set the initial angles that are taken on stories.

The research did not find examples where oppositional voices (outside the Labour party) were able to drive the direction of coverage in the same manner. The data also shows that there was no space available to Keynesian or heterodox economists, academics, Labour unions or other representatives of civil society who might have advocated countercyclical or anti-austerity policies. In fact trade unions were given more space to contest austerity in the right-wing press than they were on the News at Ten during this period.

CONCLUSION: THE AUSTERITY CONSENSUS

The analysis of print and broadcast reporting highlighted some important areas of divergence between the BBC and press coverage, but what was more striking was the commonalities in sourcing and the range of explanations offered. In terms of how the rise in the deficit was explained; all newspapers highlighted (to varying degrees) the impact of the recession and falling tax revenues. All also discussed the impact of the bank bailouts, and all (except the *Mail*) mentioned that deficit spending was helping to maintain demand during the recession. However it was only in the right-wing press that the false argument that the deficit had been caused by historical overspending was given significant space. BBC reporting provided an accurate picture of what was driving the deterioration in the public finances by concentrating primarily on the impact of the recession on tax receipts. However what was missing from all accounts was discussion of the private debt dynamics—the increase in personal debt prior to the recession and the impact of deleveraging afterwards—that were contributing to the recession. This was part of a broader trend where public debt was given far more attention and seen as far more problematic than private debt.

In terms of how the deficit was framed there was a strong emphasis in all parts of the media on the 'record' or 'unprecedented' scale of the deficit but very little information about the historically low levels of debt that the UK was carrying coming into the recession and no mention of the maturity profile of UK gilts. The right-wing press also featured a number of false international comparisons which were not present either in the left leaning press or on the BBC. In discussing the consequences of the deficit there was a remarkable consensus that stretched across the right- and left-wing press and the BBC. This was that the deficit threatened future debt refinancing, interest rates, sterling and the country's credit rating. Economists or other analysts who questioned this consensus were not featured in television coverage and barely appeared in newspaper accounts. One possible reason for the consensus was the high level of routine access given to City sources whose views were treated as authoritative accounts by many journalists. Wren-Lewis (2015a: 31) argues that this reliance on City voices produces 'mediamacro' coverage which 'tend[s] to reflect the economic arguments of those on the right: regulation is bad, top rates of tax should be low, the state is too large, and budget deficits are a serious and immediate concern'. 'In the case of UK austerity', Wren-Lewis argues 'it has allowed the media to portray the reduction of the government's budget deficit as the overriding macroeconomic priority, when in reality that policy has done and may continue to do considerable harm' (Wren-Lewis 2015a: 32).

In discussion of the deficit the main differences between press and broadcasting were in tone and tenor rather than in their interpretation of events. Whilst all parts of the media endorsed the deficit dangers highlighted above, the warnings were more dramatic in the right of centre press. This part of the media also put the most threatening spin possible on ambiguous events which were then linked to arguments in favour of shrinking the state. In contrast, the *Guardian* stood out as the only media outlet to sometimes feature balanced accounts which questioned some of the negative reporting of the deficit.

In terms of how to respond to the rise in the deficit, again there was a strong consensus across all parts of the media that cuts to public spending and increases in regressive taxation had to be the primary policy response. In the press these appeared in news accounts and strongly worded editorials and comment pieces. On television such views were expressed by Conservative politicians, the IFS, business lobby groups as well as City voices and other elite financial sources.

Whilst calls for cuts to public spending and regressive tax increases dominated coverage alternative measures such as investing for growth in new/green technologies, cracking down on tax havens or introducing wealth, property or transaction taxes were completely excluded from BBC and almost all press coverage (Dolphin 2009). Once again the *Guardian* operated as a outlier, being the only organisation to, on occasion, raise these possibilities.

In the next chapter, I will examine how these patterns in reporting contributed towards public acquiescence to austerity.

NOTES

1. For further discussion of the impact of MER on growth see Menegatti and Roubini (2007) or McBride (2006).
2. The differences between the figures provided by Wren-Lewis (2013b) and Keep (2017a) reflect minor adjustments to GDP, debt and deficit figures made over time by the ONS and OBR.
3. The Thatcher administration covers the entire period from 1979–1989, the Major administration 1990–1996 and New Labour 1997–2010. Since the

different governments changed in the middle of years these estimates are only approximations and are not completely accurate.

4. The Zero Lower Bound refers to the fact that (conventional) monetary policy loses its power when interest rates approach zero. This is because rates can no longer be cut in order to stimulate demand and investment in the economy. As interest rates hit the ZLB governments who wish to raise economic activity are forced to rely either on (1) fiscal policy, or (2) unconventional monetary policy such as bond buying (quantitative easing) or measures such as monetising deficits or helicopter money (Reichlin et al. 2013).

5. The idea that entrepreneurs, and the private sector more generally, create the wealth that is then consumed by the public sector and other parts of the economy is a key staple of right-wing ideology—see for instance Wright (2015). As the audience study shows (see p. x) it is also a narrative that has been influential in how the public see the process of wealth creation. However as Blagden (2015) notes it ignores how wealth creation is a collective endeavour built on a wide variety of actors in both the private and public sector: 'The total wealth generated by any business is a product of *all* of the capital, both financial *and* human, that has been invested in it. The business owner's personal labour is part of this, but it is not all. The midwives who bring a company's workers (including its owners) into the world, the teachers who give its workers (including its owners) their literacy and numeracy, the university academics who refine its high-skilled workers' (including its owners') analytical skills and conduct productivity-boosting foundational research, the construction workers providing the infrastructure for business and wider daily life, the doctors who preserve the workers' (including the owners') economic effectiveness both prior to and whilst working for the business, the police and military personnel who create a secure environment for all past and present economic activity, and indeed, the company's own payroll employees are all intrinsic parts of the wealth creation process.' For a discussion of the role of the state in high-technology based capital accumulation see Mazzucato (2011).

References

Akam, S. (2016, March 15). The British Umpire: How the IFS Became the Most Influential Voice in the Economic Debate. *Guardian*. Available at: https://www.theguardian.com/business/2016/mar/15/british-umpire-how-institute-fiscal-studies-became-most-influential-voice-in-uk-economic-debate. Date accessed 9 July 2018

Alloway, T. (2011, April 5). The Importance of Debt Maturity. *Financial Times*. Available at: https://ftalphaville.ft.com/2011/04/05/536631/the-importance-of-debt-maturity/. Date accessed 9 July 2018.

Andersen, A. L., Duus, C., & Jensen, T. L. (2014). *Household Debt and Consumption During the Financial Crisis: Evidence from Danish Micro Data* (Danmarks National Bank Working Paper No. 89).

Ashcroft, M. (2010). *What Future for Labour?* Available at: http://lordashcroft-polls.com/2010/09/what-future-for-labour/. Date accessed 9 July 2018.

Bank of England. (2018). Mortgage Equity Release Data. Available at: https://www.bankofengland.co.uk/boeapps/database/fromshowcolumns.asp?Travel=NIxAZxSUx&FromSeries=1&ToSeries=50&DAT=RNG&FD=1&FM=Jan&FY=1997&TD=31&TM=Dec&TY=2027&FNY=Y&CSVF=TT&html.x=66&html.y=26&SeriesCodes=LPQBE92,LPQB9LX,LPMVTVJ,LPQVTVJ,LPQBL2J,LPMVTYG,LPQVTYG,LPMVTYI&UsingCodes=Y&Filter=N&title=Housing%20Equity%20Withdrawal. Date accessed 9 July 2018.

Bardens, J., & Webb, D. (2012). *Government Borrowing and Debt: International Comparisons*, SN/EP/6504. London: House of Commons Library.

BBC. (2009). *Is UK Government Debt Really that High?* Available at: http://news.bbc.co.uk/1/hi/business/8415703.stm. Date accessed 9 July 2018.

Benito, A., & Power, J. (2004). Housing Equity and Consumption: Insights from the Survey of English Housing. *Bank of England Quarterly Bulletin,* (Autumn), 302–309.

Blagden, D. (2015). Labour Must Abandon the Dangerous Language of 'Wealth Creators'. *New Statesman.* Available at: https://www.newstatesman.com/politics/2015/05/labour-must-abandon-dangerous-language-wealth-creators. Date accessed 9 July 2018.

Blastland, M. (2008). *The Myth of Record Debt.* Available at: http://news.bbc.co.uk/1/hi/magazine/7733794.stm. Accessed 12 July 2018.

Brittan, S. (2009, October 2). A Cool Look at the Current Deficit Hysteria. *Financial Times.*

Catte, P. (2004). *Housing Markets, Wealth and the Business Cycle* (OECD Economics Department Working Papers No. 394). Available at http://ec.europa.eu/economy_finance/events/2005/bxlworkshop2111/contributions/girouard_paper_en.pdf. Accessed 12 July 2018.

Chang, H. J. (2010a, May 3). The UK Needs a Selective Industrial Policy. *Guardian.*

Chang, H. J. (2010b, October 19). Time to Broaden the Debate on Spending Cuts. *Guardian.*

Chu, B. (2014, September 16). Bank Blames High Household Debt for Depth of Britain's Recession. *Independent.* Available at: http://www.independent.co.uk/news/business/news/bank-blames-high-household-debt-for-depth-of-britain-s-recession-9734758.html. Date accessed 9 July 2018.

Chu, B. (2015, April 1). Two Thirds of Economists Say Coalition Austerity Harmed the Economy. *Independent.* Available at: http://www.independent.co.uk/news/business/news/two-thirds-of-economists-say-coalition-austerity-harmed-the-economy-10149410.html. Date accessed 9 July 2018.

Clark, T., & Reed, H. (2013, April 4). If Britain Is Broke It Has Been for Most of the Last 300 Years. *The Guardian*.

Coppola, F. (2013). *Government Debt Isn't What You Think It Is*. Available at http://coppolacomment.blogspot.co.uk/2013/01/government-debt-isnt-what-you-think-it.html. Date accessed 9 July 2018.

Dolphin, T. (2009). *Time for Another People's Budget*. Available at https://ippr.org/files/images/media/files/publication/2011/05/peoples_budget_1687.pdf. Date accessed 12 July 2018.

Dynan, K. (2012, Spring). *Is a Household Debt Overhang Holding Back Consumption?* Brookings Papers on Economic Activity.

European Central Bank. (2017). *Debt Sustainability Analysis for Euro Area Sovereigns: A Methodological Framework* (Occasional Paper Series 185). Available at: https://www.ecb.europa.eu/pub/pdf/scpops/ecbop185.en.pdf. Date accessed 9 July 2018.

Giroud, X., & Mueller, H. M. (2015). *Firm Leverage and Unemployment During the Great Recession* (NBER Working Paper No. 21076).

Hunter, P. (2015). *Red Alert: Why Labour Lost and What Needs to Change*. Smith Institute. Available from: https://smithinstitutethinktank.files.wordpress.com/2015/07/red-alert-why-labour-lost-and-what-needs-to-change.pdf. Accessed 9 July 2018.

Hutton, W. (2009, July 5). Hail the Man Who Argues Britain Should Stop Worrying About Its Debt. *Observer*.

Institute for Fiscal Studies (IFS). (2010). *Public Spending Under Labour*. Available from: http://www.ifs.org.uk/bns/bn92.pdf. Accessed 9 July 2018.

Institute for Fiscal Studies (IFS). (2012). *Revenues Including Forecasts*. Available from: http://www.ifs.org.uk/ff/revenues.xls. Accessed 9 July 2018.

International Monetary Fund. (2000). *Debt- and Reserve-Related Indicators of External Vulnerability*. Available at https://www.imf.org/external/np/pdr/debtres/debtres.pdf. Accessed 9 July 2018.

Irwin, G., Byrne, D., Murphy, R., Reed, H., & Ruane, S. (2009). In Place of Cuts. *Compass*. Available at: http://www.compassonline.org.uk/wp-content/uploads/2013/05/Compass-in-place-of-cuts-WEB2.pdf. Accessed 12 July 2018.

Johnson P. (2015, April 22). There Is No Magic Money Tree: Parties Should Stop the Pretence that 'Someone Else' Can Always Pay. *The Times*.

Keep, M. (2017a). *Government Borrowing, Debt and Debt Interest: Historical Statistics and Forecasts* (House of Commons Briefing Paper Number 05745). Available at: http://researchbriefings.files.parliament.uk/documents/SN05745/SN05745.pdf. Accessed 9 July 2018.

Keep, M. (2017b). *The Budget Deficit: A Short Guide* (House of Commons Briefing Paper Number 06167). Available at: http://researchbriefings.files.parliament.uk/documents/SN06167/SN06167.pdf. Accessed 9 July 2018.

Koo, R. C. (2009). *The Holy Grail of – Lessons from Japan's Great Recession*. London: John Wiley.

Koo, R. C. (2011). The World in Balance Sheet Recession: Causes, Cure, and Politics. *Real World Economics Review, 58*, 19–37.

Krugman, P. (2009a). Deficit Hysteria. *New York Times.* Available from: https://krugman.blogs.nytimes.com/2009/11/23/deficit-hysteria/. Accessed 9 July 2018.

Krugman, P. (2009b). Invisible Bond Vigilantes. *New York Times.* Available from: http://krugman.blogs.nytimes.com/2009/11/19/invisible-bond-vigilantes/. Accessed 9 July 2018.

Lilico, A, O'Brien, N., & Atashzai, A. (2009). *Controlling Public Spending: The Scale of the Challenge.* Available at: https://policyexchange.org.uk/wp-content/uploads/2016/09/controlling-public-spending-jun-09.pdf. Accessed 12 July 2018.

Mazzucato, M. (2010, October 9). How to Build an Ideas Factory. *Guardian.*

Mazzucato, M. (2011). The Entrepreneurial State. *Renewal, 19*(3/4), 1–11.

McBride, B. (2006). *GDP Growth: With and Without Mortgage Extraction.* Available at: http://www.calculatedriskblog.com/2006/09/gdp-growth-with-and-without-mortgage.html. Accessed 9 July 2018.

McKinsey Global Institute. (2010). *Debt and Deleveraging: The Global Credit Bubble and Its Economic Consequences.* Available at http://www.mckinsey.com/~/media/McKinsey/Global%20Themes/Employment%20and%20Growth/Debt%20and%20deleveraging/MGI_Debt_and_deleveraging_full_report. Accessed 9 July 2018.

Menegatti, C., & Roubini, N. (2007). *The Direct Link Between Housing and Consumption: Wealth Effect and Home Equity Withdrawal.* Available at http://www.economics.uni-linz.ac.at/members/Riese/files/SS08/239315/topic2_wealth_effect/Roubini_redir.pdf

Mian, A., Rao, K., & Sufi, A. (2013). Household Balance Sheets, Consumption, and the Economic Slump. *Quarterly Journal of Economics, 128*(1), 687–726.

Moore, E. (2016, July 11). Gilt Yields Sink to New Lows. *Financial Times.*

Murphy, R. (2015). *The Institute for Fiscal Studies Fisked.* Available at: http://www.taxresearch.org.uk/Blog/2015/04/28/the-institute-for-fiscal-studies-fisked-2/. Accessed 9 July 2018.

Murphy, R. (2016). *The Conservatives Have Been the Biggest Borrowers Over the Last 70 Years.* Available at: http://www.taxresearch.org.uk/Blog/2016/03/13/the-conservatives-have-been-the-biggest-borrowers-over-the-last-70-years/. Accessed 9 July 2018.

Negrine, R. (1994). *Politics and the Mass Media in Britain.* London: Routledge.

Neild, R. (2010). *The National Debt in Perspective.* Newsletter of the Royal Economic Society. Available from: http://www.res.org.uk/view/arti- cle5jan-12Correspondence.html. Accessed 9 July 2018.

Office for National Statistics. (2011). *Inclusion of Royal Bank of Scotland and Lloyds Banking Group in the Public Sector Finances.* Available at: http://webarchive.nationalarchives.gov.uk/20160108004529/http://www.ons.gov.uk/ons/guide-method/method-quality/specific/economy/public-sector-finances/inclusion-of-rbs-and-lloyds-banking-group-in-the-public-sector-finances.pdf. Accessed 9 July 2018.

Organisation for Economic Cooperation and Development. (2012). OECD Economic Outlook, Issue 2, No. 92. Available at https://doi.org/10.1787/888932751006. Accessed 9 July 2018.

Pawson, H., & Wilcox, S. (2013). *UK Housing Review 2013*. Dorking: Chartered Institute of Housing. Available at: https://www.ukhousingreview.org.uk/ukhr13/index.html. Accessed 9 July 2018.

Pettifor, A. (2009, September 25). An Alternative G20 Model. *Guardian*.

Pettifor, A. (2017). *The IFS: Viewing the Economy Through Wrong End of a Telescope*. Available at: http://www.primeeconomics.org/articles/the-ifs-viewing-the-economy-through-wrong-end-of-a-telescope. Accessed 9 July 2018.

Philo, G. (2010, August 15). Deficit Crisis: Let's Really Be in It Together. *Guardian*.

Public and Commercial Services Union. (2010). *There Is an Alternative to Public Spending Cuts*. Available at http://www.pcs.org.uk/en/campaigns/campaign-resources/there-is-an-alternative-the-case-against-cuts-in-public-spending.cfm. Accessed 9 July 2018.

Reich, R. (2009, August 31). Why the Deficit Hysteria? I Only Wish We'd Borrow More. *Guardian*.

Reichlin, L., Turner, A., & Woodford, M. (2013). *Helicopter Money as a Policy Option*. Available at: http://voxeu.org/article/helicopter-money-policy-option. Accessed 9 July 2018.

Rodrigues, V., & Foley, S. (2013, February 22). UK Loses Triple A Credit Rating. *Financial Times*.

Rosewell, B. (2009, October 7). We Must Use Debt to Create the Assets We so Sorely Need [Letter to the Editors]. *Financial Times*.

Semetko, H. (1996). Political Balance on Television—Campaigns in the United States, Britain, and Germany. *The International Journal of Press/Politics, 1*(1), 51–71.

Sikka, P. (2008, November 24). Rebalancing the Books. *Guardian*.

Sikka, P. (2009, July 2). There Are Alternatives to Public Spending Cuts. *Guardian*.

Taylor, C., Farrugia, B., O'Connell, J., et al. (2009). *How to Save £50 Billion*. Institute of Directors/Taxpayers' Alliance. Available from: https://d3n8a8pro7vhmx.cloudfront.net/taxpayersalliance/pages/211/attachments/original/1427715115/50bil.pdf?1427715115. Accessed 10 July 2018.

Trade Union Congress. (2016). *Record High for Family Debt Shows that We Don't Have a Recovery that Works for All, Says TUC*. Available at: https://www.tuc.org.uk/news/record-high-family-debt-shows-we-don%E2%80%99t-have-recovery-works-all-says-tuc. Accessed 10 July 2018.

Webb, D., & Bardens, J. (2012). *Government Borrowing, Debt and Debt Interest Payments: Historical Statistics and Forecasts*, House of Commons Library, SN/EP/5745. Available at: https://www.files.ethz.ch/isn/151100/SN06054.pdf

Webb, D., & Bardens, J. (2013). Government Borrowing, Debt and Debt Interest Payments: Historical Statistics and Forecasts, House of Commons Library, SN/EP/5745.

Weeks, J. (2017). *Assessing the Manifestos – The IFS Fails the Test*. Available at: http://www.primeeconomics.org/articles/assessing-the-manifestos-the-ifs-fails-the-test. Accessed 10 July 2018.

World Bank. (2017). *Household Final Consumption Expenditure as a % of GDP*. Available at: https://data.worldbank.org/indicator/NE.CON.PETC.ZS. Accessed 10 July 2018.

Wren-Lewis, S. (2013a). *Ken Rogoff on UK Austerity*. Available at: http://mainlymacro.blogspot.co.uk/2013/10/ken-rogoff-on-uk-austerity.html. Accessed 10 July 2018.

Wren-Lewis, S. (2013b). Aggregate Fiscal Policy Under the Labour Government, 1997–2010. *Oxford Review of Economic Policy, 29*(1), 25–46.

Wren-Lewis, S. (2015a). The Austerity Con. *London Review of Books, 37*(4), 9–11.

Wren-Lewis, S. (2015b). *A Criticism of the IFS*. Available at: https://mainlymacro.blogspot.co.uk/2015/04/a-criticism-of-ifs.html. Accessed 10 July 2018.

Wren-Lewis, S. (2017). *But Do the Numbers Add Up?* Available at: https://mainlymacro.blogspot.co.uk/2017/05/but-do-numbers-add-up.html. Accessed 10 July 2018.

Wright, B. (2015, April 1). Labour is Foolish to Dismiss the Nation's Job and Wealth Creators. *Daily Telegraph*. Available at: http://www.telegraph.co.uk/finance/economics/11510391/Labour-is-foolish-to-dismiss-the-nations-job-and-wealth-creators.html. Accessed 10 July 2018.

Yougov. (2012). *Class Survey Results*. Available at http://classonline.org.uk/docs/YouGov-Class_Polling_Results_120522_Economic_Policies.xls. Accessed 10 July 2018.

CHAPTER 5

The Deficit Debate: Audience Studies

INTRODUCTION

This chapter examines the public reaction to the deficit debate that took place in 2009. It draws on 16 focus group discussions which explore how the notion of the public deficit was understood by audiences and what measures they thought were appropriate to address it. The focus groups discussed in this chapter involve the same people featured in Chap. 3 where information about their demographic composition and patterns of media use can be found. Before engaging in focus group discussions the participants completed questionnaires which asked them about their views on what had caused the rise in public debt and what measures they had heard discussed to address it. These answers were then used as the starting point for discussions.

WHAT CAUSED THE RISE IN THE DEFICIT?

In their written responses just over a fifth of the respondents either stated that they didn't know what had caused the rise in public debt or provided answers which confused government debt with consumer or bank debt. Stanley (2014: 909), who found similar conflation of government and household debt in his research, suggests that these confusions helped to cement the metaphor of the state as household by linking the idea that we 'had all been living beyond our means' to the need to cut state spending. Of the remainder, one in eight (5/56) identified the role of the recession,

M. Berry, *The Media, the Public and the Great Financial Crisis*,
https://doi.org/10.1007/978-1-137-49973-8_5

or global recession (2/56). In our discussions, the role of the recession in driving up government debt was raised in three of the 16 focus groups. One respondent spoke of 'spending to keep the country out of recession' (Middle class group, Coventry) whilst another, who worked in accountancy, provided an informed explanation:

> In terms of the income that the government receives then their tax take has been reduced because I think a lot of their income hypothetically, well not hypothetically, a lot of their income comes from bonuses from the finance sector and that has reduced as a result of banks being bailed out and bonuses being reduced there. That's not the prime factor but a combination of the tax revenues have decreased and in addition they have had to use more funding to underwrite the banking sector. (Middle class group, Warwickshire)

However just under 70 per cent of written responses (38/56) saw the rise as attributable to increased public spending and this came across strongly in the focus groups.

Table 5.1 provides details of the ten most frequently cited areas of public spending which were identified as contributing to the rise in public debt in individual written responses. It is not surprising that the costs of bailing out the financial sector were commonly seen as driving the rise in public debt when the banking crisis—which had only taken place less than a year before the focus groups—was still fresh in many participants'

Table 5.1 Elements of public spending identified as being responsible for the rise in public debt (individual written responses)

1	Banks/Bank Bailouts
2	Wars/Military Spending
3	Immigration/Asylum Seekers
4	Welfare/Benefits claimants
5	MPs pay and expenses
6	Foreign Aid
7=	Quangos
7=	More public sector workers
7=	Servicing historic debt
10=	Benefit fraud
10=	Olympics
10=	Health
10=	Education
10=	Policing

memories. However, most people in the focus groups saw the rise in government debt as being the result of a long period of Labour overspending. One participant argued that it was due to 'historical overspending as well even before the crisis happened there has been overspending by government and increasing the debt and the problems trying to service that debt' (Low income group, Glasgow). In another group a participant said:

> Over the last ten years national debt has been building, building into you know the amount owed by us as a nation has been growing it had to reach a tipping point. (Middle class group, Warwickshire)

The visibility of the long wars in Afghanistan and Iraq meant they were widely seen as a contributory factor. However, what wasn't expected was that in 9 out of the 16 focus groups the view that immigration and asylum were to blame for the rise in public debt was firmly expressed. This perspective was particularly strong in groups of low income or older participants where it was often the first factor that was identified. In one group a participant spoke of immigrants 'taking all the money and bleeding it dry' (Low income group, Glasgow). In another group a participant spoke of how letting in more people meant that the 'books are not going to balance':

> We can't afford to keep them right there's people paying tax for 40 year and then there's somebody comes in here with a full family and they're getting the benefits, the same benefits that someone's been here for fifty year and then at some point the books are not going to balance. (Low income group, Glasgow)

It was clear from the group discussions that a key source of such beliefs was reports in the press which focused on benefit payments made to immigrants and asylum seekers—though participants also pointed to personal experience as well. Many respondents across the sample believed that immigrants and asylum seekers were only coming to the UK so they could live a life on benefits:

Respondent 1:   Social services are paying out so much money if you sit back and see how much people are getting per week, just sitting back you know thinking 'luxury, luxury'
Respondent 2:   Yeah

Respondent 1:	And we're going to work, working hard you know and everything else paying our taxes even though we're pensioners we've still got to pay our taxes.
Moderator:	Do you think most of the immigrants who come over have been just going on benefits?
Respondent 2:	Yeah, they have.
Moderator:	What makes you say that – is it something you read in the paper or is it personal experience?
Respondent 2:	I've read quite a lot of it but it's also from experience. (Senior citizens group, Surrey)

And in another group:

Respondent 1:	What about the immigrants coming into this country and all and all the houses they're getting
Respondent 2:	The asylum seekers a lot of money on that too.
Moderator:	So you think a big part of the money that we owe has gone on immigrants and asylum seekers?
Respondent 1:	Oh aye definitely
Moderator:	Would you all agree with that?

[All five in focus group lift hands and indicate agreement]. (Low income group, Glasgow)

Another participant spoke of 'billions of pounds that the government hands out willy nilly' in family allowance to immigrants 'for children that are not even in this country' (Senior citizen's group, Glasgow). In another group participants brought up instances of benefit fraud by immigrants that they had read about in the press:

| Respondent 1: | You see the social security and all that there's millions and millions of people coming into Britain and they're claiming three or four times and that must be costing a fortune in money and they've got houses here and houses there. |
| Respondent 2: | Look at that one a month ago in the paper she had ten passports for claiming for ten people. It was all illegal immigrants and she was claiming that they had kids and all the rest of it. (Low income group, Glasgow) |

Three conclusions flow from these findings. First, public understanding of the contours of public spending is extremely limited. Total benefit fraud in 2008–2009 was estimated by the DWP to £1.1 billion or 0.8 per cent of benefit spending. Family allowance claimed by EU migrants in 2012 was estimated to be £55 million or 0.035 per cent of total benefit spending (Migration Watch 2013). Neither were significant factors in the rise in public debt post-2007 but loomed large in the minds of many of our participants. Second, people tended to see the economy as a container which some people were seen as contributing to and others were seen as draining. Responsible people were seen to be putting in at least as much as they took out (see also below on 'paying' and 'drawing' 'classes'). This finding is supported in other research which noted that seeing the economy in this way had the effect of 'reinforcing the demonisation of groups who are portrayed as draining the pot, like immigrants and benefit claimants' (New Economics Foundation 2018: 28). Third, without an understanding of how public spending breaks down citizens will overestimate the contribution of issues that have high visibility in the media, especially if media accounts focus on emotive and atypical cases whose existence is then taken to be widespread. So the strong emphasis given in the press to highly charged accounts of benefit fraud by immigrants led our respondents to massively overestimate the impact that it had on the public finances. In a similar vein, another issue with high media visibility – MPs expenses – were seen in a number of focus groups to have contributed to the deficit. Yet total MPs expenses in 2008–9 were £102 million or 0.015 per cent of total public spending (Mason 2013).

It was also the case that benefit spending more widely was frequently seen as a major cause of the rise in public debt. In a Glasgow group one respondent argued that the 'amount that goes on it is ridiculous' with another agreeing, stating that 'it encourages people to go on the dole...it doesn't encourage people to work because if you have to feed a family of four, you need to earn quite a lot of money to keep them but on the dole you get everything free' (Low income group, Glasgow). In another group participants discussed how the rise of a 'benefits culture' had contributed to the rise in national debt.

Respondent 1:   I think this country's got into a benefits culture.
Respondent 2:   Yes definitely.

Moderator: And you see that as a big reason why the country owes
                      so much money?
Respondent 2:   Yes.
Respondent 1:   Yeah. (Senior citizen's group, Surrey)

In another group a clear distinction was made between the 'paying' and
the 'drawing' classes—a striking precursor to Coalition narratives of 'striv-
ers and shirkers' and 'alarm clock Britain'—reflected in intergenerational
unemployment:

Respondent 1:   I think you have a huge disparity in that there a big
                      problem in this country between those who will never
                      leave the paying classes and those who will never leave
                      the drawing classes and I think the younger genera-
                      tion particularly feel a civil war brewing because they
                      spend all their lives going to work to pay for other
                      people's children and quite sensibly decide they can't
                      afford their own because they've got everybody else's
                      to pay for.
Respondent 2:   Unless they're on benefits then they've got lots.
Respondent 1:   This is the whole point, isn't it? You're in one cate-
                      gory or the other and if you're going to spend your
                      life in the paying class you are precluded from living
                      your life as you want to by the high amount of tax you
                      pay.
Respondent 2:   You start paying tax far too early.
Respondent 1:   This is what is aggravating people. They see that
                      there are people who are never going to *third genera-
                      tion families who've never been to work* and they live
                      equally well than those people who get out of their
                      beds at six o'clock in the morning and go to work
                      and then catch to pay for everything. (Middle class
                      group, Coventry)

However, research from the Centre for Market and Public Organisation
at Bristol University found that intergenerational unemployment was
rare. Workless parents and grown up children living together were found
to make up 0.9 per cent of households whilst the proportion of

households where two generations had never worked was 0.1 per cent (Macmillan 2011). As for families where three generations had never been employed, researchers from the Joseph Rowntree Foundation couldn't find a single case in the most deprived areas of Teeside and Glasgow (Shildrick et al. 2012). Yet such alleged cases could be found in the newspapers which the respondents in the Coventry focus group consumed:

> Headline: Meet the families where no one's worked for THREE generations – and they don't care

> Known as the 'Shameless' family among horrified neighbours, the McFaddens 'boast' three generations of adults who are not working. All ten members of the clan share a council house and live off benefits amounting to around £32,000 a year. And very happy they are, too… What a damning verdict on our claim-it-all society, a grotesque mirror of the dark television drama Shameless. (*Mail*, 21 March 2008)

The views on welfare in our sample are supported by data from the British Social Attitudes Survey which found a substantial hardening in attitudes towards those on benefits during New Labour's period in office. In 1997 only 28 per cent of the population agreed with the statement that 'benefits are too high and discourage work' but by 2008 this had risen to 61 per cent (Taylor-Gooby and Taylor 2015). Yet the widespread perception that benefit spending—and particularly spending on the unemployed— had increased under New Labour is not borne out by evidence. As the IFS (2010: 8) note, 'spending on social benefits absorbed 13.1 per cent of national income (33.0 per cent of public spending) in 1996–97 but only 11.1 per cent of national income (27.1 per cent of spending) in 2007–08'. Furthermore whilst pension spending which is broadly popular with the public saw substantial real terms increases, the value of benefits for the unemployed such as Unemployment Benefit/Job Seekers' Allowance or Income Support were either static or fell in real terms (Rutherford 2013).

The ability of press accounts to influence perceptions of what caused the rise in public debt could also be seen in the linking of the deficit with other issues which have been a frequent focus of negative newspaper coverage over many years such as quangos, foreign aid and the EU (Deacon and

Monk 2001; Anderson and Weymouth 1999). In one group a respondent stated that the EU 'costs millions, trillions even' (Middle class group, Warwickshire) and in another group:

Respondent 1:	We haven't mentioned the EU at all and an enormous amount of money goes into there. On the radio today they said it was going up by 60 per cent
Moderator:	So you think the EU was a big element [in the rise in the deficit]?
Respondent 1:	It's a black hole.
Respondent 2:	It's a huge drain, isn't it?
Moderator:	Is the EU a huge drain on the country?
Respondent 1:	Yes. (Middle class group, Coventry)

In a similar vein a number of respondents mentioned public sector pensions. One commented:

> I think pensions, public sector pensions are taking a huge tranche out of income into the coffers if you like because we've now reached the baby boomers, my age group are now drawing huge tranches of money out of public funding either at local level or at national level. (Middle class group, Coventry)

In articulating their views on the expansion of the public sector under New Labour many felt that the extra money had not been well spent particularly in areas like the NHS. One participant said that there had been 'some improvement but not a great deal' and that the money hadn't gone 'on what you want to see it go on: more beds, hospitals, more nurses, more doctors'. (Low income group, Glasgow). Such views do not correspond with what actually happened when Labour was in power when there was a sharp increase in the number of doctors, nurses and hospital beds (IFS 2010). Participants also reproduced arguments that regularly appeared in the right-wing press which alleged overspending, waste and the creation of 'non-jobs' (see Chap. 6). In one of our groups a participant complained about the number of equal opportunities officers and argued that 'there must be thousands of people in local government who haven't really got a job' (Middle class group, Warwickshire) Here is a selection of quotations where respondents cited issues around waste or overexpansion of the public sector as driving the rise in government debt:

Government had been 'too expansionist' with 'too many working for council' (Senior citizens, Coventry)

They've expanded so much of the public sector that they're now going to have to go the other way aren't they (Middle class group, Coventry)

The 'welfare state is bloated' (Low income group, Glasgow)

'Bad management' and 'waste' (Senior citizens, Glasgow)

'Mismanaged budgets' and 'council waste' (Low income group, Glasgow)

'Not managing their spending' and 'local government waste' (Middle class group, Warwickshire);

One respondent spoke of how newspaper accounts had led her to see the relationship between the public and private sector as being essentially a parasitic one where the private sector generated all the taxes which the public sector then spent- again a striking echo of how the relationship is sometimes reported in the press (see Chap. 6)

> I have read recently how much public sector jobs have risen in the last ten years. So basically Labour has created a lot of public sector jobs which have to be funded and also pensions are rising for the public sector and if you look for example at councils a lot of their income or a high percentage of their income is spent on policeman's pensions. It's very bizarre. I think that has a lot to do with it as well the public sector has grown hugely in this country whereas it is the private sector which pays the taxes has not grown as much at all. (Low income group, Surrey)

The evidence from opinion polls suggests that such views were widespread. An Ipsos-Mori poll (2009) conducted around the same time as the focus groups found that 63 per cent agreed with the statement 'there are many public services that are a waste of money and can be cut'. Although that this perception was widespread it was significantly more common amongst older voters (net agree 55+ 48 per cent vs. 29 per cent for under 55s), Conservative voters (net agree 53 per cent versus 14 per cent for Labour voters) and those on low incomes (net agree ABC1 32 per cent versus 41 per cent for C2DEs). It is also a sentiment more widely shared by tabloid readers (net agree 46 per cent) as opposed to those who consume broadsheets (net agree 27 per cent). Since the two most popular broadsheets (*Daily Telegraph* and *The Times*) regularly feature allegations of widespread public waste, and the tabloid category includes the left leaning *Mirror*, if the data was fine grained enough to separate out the readers of different newspapers the cleavages would almost certainly be starker.

Overall, the results from our focus groups suggest that many people were deeply confused about what had caused the rise in the UK deficit and public debt. Only a small minority were able to correctly identify the role of the recession and how this had depleted the tax base. The bulk of people in the focus groups instead thought that the most significant issue was increased public spending. When respondents identified which areas of public spending were responsible they tended to point to areas such as immigration, unemployment benefits, public sector pensions, quangos, waste, non-jobs, foreign aid and MPs expenses. This was due, in part, to the high visibility of these topics in the press and the power of the repetition of emotionally charged messages. As we will now see, when respondents were asked how the deficit should be reduced they tended to back policies which addressed the causal factors they had identified.

How to Reduce the Deficit?

On the questionnaire focus group members were asked what proposals they had heard for reducing the deficit. This allowed us to see what people had retained from media accounts which then could be used as a starting point for discussion to see whether participants agreed with such measures. Just over a quarter of respondents (15/56) either hadn't heard of any measures for bringing down the deficit or confused public debt with corporate or household debt. Of the rest most identified some form of public spending cut (23/41) or tax rise (15/41). Table 5.2 provides a list of all the measures identified in written responses.

The measures that individuals had heard about for reducing the deficit closely map—both in occurrence and frequency—what appeared in broadcasting and the press (see Chap. 4). In this way the media was able to determine which solutions the public were aware of. However this doesn't necessarily mean that people accepted the legitimacy of those policies or

Table 5.2   Measures for reducing public debt (individual written responses)

1	Public Spending cuts (unspecified)
2	Tax rises (unspecified)
3	Freeze/Reduce Public sector wages
4	Reduce Public sector employees
5	Reduce spending hospitals/schools
6	Reduce infrastructure spending
7=	Reduce benefits
7=	Scrap ID Cards
7=	Scrap Trident
7=	Grow economy/get people back to work
7=	Introduction of 50% income tax rate
11=	Put up retirement age
11=	Cut quangos
11=	Reduce public sector pensions
11=	Increase VAT

were unable to go beyond them and suggest alternatives. In our focus groups there wasn't any enthusiasm for cuts to frontline services such as health, education or policing despite these arguments being strongly made in press accounts. This is borne out in large scale polling which found that when respondents were asked 'which two or three, if any, of the main areas of public spending should be cut to restore public finances' only a small minority identified the police (8 per cent), schools (3 per cent), the NHS (2 per cent) or care for the elderly (1 per cent) (Ipsos-Mori 2009). On the whole, participants retained a strong attachment to core elements of the welfare state even if they harboured doubts about the size and efficiency of the public sector.

An important reason why our respondents objected to cuts was because of worries that they themselves would be adversely affected. So in one of our low income groups of janitors and secretaries a participant argued that 'the lower paid like us will suffer should any public sector be cut' before citing the example of gardeners he knew who were being 'screwed' by being forced to work weekends 'and they wouldn't be getting any enhancement for it' (Low income group. Glasgow). Others questioned the feasibility of some of the measures being discussed. For instance, one respondent mentioned Ian Duncan Smith's plans to 'streamline' the benefits system so 'you won't need the number of civil servants to administer the scheme' but another objected that 'I think that's too simplistic'

(Senior citizens groups, Glasgow). Others objected to measures like raising the retirement age because they were perceived to be 'grossly unfair'
when people had paid their national insurance contributions over many
years (Senior citizen group, Surrey). Notions of fairness also influenced
how people felt about reductions in public sector pensions. Although a
number of people voiced the opinion that they should be reduced this was
sometimes contested. For instance in one group a respondent echoed an
argument prominent in newspaper accounts—that 'gilt edged' public sector pensions were being unfairly subsidised in comparison to those in the
private sector and should be reduced:

> I think the pensions should be cut because the only people who seem to be
> getting these gilt edged final salary schemes are civil servants. The whole
> private sector seems to going onto purchasing cheaper pension schemes so
> why should they sort of be different. I remember reading the amount of our
> council tax that goes to pensions, it's phenomenal. (Middle class group,
> Warwickshire)

However another person in the group raised the point that 'public sector
staff often get paid less so you've got to factor that in' whilst a third
argued that people had joined the public sector partly because of the
pension scheme and 'you don't penalise in retrospect'. However this
third respondent also argued that something had to be done because
'these costs are going out of control' and the discrepancy between public, where people had a 'cast-iron guarantee', and private provision would
inevitably 'divide people'. The public then are not just sponges who
absorb media accounts passively. Questions of logic or fairness can mediate the reception of media messages in complex and contradictory ways.
Nevertheless, the media were effective in drawing attention to certain
areas of public spending and influencing perceptions of what was seen as
'affordable'.

The issue of affordability was closely linked in many respondents' minds
with what was seen the scale of the debt which reflected the threatening
narratives that were common in the press (see Chap. 4). One participant
who despite having voted Labour described them as a 'worst government
in the last 100 years or whatever' who had 'led the country into a disaster
owe money all over the damn place, got this national debt that's zooming
up' (Middle class group, Warwickshire).

Press accounts also appeared to influence the belief—against reflected in large scale polling—that there was so much waste in the public sector that the books could be balanced through efficiency saving without damage to front line services (Ipsos-Mori 2009). A common complaint was that the public sector employed too many consultants or managers, as one respondent put it 'you go into any hospital there are nearly as many administrators as there are doctors or nurses, they could do away with them, they didn't have them years ago' (Senior citizens, Glasgow). And in another group:

Respondent 1:	You've got to protect the public services, the local libraries, the local swimming baths.
Respondent 2:	Julian don't you believe there's a lot of wastage? Look what they've done to the police, they've amalgamating areas into one, they could do with one HR, one personnel, one this one that.
Respondent 1:	What I'm saying is
Respondent 2:	And they could save a lot of money in all areas. They got an overflow of managers. (Middle class group, Coventry)

This perception of widespread waste and inefficiency also meant that respondents could be dismissive of significant areas of public spending. For instance, a key aspect of New Labour education policy had been a substantial increase in the number of teaching assistants which had risen from 34,800 in 1997 to 125,200 in 2008 (IFS 2010). However, one respondent cited a study he had heard about in the media which had found that the rise in the number of teaching assistants had only had a 'marginal' impact on education results. If the change had only been marginal, he argued, then 'get rid of them all' (Middle class group, Warwickshire).

There was also a tendency for participants to draw on anecdotes which linked personal experience to perceptions of public waste. For instance, senior citizens in one group objected to 'North Lanarkshire virtually landscaping roundabouts' whilst there wasn't 'enough money for a full time warden' in their sheltered housing (Senior citizens group, Glasgow). In another group a participant cited the experience of a friend who worked in a hospital where computers had been stolen:

Respondent 1:	So many spurious things they spend money on.
Respondent 2:	The waste is horrendous there, isn't it?
Respondent 3:	Yeah.
Moderator:	So you think a lot of this deficit could be cut by what do you mean by waste – tell me what you mean?
Respondent 2:	It's not just waste I had a friend at work at a hospital in Coventry and they had complete new computers one night and a few nights later someone had broken in and taken them all. Now that is waste indirectly because if they had had proper security or whatever someone knew they were there. (Middle class group, Coventry)

Experience—often recounted through anecdotes with high social currency—and media narratives thus served to mutually reinforce each other. Media accounts give meaning to personal experience, which itself confirms the validity of media accounts. As Stanley noted, when discussing his own focus groups on austerity, these processes then worked to justify cuts to public spending:

> The crisis of debt (which must be caused by overspending) gives sense to concrete experiences. Experiences in which public money is deemed to have been wasted 'stick' and later help make sense of, and to an extent, confirm stories of state indebtedness and overspending. Second, these anecdotes are used to excuse and justify the potentially harmful consequences – whatever they may be – of reluctantly accepting spending cuts. If one makes the connection between state indebtedness (and thus overspending) and inefficiency and profligacy, then it gives the sense of something palpable and relatively harmless to be cut. (Stanley 2014: 910)

As previously noted, ideas about how to reduce the deficit were constrained by low levels of understanding of the scale and composition of public spending and a tendency to focus on items that had high personal or media visibility. So, for instance, a respondent in one of our Glasgow groups argued that methadone programmes and cosmetic surgery on the NHS cost a 'huge' amount of money and should be stopped (Senior citizens group, Glasgow). In another when the possibility of tax rises was mooted a respondent replied 'I don't understand why they are talking about doing things like that when they are irresponsibly spending billions of pounds on things like the Millennium Dome' (Low income group, Surrey).

At times, respondents were able to go beyond proposals in the media and formulate their own ideas for how the deficit could be reduced. However these were still strongly influenced by information that had been picked up from the media and nowhere was this more obvious than over immigration. As noted earlier the high visibility of media accounts of benefit fraud and welfare payments given to migrants led people to assume that this must have been a key reason why the public deficit had risen. Unsurprisingly many respondents thought reducing immigration would reduce public debt:

Respondent 1:	I'm sure I read something recently to say that something like 2 passports every five minutes or something are getting handed out to people that are coming into this country so I think let's just solve the problems we've got now with everybody that we've got here and maybe help people who are homeless as well rather than bringing more people who are homeless and helping them as well. Is that really going to ease it long term it won't but short term it might because you getting money from the EU or whatever for allowing people in.
Moderator:	So you think stopping the number of people coming in would be one way of saving money so that we don't owe so much money.
Respondent 1:	Yes.
Respondent 2:	There's a lot of them who come into this country and before they come in they say they have got jobs to come to, and you know a lot of them come here and they don't have jobs to come to.
Respondent 3:	Aye.
Respondent 2:	But nobody follows up on that so that they immediately go onto benefits of every type. They get all their allowances, they get help with everything. (Low income group, Glasgow)

And in another group:

Moderator:	What should be done to reduce the deficit?
Respondent 1:	They've got to stop all these immigrations coming in.
Moderator:	Do you think that's a very big part of it?

Respondent 1:	I think that's a lot to do with it.
Respondent 2:	Yeah.
Respondent 1:	Yes I do.
Moderator:	If you had to put an idea of the proportion of it what sort of proportion would it be.
Respondent 2:	I think it would be quite high
Moderator:	Would it be a half, a quarter?
Respondent 2:	I would say three quarters because I live in Thornton Heath and believe you me you go there now and honestly it's
Respondent 1:	Mmmm.
Respondent 2:	We're the odd one out. (Senior citizen group, Surrey)

It was clear from the solutions raised in our focus groups that the media were very successful in setting the agenda for what people saw as viable responses. To test whether the opposite was true—would policies with little media visibility be unfamiliar to people?—participants were asked whether they had heard of alternative policies such as a Land Value Tax or a Financial Transactions Tax which had been advocated by some think tanks and pressure groups (see Chap. 4). Most people said they had not heard of these but some claimed to know what they were. However when asked to explain them, not a single person in any focus group could actually provide an account which approximated either tax. This for instance was one of the few accounts of the Land Value Tax:

> What I understand is if you have a field and that field is lying fallow it's got no value as such but if Joe Wicks decides he wants to put a big housing estate on that then suddenly that land is worth a lot of money so therefore I own that useless land which is now worth a lot of money. I will be paid by Joe Wicks to use my land or sell him that land which is useless to me but I have made, for nothing, a big profit and I should pay a huge tax on that. (Middle class group, Coventry)

When we then explained to people in our focus groups what these taxes involved they were generally popular. The inequity in the taxation of land and housing was seen as being particularly unfair by many respondents. One focus group member who had grown up in Germany remarked:

The first thing I noticed in this country with the council tax how unfair it is and how they are taking from the little people the money. Just a little example in our road is a house it is huge it has two acres of land swimming pool everything two people live in the house their council tax I know for sure is about £50 more than what I pay for a little semi-detached house which has maybe a 1/50 of amount of land they have. (Low income group, Surrey)

The proposal for a financial transactions tax was also positively received reflecting the findings of opinion polling (YouGov 2012). However, as respondents in one of our Glasgow groups argued they rarely heard about such proposals because they tended to be confined to 'specialist programmes' rather than the main news bulletins or the newspapers:

Respondent 1:   A lot of these sort of things are on specialist programmes.
Respondent 2:   Bits and pieces
Respondent 1:   I only pick up things I hear on the news channels or in the papers but the kind of thing you are talking about you would maybe get a specialist programme doing that. (Low income group, Glasgow)

However there was a widespread view that the media—and public broadcasting in particular—should be featuring alternative accounts and not just reproducing the perspectives of leading politicians. For instance in discussion on the Land Value Tax:

Moderator: Should the media introduce and discuss these things even if they're not part of the policy of one of the major parties?
Respondent 2:   Absolutely.
Respondent 1:   Yeah.
Respondent 3:   Yes.
Respondent 2:   The media should not just be some control where it goes in just one direction. (Low income group, Surrey)

And on the financial transaction tax:

Moderator:	Would you like to hear the media discuss that?
Respondent 1:	Yes.
Respondent 2:	Yes I think so.
Respondent 3:	Yes I would because that's the first I've heard about it.
Respondent 1:	Yes because the more ways we hear about ways of dealing with this it's easier then to sort of ...it is to make up your mind about what you think is the best. But that doesn't come to the fore ... this is how we could deal with it. It's all airy fairy you know but it's all about time it's about this and it's about that and all the experts are coming on but nobody is really producing anything which would let you to think about it, whether that would that be good or not.
Respondent 3:	You see that's the first I ever heard about that tax. (Senior Citizens, Glasgow)

However the widespread support for taxation directed towards the better off, again reflected in opinion polling (YouGov 2012; Ashcroft 2010; Philo 2010), was tempered by four factors. The most widely expressed reservation—which was raised in 12 of the 15 focus groups—was the perception that there was no political will amongst the main parties to tax the rich. Many believed that the well off would use their influence to make sure such legislation was blocked, thought that politicians were hand in glove with the rich or saw those at Westminster themselves benefiting from the current tax system. As one respondent put it 'they'd close ranks' with a second adding:

> I would certainly say the Land Tax go for it that sounds brilliant because a lot of these folks are the owners but the way that the political situation is set up at the moment it would be very hard to get that through. The way that Westminster runs, it's the protection of their own interests really. (Low income group, Glasgow)

This was part of a widespread collapse of faith in politicians amplified by the MPs expenses scandal which had taken place only a few months before the focus groups were conducted. However, it was not only the expenses scandal which had negatively impacted perceptions of politicians, spin was also a significant factor with one participant describing MPs as being like 'elevated used car salesmen' (Low income group, Surrey). The widespread loss of faith in elected representatives left most people in the focus groups feeling hopeless and disempowered. As one participant put it: 'I feel like a fly in amber I just feel stuck' (Low income group, Glasgow). The secondly most widely cited reservation (cited in 11 of 15 focus groups) was the perception that the rich would always find a way to avoid taxes, either through loopholes or by moving money offshore to tax havens. Participants would usually cite examples they had heard about in the press such as Terry Wogan's investment in woodlands or the activities of famous footballers such as Ally McCoist who was said to have got 'divorced as a company…Ally McCoist Ltd' (Low income group, Glasgow). The third most frequently cited objection (cited in three focus groups) was that the rich would leave the country and take their wealth with them, reflecting arguments that were made at the time in newspapers. Also cited in three focus groups was the opinion that the rich didn't have enough money to make a substantial difference, again an argument we encountered in media accounts (see Chap. 4). As one participant put it 'it's the same with the earnings pyramid people say well we'll put a huge tax on the top but in fact really most of the taxes come from the great body of the people down below, and so a small increase on those can reap more reward than taxing those people at the top' (Senior Citizens, Coventry). One participant put forward the argument, which was contested by her husband, that some wealthy people had to pay so much in 'death duties' that a Land Value Tax might be unviable:

Respondent 1:	They should be talking about it [Land Value Tax] but I think you have to be careful because some of these big estates are bankrupt, aren't they?
Respondent 2:	Oh yeah half of Mayfair's bankrupt.
Respondent 1:	No not Mayfair I'm talking about people in the country. Somebody dies and the death duties are absolutely phenomenal and they can't inherit they just inherit debts. They're losing out these one percent people. (Middle class group, Coventry)

The press are likely to be have been a key source of such beliefs. The speaker who raised the issue of 'death duties' was a regular reader of the *Mail* which has conducted a long campaign against the alleged iniquities of inheritance tax. A Nexis search for the string 'death duties OR death taxes' produced 425 articles between the election of Labour in 1997 and the time of the focus groups. Some of these focused on emotive stories such as the case of a one man's struggle to hold onto a long held family farm in the face of 'death duties' and bankruptcy (*Mail on Sunday*, 27 February 2000). Some articles even suggested that 'death duties' were so onerous that the 'middle classes couldn't afford to die'

> The middle classes can't afford to die: MY FRIEND Jane says she can't afford to die (Headline)
> A single mother with two children and no other close relatives, Jane confessed recently she is terrified of something happening to her in the next few years because her boys would lose their home....The house is the family's only asset and, unbelievably, a portion of it would be taken from Jane's boys by the Government if anything happened to their mum. When we think of death duties, we think of a Rembrandt or two being flogged off to enable some dissolute duke to hang on to the stately pile. We don't think of an ordinary family being mugged in a time of grief by the Treasury. (*Mail*, 23 August 2006)

Having presented the empirical data on audience knowledge and beliefs the chapter will conclude by reflecting on the role of the media in shaping responses to the deficit.

Conclusion: The Media and the Public Turn to Austerity

In Chap. 2 this book explored how a banking crisis rooted in risk taking, excessive leverage and the overextension of credit precipitated the worst downturn since the Great Depression. Yet within less than 18 months, discussion of the role of the banking crisis had been eclipsed by concerns over the public finances, with a majority of the public consenting to cuts to the welfare state. Underlying this acquiescence was the widespread belief that the problems with the public finances represented a crisis and were a result of historic Labour overspending.

Amongst the media and political classes the dominant explanation for how this happened was that the Conservatives together with the Liberal Democrats had been very effective at selling the message of

Labour overspending through the metaphor of 'maxing out the credit card' whilst Labour failed to contest this narrative (e.g. Gamble 2015; Ussher 2015; Wintour 2015). Many commentators identify the period when this account became widely accepted as being just after the 2010 election when a demoralised Labour party turned in on itself in the process of electing a new leader, allowing the Conservatives free rein to establish this narrative (e.g. Ussher 2015; Elliott 2017). Although the Conservative strategy was highly effective—and Labour's decision not to seriously contest this narrative was a major blunder—as an explanation as to why this explanation stuck it is at best a partial and at worst a misleading explanation of what happened. One problem is that it gets the chronology wrong. As the focus groups reported in this chapter and polling demonstrated this narrative had become widely accepted well before the 2010 election (YouGov 2010a). A second problem with the account is that it doesn't recognise the pivotal role of the media.

As the analysis in Chap. 4 demonstrated both broadcasting and the press constructed—to varying degrees—a narrative that the deficit represented a major economic threat which necessitated quick and sharp cuts to the welfare state. Analysts who contested what some economists described as 'deficit hysteria' were rarely featured in coverage (Brittan 2009; Krugman 2009; Reich 2009). This meant that the overwhelming majority of citizens were only exposed to one perspective on the deficit which was highly negative and alarmist, with many press accounts going as far as to predict national bankruptcy. The views of our focus group members corresponded closely to these consistent messages that the deficit represented a 'crisis' which threatened economic stability and so needed to be addressed urgently. Later polling confirmed these findings, particularly amongst the key electoral constituency of swing voters (YouGov 2010a, b; Ashcroft 2010). Ashcroft's (2010) polling found that 72 per cent of swing voters agreed with the statement that 'The deficit is the most serious problem facing Britain's economy and needs to be dealt with urgently, beginning this year'. These findings also reflect the fact that media coverage gave far more weight to arguments in favour of accelerated deficit reduction than the view of some macroeconomists—that an early fiscal tightening would be damaging to employment, growth and deficit reduction. In fact, the dangers of cutting in a weak economy—which received relatively little media attention in comparison to the alleged dangers created by the deficit—were also reflected in polling which saw a majority of respondents believe that cutting spending to reduce the deficit would benefit the economy rather than damage it (YouGov 2010b).

The impact of media accounts could also be seen in perceptions of how to respond to the crisis. One of the clearest findings in the content analysis in Chap. 4 was the strong consensus across all newspapers and broadcasting that cuts were unavoidable, a perspective which came across clearly in my focus groups and commanded majorities in polling (YouGov 2010b; Ashcroft 2010). Furthermore, the policies that our participants had heard of for reducing the deficit closely corresponded to those that appeared in the press and on television news. In this sense media accounts set the public's agenda for how the deficit could be addressed—even if some of the measures being proposed in the media, such as cuts to health or education, were resisted by our participants. Conversely, alternative policies which received almost no media attention such as investing for growth or raising taxes on the wealthy weren't recognised by our participants. This does not mean that had such policies been discussed by the media then austerity could have been avoided. Clearly there was a strong consensus across a wide range of political, financial and economic elites that public spending was going to be cut sharply. However, had journalists pointed out that there were alternatives to reductions in public spending this would have made it harder for politicians to hide behind the claim that they had no choice but to enact unprecedented cuts to the welfare state (Taylor-Gooby and Stoker 2011).

It was also the case that reception processes were mediated by social values. As our focus groups and Stanley's (2014: 906–907) work in this area demonstrated arguments about the need to reduce public debt worked so effectively because they resonated both with strongly held moral beliefs that 'one pays back one's debts' and the perception that during the boom 'we'—both citizens and the state—had 'lived beyond our means'. At other times personal experience, specialist knowledge or a belief in fairness, mediated the reception of media messages. However, in an environment in which there was a very low level of public understanding of the composition of public expenditure—itself partly a consequence of the lack of discussion of the constitutive elements of public spending in the media—participants tended to misidentify issues which had high and sustained media visibility when attempting to understand where the deficit originated. This was especially the case in relation to issues such as immigration or welfare which generated significant resentment. As this research and other has demonstrated this resentment is based around a 'legitimacy gap' where people self-define themselves as 'hard working tax-payers' who are seen to prop up undeserving welfare recipients, migrants and a profligate state (Seabrooke 2007; Kidder and Martin 2012; Stanley 2014). For those who are themselves are on low incomes or in insecure employment—like many members of my focus groups—the impulse to differentiate themselves from those stigmatised as the 'undeserving poor' can be particularly strong (Shildrick and MacDonald 2013).

The next chapter will explore how such beliefs and attitudes contributed to the public acquiescence to austerity via longer term patterns of media socialisation. These meant that coming into the GFC the public already held a set of beliefs and views that meant that they were susceptible to arguments in favour of cutting parts of the welfare state.

REFERENCES

Anderson, P. J., & Weymouth, T. (1999). *Insulting the Public? The British Press and the European Union*. London: Longman.

Ashcroft, M. (2010). *What Future for Labour?* Available at: http://lordashcroft-polls.com/2010/09/what-future-for-labour/. Date accessed 9 July 2018.

Brittan, S. (2009, October 2). A Cool Look at the Current Deficit Hysteria. *Financial Times*.

Deacon, D., & Monk, W. (2001). 'New Managerialism' in the News: Media Coverage of Quangos in Britain. *Journal of Public Affairs, 1*(2), 153–166.

Elliott, L. (2017, March 12). Labour Must Learn to Win if It Wants to Shape the UK's Economic Future. *Guardian*. Available at: https://www.theguardian.com/business/2017/mar/12/labour-must-learn-to-win-if-it-wants-to-shape-the-uks-economic-future. Accessed 9 July 2018.

Gamble, A. (2015). The Economy. *Parliamentary Affairs, 68*(1), 154–167.

Institute for Fiscal Studies (IFS). (2010). *Public Spending Under Labour*. Available from: http://www.ifs.org.uk/bns/bn92.pdf. Accessed 9 July 2018.

Ipsos-Mori. (2009). *Public Spending Index – June 2009*. Available from: https://www.ipsos.com/sites/default/files/migrations/en-uk/files/Assets/Docs/poll-public-spending-charts-june-2009.pdf. Accessed 9 July 2018.

Kidder, J. L., & Martin, I. W. (2012). What We Talk About When We Talk About Taxes. *Symbolic Interaction, 35*(2), 123–145.

Krugman, P. (2009). Deficit Hysteria. *New York Times*. Available from: https://krugman.blogs.nytimes.com/2009/11/23/deficit-hysteria/. Accessed 9 July 2018.

Macmillan, L. (2011). *Measuring the Intergenerational Correlation of Worklessness.* The Centre for Market and Public Organisation Working Paper No. 11/278. Available at: https://www.bristol.ac.uk/media-library/sites/cmpo/migrated/documents/wp278.pdf. Accessed 13 July 2018.

Mason, R. (2013, September 12). MPs' Expenses Rise to Almost £100m. *Guardian.* Available at: https://www.theguardian.com/politics/2013/sep/12/mps-expenses-rise-record-high. Accessed 13 July 2018.

Migration Watch. (2013). *UK Child Benefit and Non-UK Resident EU Children.* Available at: https://www.migrationwatchuk.org/briefing-paper/288. Accessed 9 July 2018.

New Economics Foundation. (2018). *Framing the Economy: How to Win the Case for a Better System.* Available at: http://neweconomics.org/wp-content/uploads/2018/02/Framing-the-Economy-NEON-NEF-FrameWorks-PIRC.pdf. Accessed 9 July 2018.

Philo, G. (2010, August 15). Deficit Crisis: Let's Really Be in It Together. *Guardian.*

Reich, R. (2009, August 31). Why the Deficit Hysteria? I Only Wish We'd Borrow More. *Guardian.*

Rutherford, T. (2013). *Historical Rates of Social Security Benefits.* House of Commons Library SN/SG 6762. Available from: http://researchbriefings.files.parliament.uk/documents/SN06762/SN06762.pdf. Accessed 9 July 2018.

Seabrooke, L. (2007). The Everyday Social Sources of Economic Crises: From 'Great Frustrations' to 'Great Revelations' in Interwar Britain. *International Studies Quarterly, 51*(4), 795–810.

Shildrick, T., & MacDonald, R. (2013). Poverty Talk: How People Experiencing Poverty Deny Their Poverty and Why They Blame 'the Poor'. *The Sociological Review, 61*(2), 285–303.

Shildrick, T., Macdonald, R., Furlong, A., Rodden, J., & Crow, R. (2012). *Are 'Cultures of Worklessness' Passed Down the Generations.* Joseph Rowntree Foundation. Available at: https://www.jrf.org.uk/file/43209/download?token=12LE8LK8&filetype=full-report. Accessed 10 July 2018.

Stanley, L. (2014). 'We're Reaping What We Sowed': Everyday Crisis Narratives and Acquiescence to the Age of Austerity. *New Political Economy, 19*(6), 895–917.

Taylor-Gooby, P., & Stoker, G. (2011). The Coalition Programme: A New Vision for Britain or Politics as Usual? *The Political Quarterly, 82*(1), 4–15.

Taylor-Gooby, P., & Taylor, E. (2015). Benefits and Welfare: Long-Term Trends or Short-Term Reactions? *British Social Attitudes, 32.* Available at: http://www.bsa.natcen.ac.uk/media/38977/bsa32_welfare.pdf. Accessed 10 July 2018.

Ussher, K. (2015). Labour Did Not Cause the Economic Crisis – It Must Counter the Myth That It Did. *Guardian*. Available from: https://www.theguardian.com/commentisfree/2015/may/18/labour-economic-crisis-tories. Accessed 10 July 2018.

Wintour, P. (2015, June 3). The Undoing of Ed Miliband – And How Labour Lost the Election. *Guardian*. Available at: https://www.theguardian.com/politics/2015/jun/03/undoing-of-ed-miliband-and-how-labour-lost-election. Accessed 10 July 2018.

YouGov. (2010a). *Economy*. Available at: https://d25d2506sfb94s.cloudfront.net/today_uk_import/YG-Archives-Pol-Channel4Economy-100329.pdf, https://d25d2506sfb94s.cloudfront.net/today_uk_import/YG-Archives-Pol-Channel4Economy-100329.pdf. Accessed 10 July 2018.

YouGov. (2010b). *Unavoidable Cuts*. Available at: https://yougov.co.uk/news/2010/10/19/unavoidable-cuts-story/. Accessed 10 July 2018.

YouGov. (2012). *Class Survey Results*. Available at: http://classonline.org.uk/docs/YouGov-Class_Polling_Results_120522_Economic_Policies.xls. Accessed 10 July 2018.

CHAPTER 6

Long-term Media Socialisation and Support for Austerity

INTRODUCTION

In the previous two chapters this book explored how during the critical period in 2009, when public acceptance of the necessity for public sector cuts began to solidify, the media helped establish key elements of audience belief. These included the view that the deficit represented an economic crisis that needed to be addressed quickly and that cuts to public spending were unavoidable. The results from the focus groups in Chap. 5 showed that participants largely attributed the deficit to Labour overspending and in particular to areas such as waste and inefficiency, bank bailouts, foreign wars, immigration, welfare and the EU. The focus group and polling also showed that these were areas where, if cuts had to be made, people would prefer the axe to fall (Yougov 2010a).

At one level, these findings demonstrate that there was a great deal of confusion over the relationship between growth, recessions and public borrowing. Most people saw the economy as analogous to a household budget where rising debt indicated that there had been a sustained period of overspending, rather than a sudden collapse in tax revenues caused by a recession. At another level, the findings point to fundamental misunderstandings about the contours of public spending and where Labour's extra public investment had gone. Aside from the bank bailouts none of the issues cited by our participants contributed significantly to the public deficit. In fact, most evidence suggests one of the most frequently (and passionately) cited factors, immigration, was actually a net contributor

© The Author(s) 2019
M. Berry, *The Media, the Public and the Great Financial Crisis*,
https://doi.org/10.1007/978-1-137-49973-8_6

to the public purse and that attempts to restrict immigration—the favoured response of many of our participants—would actually make it harder to reduce the deficit (Vargas-Silva 2017; OBR 2013).

However, recognising that the public struggled to estimate the constituent elements of public spending—or understand how growth and recession impacted the public finances—doesn't adequately explain why the focus groups consistently misidentified these casual factors. Since these factors have had consistently high media visibility and focus group members repeatedly pointed to news stories which mentioned them it is plausible to assume that the media were important in helping to establish their salience. Whilst the content analyses in Chap. 4 showed they were present in 2009 press accounts, they did not appear spontaneously at this point. Instead they represented themes which had been present in many newspaper articles in the preceding years.

This chapter will examine how two key beliefs common in my focus groups had become increasingly prominent themes in press reporting in the period following Labour's re-election in 2001. These were the belief that much of Labour's post-2001 spending increases had been wasted and that public sector pensions, immigration and welfare had become increasingly unfair and unsustainable burdens on the taxpayer. To locate the development of these narratives Nexis searches going back to 2000 were conducted in four right-wing national newspapers.

'Inefficiency', 'Waste' and 'Non-jobs' in the Public Sector

In my focus groups (and opinion polls) many participants believed that there was a great deal of waste in the public sector and it was clear that personal experience sometimes interacted with media accounts to reinforce this view (Ipsos-Mori 2009). Local government, in particular, was repeatedly cited as an area that was inefficient and opinion polling showed that voters prioritised this as an area where public spending cuts should be made (Yougov 2010a). However polling also demonstrated that a widespread belief in public sector inefficiency helped legitimise the idea that cuts to public spending could be made without damaging 'frontline' services. Research in June 2009 found that 79 per cent of those polled agreed with the statement that 'making public services more efficient can save enough money to help cut government spending without damaging services the public receive' (Ipsos-Mori 2009). This belief was likely to have been a significant factor in helping to smooth both the introduction of austerity policies and the election of the Conservatives —since by a significant margin they were seen as the party most likely to get 'good value' in public spending (Ipsos-Mori 2009).

The argument that the public sector is inherently inefficient has been a core element of the New Right's long-standing critique of the state (Gamble 1994; George and Wilding 1994; Crouch 2011). To the Thatcherite right the public sector is bureaucratic, riddled with waste and beholden to 'producer' interests. To locate the development of these narratives in the press, Nexis searches were run using the search string 'public sector OR public spending AND bloated OR inefficien* OR waste*'. Table 6.1 shows the number of articles for each year from 2000 to 2009. Due to a problem with Nexis returning *Express* articles for the three years between 2006 and 2008 the results from that newspaper are presented below all graphs in tables.

As can be seen in Fig. 6.1 and Table 6.1 there was an approximately 600 per cent increase in these kinds of newspaper articles between 2000 and 2009 during the period when Labour increased spending, primarily on health, education and transport. This rise in negative reporting had two phases—an initial increase after 2000 and then another sharp rise after the financial crisis began in 2008. What is striking is how this increase happened in all right-wing newspapers—*The Times* has not been included in these analyses but it too saw an increase from 36 articles in 2001 to 212 in 2009. Effectively, this section of the press responded to the sharp rise in public spending by arguing it had been squandered and when the financial crisis hit these arguments were ratcheted up another notch. Another key device was to juxtapose the private sector as the part of the economy which allegedly generated the growth and wealth against the public sector which was presented as parasitic. As the focus group discussions in Chap. 5 showed this view had become accepted by some participants. Headlines illustrating these narratives included:

Table 6.1 *Express* articles using search string 'public sector OR public spending AND bloated OR inefficien* OR waste*'

2000–2001	2001–2002	2002–2003	2003–2004	2004–2005	2005–2006	2009–2010
13	8	10	27	29	25	96

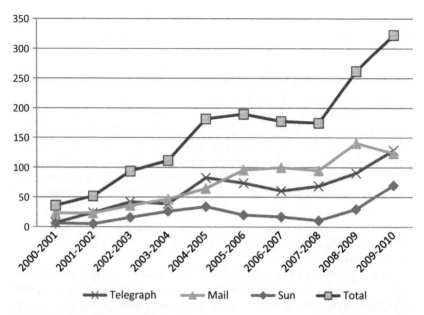

Fig. 6.1 Articles generated using search string 'public sector OR public spending AND bloated OR inefficien* OR waste*'

Brown reveals his other mistress – the wasteful, money-draining NHS (*Telegraph*, 30 September 2003)

Pork-barrel Labour (*Telegraph*, 21 June 2006)

£20BN RED TAPE AND PAY RISES SWALLOW UP MONEY FOR SERVICES: YOUR CASH GOES DOWN THE DRAIN (*Express*, 26 April 2004)

OVERBLOWN BUREAUCRACY IS OUT OF CONTROL; HOW BLAIR'S BLOATED BRITAIN IS COSTING TAXPAYERS A FORTUNE (*Express*, 16 September 2004)

The Monster Devouring Britain: Despite the recession, the Guardian yesterday carried its biggest ever public sector advertising section for jobs. And guess what you'll be paying for them all (*Mail*, 6 September 2001)

Taxpayers' £800m wasted on Jobzilla (*Mail*, 29 December 2006)

£20BN A YEAR DOWN DRAIN (*Sun*, 26 April 2006)

THE WASTED BILLIONS WE ALL COULD SHARE (*Sun*, 23 October 2003)

Extracts which illustrate these narratives include, for example:

> Public spending, which Gordon Brown calls 'investment', is not investment at all. It earns no returns, does not produce wealth and causes inflation. Private (real) investment does the opposite of all those things. So wasteful and inefficient is public spending that any sensible government must introduce massive (and hugely expensive) bureaucratic checks and internal audits, as Alan Milburn plans to do in the NHS, to simulate the ultimate check of bankruptcy that any private business would face under bad management. (*Telegraph*, 24 April 2002)

> OVERPAID, irresponsible and contemptuous of the public, a new breed of fat cat is making its expensive presence felt across the country. But these bloated creatures are not the boardroom capitalists who feature so prominently in trade union rhetoric. Instead, they hail from the supposedly progressive, caring public sector. The highest levels of the British state machine, from the NHS to local government, are now filled with bureaucrats who are remarkably skilled at getting their claws into taxpayers' wallets and creaming off funds intended for frontline services – for themselves. (*Mail*, 25 September 2003)

> A mind-boggling 6,526,000 people are on the public payroll – more than one in four of the total workforce, compared with fewer than one in five in America. They include soldiers, teachers, judges nurses – and MPs. Not one of them contributes to the generation of national wealth. Yet they all consume that wealth, often by inefficient and bureaucratic work practices. Every three workers in manufacturing and service industries have to shoulder the burden of one public sector worker's pay and pension. (*Sun*, 23 October 2003)

And from 2009 when these narratives peaked in number:

> Every encounter with the bloated monster of Brownian big government – not to mention John Prescott's grotesque legacy at regional and local level – tells us that it is riddled with waste, inefficiency and executive perks. (*Telegraph*, 17 June 2009)

If Mr Cameron wants to be remembered as a genuinely courageous public figure rather than merely as a camera-friendly celebrity, then he should devote his attention to slashing our gigantic public sector, with its vast swathes of pen-pushers, time-servers, quangos and leeches. (*Mail*, 28 July 2009)

BRITAIN'S bloated public sector is set to get even fatter, Chancellor Alistair Darling revealed yesterday...Much of the cash will go on benefits, public-sector wage rises and pensions, plus perks like MPs' expenses...Susie Squire, of the TaxPayers' Alliance, said: 'Our public sector is more bloated and wasteful than ever'. (*Express*, 23 April 2009)

The gravy train is out of control across all tiers of government – national, local and European. Town halls waste millions. The public sector is crying out for reform. Pointless pseudo-government quangos mop up £70 BILLION a year and employ 50,000 people hand-picked by the party in power. (*Sun*, 18 May 2009)

Another element of the narrative that the extra state spending had been wasted was the argument that Labour had created many pointless 'non-jobs', with the *Telegraph* introducing a 'Non-Job of the Week' column in 2004. This again was an argument that, as my focus groups showed, had gained traction. Figure 6.2 and Table 6.2 show the growth of this theme from 2000.

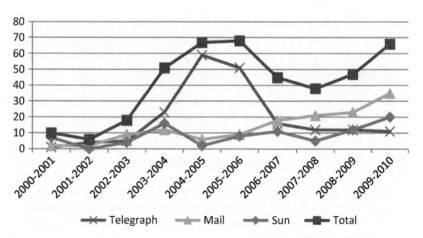

Fig. 6.2   Articles generated by Nexis search string 'non-jobs or non jobs'

Table 6.2   *Express* articles using search string 'non-job or non job'

2000–2001	2001–2002	2002–2003	2003–2004	2004–2005	2005–2006	2009–2010
1	0	3	2	6	4	24

Here is a selection of headlines emphasising this theme:

The council non-job of the year is a real waste of space (*Telegraph*, 31 December 2008)

Toothbrush adviser among the non-jobs costing councils pounds 3m (*Telegraph*, 20 April 2009)

JOBZILLA The public sector non-jobs monster destroying Britain: Yesterday, as the stock market wobbled again, and more layoffs hit the private sector, a signal event occurred: the public sector jobs supplement of the *Guardian* weighed in at a hernia-inducing 160 pages. But are any of its adverts for real jobs? And how long can Britain sustain such madness? (*Mail*, 5 September 2002)

DANCE ASSISTANTS, TREE PLANTERS, MUSEUM GUIDES ...47,000 NON-JOBS TO GET YOUNG PEOPLE INTO WORK (*Mail*, 30 July 2009)

Bureau-prats: DAFT JOBS COST TAXPAYERS £800M A YEAR (*Sun*, 29 December 2006)

WANTED: BOUNCY CASTLE ASSISTANT; Councils blow £3m on barmy posts (*Sun*, 23 March 2009)

'GOLD-PLATED PENSIONS'

As my focus groups demonstrated another aspect of concern over public spending concerned the difference between public and private sector pension provision. In the press this worked as a wedge issue by arguing that (a) private sector workers were being unfairly treated in relation to public sector workers, and (b) the scale of public sector pension provision was unafford-able. In newspaper coverage this was expressed through the claim that public sector workers were getting 'gilt-edged' or 'gold-plated' pensions—a theme that mushroomed in the early 2000s before increasing again in most newspapers once the financial crisis began (see Table 6.3 and Fig. 6.3 below).

Table 6.3 *Express* articles using search string 'gold-plated OR gilt-edged AND public sector AND pensions'

2000–2001	2001–2002	2002–2003	2003–2004	2004–2005	2005–2006	2009–2010
0	0	1	0	2	16	27

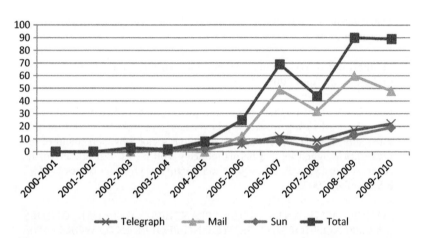

Fig. 6.3 Articles generated by Nexis for search string 'gold-plated OR gilt-edged AND public sector AND pensions'

Here are a couple of newspaper extracts that emphasise the issues of unfairness and unaffordability:

> Families paying £900 a year to maintain public sector pensions (Headline)... According to figures from the Institute of Economic Affairs (IEA), the cost of maintaining gold-plated pensions for nearly six million state employees including doctors, teachers and nurses, is more than £22.3 billion a year... The burden will be shouldered by many private sector workers whose own pension entitlements are crumbling, creating a huge divide between public and private sector...A recent report from the IEA revealed that the deficit in public sector pensions was more than a trillion pounds, meaning it would cost each taxpayer £2,000 a year if the deficit was to be paid back. (*Telegraph*, 29 December 2006)

WHO'LL SLAY THE MONSTER?: State workers prosper as never before, with millions better off than those in the private sector. But politicians desperate for their votes lack the courage to tackle a behemoth that is slowly suffocating our economy(Headline)...In a generation, Britain will be a nation divided between privileged state retirees, with their gold-plated deal, and the private sector most of whose employees have lost their defined benefits pension schemes funding it. The Lib Dems have calculated that for every £1 a private sector worker pays into his pension fund, they must fork out another 90p in tax towards the pension of a state employee. The burden on the nation is not only grossly unjust it will be insupportable 30 or 40 years from now. (*Mail*, 13 October 2007)

The development of themes around a 'wasteful' and 'parasitic' public sector contributed—as the audience studies and polling showed—to a particular strand of anti-statist opinion which could then be mined by the Conservative party. As Dorey (2014) notes, such arguments were used extensively by the Conservative party during the 2010 election campaign and provided a key part of the justification for the implementation of austerity policies.

...by positing a clear link between the scale of the fiscal crisis and the size (and thus costs) of the public sector, the Conservatives could play 'divide and-rule' by promoting resentment among private sector workers towards public sector employees, on the grounds that many of the latter allegedly enjoyed higher pay, 'jobs for life' and so-called 'gold-plated' pensions when they retired at an earlier age than workers in the non-State sector. Much of this characterisation was patently untrue, and as such, was either malicious or mischievous, for a few high profile instances of well-remunerated senior civil servants or town hall chiefs were given prominence in order to establish the popular impression that the whole public sector was awash with such generous salaries and pensions; the exceptions were depicted as the rule. Yet the Conservatives' intention was clearly to fuel hostility among private sector employees towards workers in the 'bloated' or 'parasitic' public sector, for this would not only further divert popular attention and anger away from the role of the banks and 'the City' in precipitating the economic down-turn, it would also, it was envisaged, secure wider support for cutting public expenditure. After all, if private sector workers (already experiencing redundancies and pay cuts or freezes) could be persuaded that their taxes were being used to support an allegedly comfortable, cosseted, public sector that was being relentlessly expanded by Labour, then a pledge to cut public expenditure would presumably prove more electorally attractive and justifiable. (2014: 418)

However, such campaign messages would not have had such resonance had the themes they played on not been developed over many years in newspaper articles. In this way politicians are able to leverage the ideological power of the press.

THE UNEMPLOYED AND WELFARE CLAIMANTS

The scale of antipathy to welfare claimants in the focus groups was striking, as was the belief that welfare payments were an important factor in the increase in the deficit. Such views reflect a long-term trend since the 1990s in which attitudes towards the unemployed have hardened (Taylor-Gooby and Taylor 2015; Sage 2012; Hills 2001). The public has become less concerned about unemployment, less likely to think the unemployed are 'really poor' and more likely to support punitive sanctions against the jobless (Sage 2012; Taylor-Gooby and Martin 2008). What factors might explain such shifts and how significant a role has the media played? One possible explanation is that the public responded to long period of uninterrupted growth between the mid 1990s and the GFC by believing that support for the unemployed was no longer so necessary. However, Sage (2012: 366) argues, 'the shift in such concerns... are over and above what can be explained by the economic cycle... signifying an escalating concern with people 'choosing' to be on benefits' and a 'growing conviction in welfare "dependency"'.

By 2011, Britain had the highest level of belief in the idea of 'welfare dependency'—a key theme of press coverage—in a survey of 25 European countries, with 66 per cent of Britons agreeing that 'social benefits/ services make people lazy' compared to 37 per cent of Norwegians, and only 18 per cent of Greeks (Geiger 2012). If the economic cycle doesn't adequately explain hardening attitudes towards the unemployed another possible factor was New Labour's own approach to welfare. Roberts (2017) and Connor (2007) have argued that Department for Work and Pensions' public information campaigns targeting 'benefit thieves' served to reinforce negative media images of welfare recipients by imply-ing that many people were claiming benefits they were not entitled to. Other critics have argued that New Labour's embrace of 'conditionality' and reversal of its previous opposition to workfare served to erode soli-darity with the unemployed and the welfare system (King 1999; White 2000; Jayasuriya 2002; Plant 2003; Dwyer 2004; Sage 2012). New Labour policies such as the New Deal and Welfare to Work relied on a model of 'reciprocal responsibility' where government and claim-ants were seen to possess both 'rights and responsibilities'. Labour argued such policies constituted the 'largest assault on structural unem-ployment ever taken' which would change 'the whole culture of the ben-efits system' (Labour Party 1998: 3–4, cited in Sage 2012: 360). However, critics argue that the shift from a social rights based model of welfare to one based on conditionality 'renegotiates and undermines the status of unemployed people in society' by reframing unemployment and poverty as voluntary (Sage 2012: 361). Rather than strengthening support for welfare and preventing Labour being outflanked by the right, the party's embrace of conditionality may have eroded support for the unemployed, the wider welfare system—and ultimately their own electoral prospects:

> Welfare contractualism – akin to means testing and to marketisation – appears capable of renegotiating and ultimately damaging social relations, with contracts possessing the capacity to fundamentally alter our norms and conceptions about the nature and purpose of welfare itself and the outcomes which policies produce. As Hills (2001: 4) accurately predicted a decade ago: "the emphasis on the conditional nature of benefits may have reinforced their social unacceptability and rendered them less popu-lar". This conclusion suggests that welfare contractualism – no matter how purportedly integrative or balanced – is incompatible with strengthening public support for and inter-class solidarity with the unemployed. (Sage 2012: 371)

Rodger (2003) provides a different explanation for the hardening in attitudes to welfare. He argues that the lack of an industrial strategy and a declining welfare state has led to social and economic polarisation with a growing proportion of the population excluded from economic life. This excluded group, Rodger (2003: 413) argues, is prone to 'violence and incivility' as part of a struggle for 'access to material resources' denied it by the economic system which then provides a rationale for further punitive attacks on state benefits as a strategy to restore order. Rodgers also argues that this social polarisation creates 'a post-emotional society in which knowledge of the plight of those at the bottom of the social hierarchy *is gained from a distance through the mass media* rather than through routine daily interaction' (Rodger 2003: 414).

As research has consistently demonstrated the image of welfare claimants in the press has been highly negative (e.g. Deacon 1978, 1980; Golding and Middleton 1983; Bagguley and Mann 1992; Misra et al. 2003; Briant et al. 2011; Larsen and Dejgaard 2013; Lundström 2013; Blackman and Rogers 2017; McEnhill and Byrne 2014; Morrison 2018). However as Fig. 6.4 and Table 6.4 show the hardening in attitudes towards welfare recipients coincided with a sharp increase in press narrative which portrayed benefit recipients as 'cheats', 'frauds' or 'scroungers'.

Press accounts during this period were buttressed by the proliferation of television representations of a feckless working class living on benefits. The most notable fictional example was the comedy-drama *Shameless*

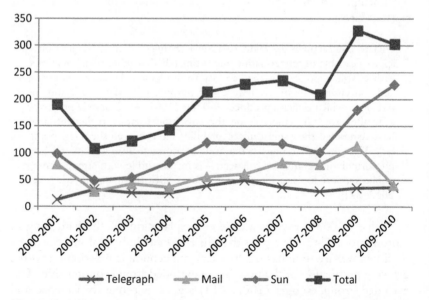

Fig. 6.4 Articles generated by Nexis for search string 'benefit cheat OR benefit fraud OR scrounger OR skiver OR welfare cheat OR welfare fraud'

Table 6.4   *Express* articles using search string 'benefit cheat OR benefit fraud OR scrounger OR skiver OR welfare cheat OR welfare fraud'

2000–2001	2001–2002	2002–2003	2003–2004	2004–2005	2005–2006	2009–2010
34	39	34	42	97	129	114

whilst in the tabloid talk show format *The Jeremy Kyle Show* featured a procession of dysfunctional and often unsympathetic low income families (Skeggs and Wood 2012). Some commentators such as Owen Jones (2011) and Tim Horton, the research director of the Fabian Society, have argued that the complex and often sympathetic portrayal of the poor and working class present in dramas such as *Auf Weidersein Pet* and *Kes* have been replaced over the last 20 years by either the kind of 'bling culture' represented by shows such as *The Only way is Essex* or a relentlessly negative, one dimensional portrayal of a 'semi-feral underclass' (Cadwalladr 2011; Haywood and Yair 2006). Jones (2011) suggests that the segregated nature of British society means that for many middle-class Britons the highly negative portrayal of the poor in mainstream television is widely believed, citing a 2006 Yougov poll that found that 70 per cent of professionals working in television thought that Vicky Pollard from *Little Britain* was an accurate representation of the white working class. As Tyler (2008) notes fictional representations of 'benefit scroungers' and 'chavs' also become spoken of as if they are real people by politicians and the media in order to stigmatise benefit recipients (see also Chap. 4) or further other agendas:

> Vicky Pollard is increasingly used as a shorthand within 'serious' debates about the decline of social and educational standards. For example, in a 2006 speech to the annual conference of the Professional Association of Teachers, Lawson, chair of the association, warned teachers that nursery nurses with few qualifications and poor social skills risked creating a generation of 'Vicky Pollards': 'I don't want to trivialise this in any way at all, but we don't want a future generation of Vicky Pollards' (2006). As 'Vicky Pollard' becomes entrenched and condemned as a negative figure she takes on a force and reality which conceals her origins as a fictional television character played by a white middle-aged man. Indeed, the movement of this fictional figure from scripted television comedy into news media, political rhetoric and onto the streets foregrounds the disturbing ease which the chav figure shapes social perception and comes to be employed in instrumental ways. (Tyler 2008: 28)

IMMIGRATION AND WELFARE

As the focus groups showed there was also widespread concern over welfare payments to migrants and asylum seekers and a belief that these payments had contributed to the deficit. Indeed the power and longevity of this concern was shown in polling shortly after the 2016 EU referendum which found that when asked to rank which issues most influenced their vote, the fourth most popular answer—and second amongst Leave voters—was 'the cost of EU immigration on Britain's welfare system' (Ipsos-Mori 2016). Research has demonstrated that migrants, refugees and asylum seekers are frequently framed by the media as an economic threat (e.g. Berry et al. 2016; Philo et al. 2013). Newspaper reporting prior to the GFC presented migrants in two distinctive and—at first glance—contradictory ways. One narrative presented migrants as displacing British workers and driving down wages, particularly for those on low incomes. Here is a selection of headlines emphasising these themes.

> 100,000 lose out to migrants in hunt for work (*Telegraph*, 18 December 2007)

> Britons 'squeezed out of workforce by foreigners' (*Mail*, 5 November 2007)

> Scandal of immigrants taking over our IT jobs (*Express*, 29 September 2009)

> Migrants 'put Brits on dole' (*Sun*, 18 September 2007)

The anti-migration theme also at times intersected with anti-welfare narratives by claiming that newcomers were taking jobs that British workers were too lazy to do because they preferred a life on benefits:

> EVERYBODY appears hot and bothered about the fact that half of the 2.1 million jobs created in the last decade have gone to immigrants. Why? If they didn't do the jobs, who would? You know the answer – nobody. And, if nobody did the jobs, our economy would come close to collapse or at least wouldn't have expanded in the enormously successful manner it has today. Even now, every other shop, pub and restaurant I pass has 'help wanted' ads.

The truth is the English don't want and will not do these jobs, and many would rather claim benefit than get out of bed. I have a new slogan for Brown – British Jobs For British Shirkers. (*Sun*, 1 November 2007)

All this stuff about skill shortages and the need for willing labour misses the point. We have millions of people unable to read and write, or paid by the State to do nothing, or employed in meaningless makework jobs. It is not necessary to submerge our culture in someone else's for temporary cheap gain. The remedy is available. Drain the swamps of the welfare state, so it is worthwhile to work again. (*Mail*, 28 October 2007)

The second narrative stressed that migrants and asylum seekers were a drain on the economy through claiming benefits, using the welfare state and fraud. As can be seen in Fig. 6.5 and Table 6.5 newspaper articles making links between immigration/asylum and the benefits system— which have traditionally been a regular feature of reporting in the right-wing press—rose significantly during the 2000s. Between 2001 and 2007 they more than doubled before falling back in 2008 and 2009.

These narratives, which were a common theme in hundreds of articles across the sample period, corresponded very closely to what I encountered in my focus groups. Furthermore most articles—with their emphasis on migrants taking out more than they put in were written in a manner that was likely to generate anger and resentment—exactly the sentiments expressed in the focus groups. Here are a few headlines from the *Sun* and *Mail* in 2007 that illustrate these themes:

Immigrants who are a drain on the taxpayer (*Mail*, 1 October 2007)

Migrants 'putting billions on council tax' (*Mail*, 1 November 2007)

Immigrants with cancer 'could swamp the NHS' (*Mail*, 3 September 2007)

Benefits bill for migrants hits £125m; One in six East Europeans is claiming help from the state (*Mail*, 22 August 2007)

Schools are stretched to breaking point by immigrant children (*Mail*, 31 May 2007)

Hundreds have left my Romanian town. What for? British benefits; Special Report (*Mail*, 21 May 2007)

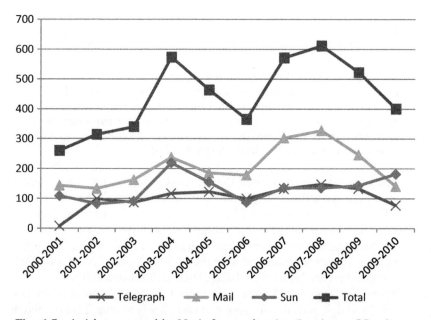

Fig. 6.5 Articles generated by Nexis for search string 'immigrant OR migrant OR asylum seeker AND benefits or welfare'

Table 6.5 *Express* articles using search string 'immigrant OR migrant OR asylum seeker AND benefits OR welfare'

2000–2001	2001–2002	2002–2003	2003–2004	2004–2005	2005–2006	2009–2010
41	68	103	207	228	142	249

We can't cope with migrants, warn GPs (*Mail*, 27 April 2007)

Stop migrant benefit farce (*Sun*, 20 September 2007)

How you can fill your boots with British benefits (*Sun*, 15 September 2007)

TERRORISTS Free homes, healthcare and benefits (*Sun*, 11 July 2007)

Refugees' £60,000 Trapeze lessons (*Sun*, 22 January 2007)

A key complaint amongst many in my focus groups which was also picked up by the Labour pollster James Morris (2017) was the claim that 'Labour came to be seen as a party that put migrants before British citizens'. This again was a recurrent theme in newspaper coverage with migrants and asylum seekers presented as getting preferential access to housing, education and even driving lessons:

Holyrood gives asylum seekers' children free university education (Headline) THE children of asylum seekers were yesterday handed a free Scottish university education – but students from the rest of the UK will continue paying thousands of pounds. (*Mail*, 9 November 2007)

Equality chief probes migrant housing 'bias' (Headline) CLAIMS that migrants are jumping housing queues are to be investigated by equality officials, it emerged yesterday. Trevor Phillips, who heads the Equalities and Human Rights Commission, said the belief that foreigners were gaining 'unfair advantages' was fuelling tensions... Critics of the social housing system say new migrants inevitably get priority for homes over long established residents because they can always show that their need, as measured by poverty and homelessness, is greater. Around one in 12 council and housing association homes are occupied by someone born abroad. (*Mail*, 3 November 2007)

Asylum children get £30 to stay at school (Headline) ASYLUM seeker children are to be handed taxpayer-funded bribes of £30 a week to stay on at school... Sir Andrew Green of pressure group Migrationwatch said: This is absolutely the wrong direction for policy. It can only encourage yet more asylum seekers, despite the fact that over 60 per cent of them are found to be bogus. (*Sun*, 4 August 2007)

Asylum seekers will get £50,000 to pay for their driving lessons (Headline) REFUGEES and asylum seekers are to be given free driving lessons at taxpayers' expense to stop them driving illegally, it emerged yesterday. They will be helped by a £50,000 scheme using public money earmarked to assist deprived areas. The Coventry Refugee Centre also plans to give them tips on car maintenance. But the idea provoked an angry response from local residents, while MPs warned that such schemes risk triggering resentment and harming race relations. (*Mail* 30 August 2005)

The theme of preferential treatment was also common in the letters pages which featured correspondence which juxtaposed the lack of resources given to groups such as military veterans, pensioners or cancer patients with support given to migrants and asylum seekers. Here is a selection of published letters illustrating these arguments:

> IN BRITAIN, it seems everything possible is done to help immigrants and asylum seekers, including a new £10 million grant. I'm a 73-year-old pensioner who went to visit my son in Spain and stayed there longer than a month. As a result, all my benefits, including my old age pension, were stopped. Had this happened to an immigrant to the UK, there would be a blockade of the pension service. (*Mail*, 25 September 2007)

> IT'S an absolute disgrace and embarrassment that a charity is being set up called Help For Heroes because the rehabilitation facilities for our injured soldiers are inadequate. We keep ex-Taliban fighters on benefits and give them legal aid and medically look after a terrorist who tried to blow up an airport, yet the soldiers have to pay community charge and income tax while they are fighting, and are away from their loved ones. If they get injured the money is not available for them to get better to the best available standards. Take the benefits away from these people who are our enemies, kick them out, give the money to our soldiers, plus everything they need. They are risking their lives for us. (*Mail*, 4 October 2007)

> Did you know we have paid illegal immigrants £36million – £ 4,000 a time – to leave Britain and set up businesses back home? Can that be right when the NHS is refusing life-saving care to cancer victims because it is too dear? Or when our troops are fighting for their country on a shoestring? (*Sun*, 17 December 2007)

> FAILED asylum seekers being bribed by the Government to return to their homelands is just another sick indictment of how those who don't contribute to our society, but sponge off the taxpayer, get preferential treatment. Meanwhile, our elderly freeze while struggling to pay their council tax and our service personnel don't get paid and have sub-standard accommodation. (*Sun*, 20 December 2007)

It is important to stress that many—if not all—of the stories reported in the press may be factually accurate but their influence works through how the stories are framed, the power of repetition and a lack of contextual information. There are many stories that could be told about the public sector, welfare spending and migration but the narratives in parts of the press focus on a relentlessly one sided negative framing of these issues. Furthermore the lack of any contextual information—for instance the total level of benefit fraud within the system or the proportion of welfare spending that is claimed by migrant workers—means that readers are left with a distorted picture of how the welfare state operates.

CONCLUSION: PRIMED FOR AUSTERITY

The audience research and polling data in Chap. 5 showed that there was a widespread perception that the deficit represented an economic 'crisis' that had been caused by Labour overspending. In forming these judgments the public did not just rely on information that was circulating at the time. Instead coming into the GFC many already believed that Labour had squandered much of the extra post-2001 investment in public services and that immigration and welfare were a major drain on state resources. Although these perceptions had little basis in reality,[1,2,3] they closely matched narratives that had become increasingly prominent in the right-wing press. From this point—seeing Labour as having overextended the state through wasteful spending whilst viewing immigration and welfare as putting a huge strain on the state—it was only then a small conceptual leap to see these issues as being linked to the rise in the deficit and to point to their reduction as being obvious solutions. Furthermore, the widespread belief that immigrants, welfare and waste contributed to the deficit helped to create the impression that deficit reduction could be achieved through a) cuts which would hit stigmatised groups, and/or b) efficiency savings which didn't impact frontline services.

Further evidence for the political impact of these press narratives can be seen in research which examined the profile of voters who abandoned Labour in the 2010 General Election. Kellner (2012) found that whilst demographic factors such as whether a voter lived in social housing, worked in the public sector or belonged to a trade union modestly predicted—in the expected direction—who abandoned Labour, a far more significant factor was the newspaper they read. Whilst loyalists (who voted Labour in 1997 and 2010) were split in roughly equal numbers between left and right leaning tabloids and broadsheets, those who deserted Labour were four and a half times more likely to be regular readers of the right-wing press. Other research found that in comparison to those who voted Labour in 2010 those who abandoned the party (but had supported them in 2005) were far more likely to favour cuts and believe that a 'lot of the extra money' Labour had spent on the NHS had been 'wasted' (Yougov 2010b). Deserters were also significantly less likely to see government as a 'force for good' in their and their families' lives, and more likely to see it 'as part of the problem not the solution'.

It is not possible to construct the kind of study which could isolate and evaluate the impact of specific media messages in a naturalistic environment. Instead we have to ask—what is the most plausible explanation for observable patterns in data? (Lewis 2008). Of course some readers choose right-wing newspapers because they correspond to their own political views. In the Yougov polling cited above (Kellner 2012), Labour deserters (and hence those more likely to read right-wing titles) were more likely to self-identify as 'centre/right of centre'. But, when participants hold *false beliefs* that closely match common themes in the media they regularly consume, the most plausible explanation is that the media helped create those beliefs. Further support for this perspective is provided by participants in my focus groups who directly cited news stories in explaining the source of their beliefs—such as the contention that the deficit was linked to welfare payments made to migrants.

Reception processes are complex and mediated through a host of factors including experience, knowledge, beliefs, group memberships and deep seated cultural values (Philo 1990, 2001, 2004). Furthermore, media are not the only factor influencing audience knowledge, beliefs, and attitudes. Distrust and hostility towards migrants may be in part a consequence of pressures on housing and public services, though even here, who is seen as responsible—the state or migrants—is likely to be influenced by the media narratives that people consume. Labour's own welfare policies may have contributed to the stigmatisation of the unemployed and the belief that welfare had become an insufferable burden on the state. Public beliefs about the 'deserving' and 'undeserving' poor were not created out of nothing in the last two decades; they have deep cultural roots going back centuries. In this sense, the press are usually most effective when they build upon and amplify pre-existing social beliefs and anxieties (Golding and Middleton 1983; Deacon 1980). This is especially so when reporting presents welfare claimants and migrants as getting preferential treatment in a highly emotive way. This tendency for the public to react negatively towards those painted as 'free riders' is also likely to have been accentuated by other factors such as deindustrialisation and entrenched poverty, the contemporary intensification of work, increased precarity of employment, and the perception of cultural and economic threat from globalisation and migration (Olsen et al. 2010; Standing 2014; Carter 2018; Krastev 2017).

Yet despite these caveats the evidence suggests that the media played an important role in the construction of public misunderstandings around public spending, welfare, and immigration which underpinned support for austerity policies that were opposed by many academic economists (Blyth 2013; Hopkins and Rosamond 2017). The next chapter examines the factors that shaped the patterns in news coverage that have been documented so far.

Notes

1. There is no evidence that most of Labour's increase in spending was wasted or that the NHS is overly bureaucratised. An LSE study found that the major public spending increases introduced by Labour led to large increases in frontline resources such as 'new hospitals, schools, equipment and ICT, 48,000 extra FTE equivalent teachers, 3500 new children's centres, more doctors and nurses, and many new programmes aimed at neighbourhood renewal' leading to substantial improvements in waiting times and pupil-teacher ratios (Lupton et al. 2013: 7). Was all this money well spent? Research from the IFS (2010) found that spending increases had been associated with a small decline in productivity of 0.3 per cent per year between 1997 and 2007. On a separate calculation of 'bang for buck' the organisation reported a larger fall of 1.3 per cent per year. However the IFS noted that measuring productivity in public services is 'notoriously difficult' and that the extra funding may 'have improved the quality of outputs in ways not measured' (2010: 11–12). Alternative research by the ONS (2013) found that productivity in public services remained broadly constant during this period. Reports concentrating specifically on the NHS report a largely positive picture. A report by the Commonwealth Fund found that the NHS was the third most efficient health systems in a study of 11 developed nations (Schneider et al. 2017). Furthermore the Nuffield Trust found that 'idea that the NHS employs an unjustifiably huge number of full-time managers is just wrong' citing research which found that the NHS employed less than half the proportion of managers compared to the economy as a whole (Dayan and Edwards 2015).

2. Labour did not increase the number of workless people living on benefits, the proportion of public spending going to social security, nor did it make it more comfortable for those reliant on welfare. The claimant count which

measures the number of people claiming benefits due to unemployment fell from 1.6 million in May 1997 to 815,200 at the end of 2007 (ONS 2017). The Labour Force Survey which includes a broader range of those who are unemployed recorded a smaller fall from just over 2 million in 1997 to 1.6 million in 2007, whilst the unemployment rate fell from 7.2 per cent to 5.4 per cent over the same period (Full Fact 2011). The broadest measure of benefits paid to those not in work, the out of work benefits numbers which includes job seekers allowance, income support and incapacity benefit also reported a fall from 5 million in 1999 (data on this measure only goes back to 1999) to just under 4.4 million in 2007 (Full Fact 2011). Social security fell from 33.0 per cent of total public spending in 1997 to 27.1 per cent in 2007 despite substantial real terms increases in benefits directed at pensioners and children (IFS 2010) In terms of the level of benefits again there is no evidence that these had increased making life more comfortable for those reliant on them. The real level of income support and incapacity benefit was static between 1997 and 2007 whilst the value of job seekers allowance fell in real terms (Rutherford 2013).

3. There is no evidence that migrants accessed out of work benefits at a level above British citizens or acted as a significant drain on public spending—if anything the balance of research finds that migrants—and particularly EEA migrants are net contributors to the state. Research from the Migration Observatory at the University of Oxford found that EU and non-EU migrants were half as likely to be claiming out of work benefits as British nationals (Full Fact 2015). EU migrants- particularly those from the post 2004 accession states- did however claim tax credits at a higher rate than UK nationals because they were more concentrated in low wage sectors (Full Fact 2015). When the net contribution of migration is calculated by subtracting the costs of the public services migrants use from the tax they pay research finds that the overall fiscal impact is small—+/− 1 per cent of GDP—with most studies finding EU migrants are net contributors (Vargas-Silva 2017). Furthermore the OBR (2013) has argued that cutting migration will actually make it harder to reduce the deficit—the exact opposite view of many participants in our focus groups—because migrants are more likely to be of working age and thus add to the tax base.

REFERENCES

Bagguley, P., & Mann, K. (1992). Idle Thieving Bastards? Scholarly Representations of the 'Underclass'. *Work, Employment & Society, 6*(1), 113–126.

Berry, M., Garcia-Blanco, I., & Moore, K. (2016). *Press Coverage of the Refugee and Migrant Crisis in the EU: A Content Analysis of Five European Countries.* Available at: http://www.unhcr.org/56bb369c9.html. Date accessed 9 July 2018.

Blackman, S., & Rogers, R. (2017). *Youth Marginality in Britain: Contemporary Studies of Austerity*. London: Policy.

Blyth, M. (2013). *Austerity: The History of a Dangerous Idea*. New York: Oxford University Press.

Briant, E., Watson, N., & Philo, G. (2011). *Bad News for Disabled People: How the Newspapers Are Reporting Disability* (Project Report). Strathclyde Centre for Disability Research and Glasgow Media Unit, University of Glasgow, Glasgow.

Cadwalladr, C. (2011, June 5). Vajazzled! How Chavs Have Replaced Working Class People on Britain's TV. *Observer.*

Carter, R. (2018). Fear, Loss and Hope: Understanding the Drivers of Hope and Hate. Available at: https://www.hopenothate.org.uk/wpcontent/uploads/2018/10/FINAL-VERSION.pdf. Accessed 16 Oct 2018.

Connor, S. (2007). We're Onto You: A Critical Examination of the Department for Work and Pensions' 'Targeting Benefit Fraud' Campaign. *Critical Social Policy, 27*(2), 231–252.

Crouch, C. (2011). *The Strange Non-death of Neo-liberalism*. London: Polity.

Dayan, M., & Edwards, N. (2015). Fact or Fiction? The NHS Has Too Many Managers. *The Nuffield Trust*. Available at: https://www.nuffieldtrust.org.uk/news-item/fact-or-fiction-the-nhs-has-too-many-managers. Date Accessed 9 July 2018.

Deacon, A. (1978). The Scrounging Controversy: Public Attitudes Towards the Unemployed in Contemporary Britain. *Social and Economic Administration, 12*(2), 120–135.

Deacon, A. (1980, February 28). Spivs, Drones and Other Scroungers. *New Society.*

Dorey, P. (2014). Faltering Before the Finishing Line: The Conservative Party's Performance in the 2010 General Election. *British Politics, 5*(4), 402–435.

Dwyer, P. (2004). Creeping Conditionality in the UK: From Welfare Rights to Conditional Entitlements? *Canadian Journal of Sociology, 29*(2), 265–287.

Full Fact. (2011). *Labour's Record on Welfare: Liam Byrne Fact-Check*. Available at: https://fullfact.org/news/labours-record-welfare-liam-byrne-fact-check/. Accessed 9 July 2018.

Full Fact. (2015). *Migration and Welfare Benefits*. Available at: https://fullfact.org/immigration/migration-and-welfare-benefits/

Gamble, A. (1994). *The Free Economy and the Strong State; The Politics of Thatcherism*. Basingstoke: Macmillan.

Geiger, B. B. (2012). *The Positive and Negative Consequences of the Welfare State*. Available at: https://inequalitiesblog.wordpress.com/2012/10/25/the-positive-and-negative-consequences-of-the-welfare-state/. Accessed 9 July 2018.

George, G., & Wilding, P. (1994). *Welfare and Ideology*. London: Harvester Wheatsheaf.

Golding, P., & Middleton, S. (1983). *Images of Welfare: Press and Public Attitude to Poverty*. London: Blackwell.

Hayward, K., & Yair, M. (2006). The 'Chav' Phenomenon: Consumption, Media and the Construction of a New Underclass. *Crime Media and Culture, 2*(1), 9–28.

Hills, J. (2001). Poverty and Social Security. What Rights? What Responsibilities? In A. Park et al. (Eds.), *British Social Attitudes: The 18th Report*. London: Sage Publications.

Hopkins, J., & Rosamond, B. (2017). Post-Truth Politics, Bullshit and Bad Ideas: 'Deficit Fetishism' in the UK. *New Political Economy, 4*, 1–15.

Institute for Fiscal Studies (IFS). (2010). *Public Spending Under Labour*. Available from: http://www.ifs.org.uk/bns/bn92.pdf. Accessed 9 July 2018.

Ipsos-Mori. (2009). *Public Spending Index – June 2009*. Available from: https://www.ipsos.com/sites/default/files/migrations/en-uk/files/Assets/Docs/poll-public-spending-charts-june-2009.pdf. Accessed 9 July 2018.

Ipsos-Mori. (2016). *Shifting Ground 8 Key Findings from a Longitudinal Study on Attitudes Towards Immigration and Brexit*. Available at: https://www.ipsos.com/sites/default/files/ct/news/documents/2017-10/Shifting%20Ground_Unbound.pdf. Accessed 9 July 2018.

Jayasuriya, K. (2002). The New Contractualism: Neo-liberal or Democratic? *Political Quarterly, 73*(3), 309–320.

Jones, O. (2011). *Chavs: The Demonization of the Working Class*. London: Verso.

Kellner, P. (2012). *Labour's Lost Votes*. Available at: https://yougov.co.uk/news/2012/10/22/labours-lost-votes/. Accessed 9 July 2018.

King, D. (1999). *In the Name of Liberalism: Illiberal Social Policy in the USA and Britain*. New York: Oxford University Press.

Krastev, I. (2017). *After Europe*. Pennsylvania: The University of Pennsylvania Press.

Larsen, C. A., & Dejgaard, T. E. (2013). The Institutional Logic of Images of the Poor and Welfare Recipients: A Comparative Study of British, Swedish and Danish Newspapers. *Journal of European Social Policy, 23*(3), 287–299.

Lewis, J. M. W. (2008). Thinking by Numbers: Cultural Analysis and the Use of Data. In T. Bennett & J. Frow (Eds.), *The SAGE Handbook of Cultural Analysis* (pp. 654–673). London: Sage.

Lundström, R. (2013). Framing Fraud: Discourse on Benefit Cheating in Sweden and the UK. *European Journal of Communication, 28*(6), 630–645.

Lupton, R., Hills, J., Stewart, K., & Vizard, P. (2013). *Labour's Social Policy Record: Policy, Spending and Outcomes 1997–2010* (Social Policy in a Cold Climate Research Report 1). Available at: http://sticerd.lse.ac.uk/dps/case/spcc/rr01.pdf. Accessed 9 July 2018.

McEnhill, L., & Byrne, V. (2014). 'Beat the Cheat': Portrayals of Disability Benefit Claimants in Print Media. *Journal of Poverty and Social Justice, 22*(2), 99–110.

Misra, J., Moller, S., & Karides, M. (2003). Envisioning Dependency: Changing Media Depictions of Welfare in the 20th Century. *Social Problems, 50*(4), 482–504.

Morris, J. (2017, February 25). Working-Class Desertion of Labour Started Before Corbyn. *Guardian*. Available at: https://www.theguardian.com/commentisfree/2017/feb/25/wings-labour-blame-electoral-collapse. Accessed 9 July 2018.

Morrison, J. (2018). *Scroungers: Moral Panics and Media Myths*. London: Zed Books.

Office for Budget Responsibility. (2013). *2013 Fiscal Sustainability Report*. Available at: http://budgetresponsibility.org.uk/docs/dlm_uploads/2013-FSR_OBR_web.pdf. Accessed 9 July 2018.

Office for National Statistics. (2013). *Public Service Productivity Estimates: Total Public Services*, 2010. Available at: http://www.ons.gov.uk/ons/rel/psa/public-sector-productivity-66estimates%2D%2Dtotal-public-sector/2010/art-public-service-productivity-estimates.html. Accessed 9 July 2018.

Office for National Statistics. (2017). Claimant Count and Vacancies Time Series Dataset. Available at: https://www.ons.gov.uk/employmentandlabourmarket/peoplenotinwork/unemployment/datasets/claimantcountandvacanciesdataset. Accessed 9 July 2018.

Olsen, K. M., Kalleberg, A. L., & Nesheim, T. (2010). Perceived Job Quality in the United States, Great Britain, Norway and West Germany, 1989–2005. *European Journal of Industrial Relations, 16*(3), 221–240.

Philo, G. (1990). *Seeing and Believing: The Influence of Television*. London: Routledge.

Philo, G. (2001). Media Effects and the Active Audience. *Sociology Review, 10*(3), 26–29.

Philo, G. (2004). The Mass Production of Ignorance: News Content and Audience. In C. A. Paterson & A. Sreberny (Eds.), *International News in the 21st Century*. Eastleigh: University of Luton Press.

Philo, G., Briant, E., & Donald, P. (2013). *Bad News for Refugees*. London: Pluto.

Plant, R. (2003). Citizenship and Social Security. *Fiscal Studies, 24*(2), 153–166.

Roberts, C. (2017). The Language of "Welfare Dependency" and "Benefit Cheats": Internalising and Reproducing the Hegemonic and Discursive Rhetoric of "Benefit Scroungers". In A. Mooney & E. Sifaki (Eds.), *The Language of Money and Debt* (pp. 189–204). London: Palgrave Macmillan.

Rodger, J. J. (2003). Social Solidarity, Welfare and Post-Emotionalism. *Journal of Social Policy, 32*(3), 403–421.

Rutherford, T. (2013). *Historical Rates of Social Security Benefits*. House of Commons Library SN/SG 6762. Available from: http://researchbriefings.files.parliament.uk/documents/SN06762/SN06762.pdf. Accessed 9 July 2018.

Sage, D. (2012). Fair Conditions and Fair Consequences? Exploring New Labour, Welfare Contractualism and Social Attitudes. *Social Policy and Society, 11*(3), 359–373.

Schneider, E. C., Sarnak, D. O., Squires, D., Shah, A., & Doty, M. M. (2017). *Mirror, Mirror 2017: International Comparison Reflects Flaws and Opportunities for Better U.S. Health Care. The Commonwealth Fund.* Available at: http://www.commonwealthfund.org/interactives/2017/july/mirror-mirror/. Accessed 9 July 2018.

Skeggs, B., & Wood, H. (2012). *Reacting to Reality Television: Performance, Audience and Value.* Abingdon/New York: Routledge.

Standing, G. (2014). *The Precariat: The New Dangerous Class.* London: Bloomsbury.

Taylor-Gooby, P., & Martin, R. (2008). Trends in Sympathy for the Poor. In A. Park et al. (Eds.), *British Social Attitudes: The 24th Report.* London: Sage Publications.

Taylor-Gooby, P., & Taylor, E. (2015). Benefits and Welfare: Long-Term Trends or Short-Term Reactions? *British Social Attitudes, 32.* Available at: http://www.bsa.natcen.ac.uk/media/38977/bsa32_welfare.pdf. Accessed 10 July 2018.

Tyler, I. (2008). "CHAV MUM CHAV SCUM" Class Disgust in Contemporary Britain. *Feminist Media Studies, 8*(1), 17–34.

Vargas-Silva, C. (2017). *The Fiscal Impact of Immigration in the UK.* Available at: http://www.migrationobservatory.ox.ac.uk/resources/briefings/the-fiscal-impact-of-immigration-in-the-uk/. Accessed 10 July 2018.

White, S. (2000). Social Rights and the Social Contract: Political Theory and the New Welfare Politics. *British Journal of Political Science, 30*(3), 507–532.

YouGov. (2010a). *Unavoidable Cuts.* Available at: https://yougov.co.uk/news/2010/10/19/unavoidable-cuts-story/. Accessed 10 July 2018.

YouGov. (2010b). *YouGov/Demos Survey Results.* Available at: https://d25d2506sfb94s.cloudfront.net/today_uk_import/YG-Archives-Pol-Demos-Govt-210510.pdf. Accessed 10 July 2018.

CHAPTER 7

The Production of GFC News

Introduction

In the previous five chapters this book examined how the GFC was reported and how this reporting influenced public knowledge and beliefs. In this chapter I explore the factors that structured the reporting of news in this area. I do so by drawing on a series of interviews conducted with print and broadcast journalists. These semi-structured interviews took place between 2015 and 2018 and were conducted as either telephone or face to face encounters. The interviews lasted between 20 minutes and an hour and a half with an average duration of approximately 45 minutes. Although the sample here is relatively small—in part because many journalists did not respond to requests to be interviewed[1]—it includes many senior editors who should have been able to provide an overview of the priorities of their respective news organisations. A number of journalists wished to speak 'off the record'. Their names are not listed below and their comments are presented in an unattributed form. The journalists who were prepared to speak on the record together with their position at the time of the GFC are listed below. One journalist Aditya Chakrabortty is listed under both columns because during interviewing he drew on his experiences working at both *The Guardian* and the BBC:

Print Journalists
Damian Reece (Head of Business, *Telegraph Media Group*)
Larry Elliott (Economics Editor, *Guardian*)

© The Author(s) 2019   229
M. Berry, *The Media, the Public and the Great Financial Crisis*,
https://doi.org/10.1007/978-1-137-49973-8_7

Aditya Chakrabortty (Senior Economics Correspondent, *Guardian*)
Dan Atkinson (Economics Editor, *Mail on Sunday*)
George Pascoe-Watson (Political Editor, *Sun*)
Kevin Maguire (Political Editor, *Mirror*)
Kevin Schofield (Westminster Correspondent, *Record*)

Broadcast Journalists
Evan Davis (BBC Economics Editor)
Robert Peston (BBC Business Editor)
Hugh Pym (BBC Economics Editor)
Aditya Chakrabortty (BBC Producer)

THE PRODUCTION OF PRINT COVERAGE OF THE GFC

Complexity, Comprehension and Servicing the Audience

The banking crisis in particular was widely seen as being one of the most challenging stories in recent economic reporting. So complex were some of the financial products at the heart of the crisis that even many bank CEOs failed to appreciate their implications and risks. It is therefore not surprising a number of journalists struggled to grasp what was happening because initially they were unfamiliar with the intricacies of different financial products. At the *Guardian*, specialist correspondents with a deep knowledge of banking had to try to bring other reporters up to speed:

> Internally on the Guardian, we found that people like me and the banking editor at the time, Jill Traynor and Nils Pratley, who writes our business analysis column, we were called in and had to try and explain to the rest of the staff what the hell was going on because no one really had the first idea what a subprime mortgage was or what a collateralised debt obligation was or CDO squared. And, be honest, a lot of us were picking up as we were going along and I deal with the macro stuff, and a lot of that micro banking stuff was brought to the party by people who were expert in those fields. (Larry Elliott, *Guardian*)

If telling such a difficult story represented a significant challenge it was one that almost all journalists thought the British press handled well. There was a widespread sense of pride in the ability of journalists to explain complex issues and a belief that the UK has a particularly strong news culture. In order to make reporting of the GFC as accessible as possible editors varied the level of complexity in different parts of the newspaper. Sections—such as the business or finance supplement—which might be expected to attract a more specialised audience with a deeper understanding of finance would be pitched at a higher level than news in the main section. As Dan Atkinson explained even within the specialist sections there would be gradations:

> Even within the financial section as well, there was a slight variation. So if you're writing for the front page of the financial section, that would be a bit more easy to understand than if you're inside the section somewhere. But certainly when you're writing for the main page, you have to write for different audiences. You can't assume anything. You use simple phrases. You don't talk about bank reserve, you talk about cash and it was a different way of operating. (Dan Atkinson, *Mail on Sunday*)

As noted in Chap. 2, most reporting explained the banking crisis in terms of individual pathology and eschewed a deeper engagement with some of its more technical aspects. However, some journalists argued that for tabloid audiences references to the greed or reckless behaviour of the bankers offered the opportunity to explain complex issues like derivatives or subprime:

> You see, that's [derivatives and sub-prime] all covered by reckless behaviour. The Northern Rock 120 per cent mortgage and so on, it's quite easy but the way they borrowed on the markets and then couldn't get any more money, it was rather like you could understand why customers wanted to take their money out of Northern Rock when other financial institutions didn't suffer it. All these questions as well, like science, engineering, medicine, right across economics, finance, politics, they may all be complex but they can all be quite easily reduced. People do that every day, that's what we do in the media. You don't need an hour of Panorama. (Kevin Maguire, *Daily Mirror*)

The bankers were the actors who were subject to the most criticism because they there were the group most directly responsible, but this was not the whole story. Journalists argued that they also fitted key tabloid news values in that they could be fitted into a simple moral story. As one journalist put it 'fat cat bankers being greedy and maybe breaking the rules or cutting corners' for 'a tabloid audience, it's a convenient way of writing a story and making it punchy and putting bad guys in the dock' (Kevin Schofield, *Daily Record*). As another interviewee noted the 'the regulatory stuff is quite a difficult story to tell' but for a host of reasons bankers made 'very satisfying villains' who could be fitted into a simple narrative:

> People like simple to understand stories, to be perfectly honest, and credit rating people, for example, didn't really make very satisfying villains, but bankers do. We've all had experience with banks from time to time, it's just part of life and now here we are, especially of course they'd been built up to such an extent. People like Frank Goodwin and all the other ones, they were very often in the business pages being praised for their daring do and buc-caneering spirit and all that sort of thing, and now it turns out that not only have they brought their own banks to their knees – or most of them – but they're going to require something like a trillion pounds worth of support from the taxpayer. The third thing, of course, is that we were given all this stuff about 25 years' worth of 'masters of the universe' who were so amaz-ingly talented and good at their jobs, that ... we were lucky to have them in our country, they could go anywhere, and had these wonderful global skills and all that and then it turns out when it all went wrong, the previously despised nation state was required to step in and bail them out. So I think they just made very satisfying villains. (Dan Atkinson, *Mail On Sunday*)

However at the *Telegraph*—where the content analysis demonstrated 'banker bashing' was more subdued than in other parts of the press—criti-cism of the finance sector was moderated by two factors. One was the belief—also expressed by journalists in other right of centre newspapers—that banks were a vital part of the British economy. The other was a stated desire to remain 'balanced' and highlight the culpability of different actors. As well as guiding the placement of stories and influencing how they were told, perceptions of the audience—and how they might respond—also affected the viewpoints that newspapers adopted. When discussing why the *Mail*—a newspaper that has tended to support the free market—was so hard on bankers, one former employee argued that a key part of the paper's success was to incite outrage: 'They will always run stories that they think will exercise their readers that's why it's such a financially suc-cessful title. It's good at identifying themes and issues that its readers are going to get angry about'. For the *Mirror's* Kevin Maguire though the key issue in focusing on banker misbehaviour was the price that it was going to extract on the newspaper's readers:

> Our users use state schools, they rely on the NHS, they want tax credits and need tax credits to boost their wages. They are the public service workers and nurses, teachers and councillors and so on. So we didn't want them to be sacrificial lambs, they didn't want to be sacrificial lambs. [That's] one of the reasons we've focused time after time on the bankers themselves and getting their snouts really back into their bonus trough very quickly after they were bailed out while other people were paying the price for what they did wrong. (Kevin Maguire, *Mirror*)

However the most developed account of how perceptions of the audience influenced reporting came from the *Sun*'s political editor George Pascoe-Watson. He explained that in order to maximise the newspaper's readership 'you need to be hitting the themes and topics that most chime with people's interests'. The *Sun*'s job he explained:

> …was to magnify and amplify things that the public found interesting and to take a view on those things, whilst also reminding the public that there are things that, on the face of it, could be quite dull and boring but actually have a massive impact on them and, therefore, are important and, therefore, the *Sun*'s job was to try and engender interest in the public in them.

The 'skill of the *Sun*', he argued, 'is to do both of those things, whereas other tabloids tend just to follow what they think is the diet that their readers are interested in'. For instance, in discussing why the *Sun* took a hard line against freedom of movement (see Chap. 6) he explained that the newspaper's focus was influenced by feedback from their audience:

Interviewer:	The *Sun* was very influential in that debate and took a very hard line, in some senses, a very critical line about free movement and I was wondering what drove that particular policy stance?
George Pascoe-Watson:	That is very easy. Sackfuls of mail and emails on a daily basis from readers right across the land saying 'I can't get a doctor's appointment, I can't get my kid into primary school', or some other reflection of a British born person being disadvantaged or being put down a waiting list or being put further back in a queue because of an influx of newcomers, and that the *Sun* had long predicted would happen but that

Tony Blair massively downplayed the impact of in quite an alarming error of judgement.

The audience—both in imagined and more tangible forms—then had powerful impacts on how reports were structured and the kinds of stories that were told by newspapers.

Ideology

This section will discuss how the economic ideology of particular newspapers—and by ideology I mean a broad set of beliefs about how the economy should be run—influenced reporting. The *Mirror*'s political editor argued that its approach to the economy was broadly Keynesian social democratic. In relation to austerity he argued that the *Mirror*'s position was that the way to get the deficit down 'was economic growth and getting the economy going, not cutting, not the economics of a leech doctor'. The *Guardian*'s economic editor offered a more structural account of what influenced his reporting of the crisis:

> I suppose my take on what was happening in the build up to 2007 was that this was a completely unsustainable model because it seemed to run counter to everything that had happened in the first 25 years after the Second World War, and the so-called 'Golden Age' ... After the neoclassical free market revolution, it seemed to me that the system essentially was going to run into a crisis because the balance of power had shifted so much towards capital, that it was a struggle for workers to actually get decent pay rises, fund their increasing living standards out of an increase in real wages. So all they could do was borrow money from a financial system which had been liberalised and was only too willing to actually lend out large sums of money to people so that they could push up asset prices and use their... to me, that was what the model was about and I just couldn't see...I just didn't think that was sustainable and I said that repeatedly. (Larry Elliott, *Guardian*)

In explaining the *Telegraph*'s ideological position on the economy its business editor explained that 'broadly there are editorial lines, I think you could say, on philosophical points around the importance of, say, discipline in public finances or the importance of choice and free markets and things like that'. These perspectives, explained Reece, were the reason why the *Telegraph* was prepared to support austerity and 'across the board' cuts to 'frontline' services despite the fact that such views were not widely shared by the public:

> I think that stance [cuts to frontline services] was entirely consistent with decades of thought on the *Telegraph* on the importance of sound public finances, and bailing out the banks was a huge commitment that any country could make but it doesn't mean you then throw out the window the idea of financial discipline. It was a school of thought that was entirely consistent basically with the *Telegraph*'s view on public finances, the need for sound finances. Did it risk alienating readers? Possibly, and absolutely and any newspaper worth its salt will always publish coverage that risks that. (Damian Reece, *Telegraph*)

This belief in the primacy of 'sound money' and 'fiscal discipline' were also key reasons, Reece explained, why the *Telegraph* had been so critical of New Labour's extra public spending in their second term. 'Prudence' and 'fiscal discipline' he argued had been the 'rallying cry' for New Labour but after 2001 'that discipline around public spending, which I mentioned earlier, is an essential tenet I suppose of the *Telegraph*'s thought, was clearly thrown out of the window and it was a return to the spend, spend, spend habits of previous Labour governments which generally ended badly'. At other times support for particular policies—in this case the *Telegraph*'s opposition to full nationalisation—was explained not so much in terms of a particular ideological position but more in terms of 'common sense':

> ...returning the banks to the private sector was going to be a priority to get them off the Government's balance sheet because governments are not good at running banks. Why should they be? There's no reason to suggest that having banks owned by the Government is a good thing. It's not, it's a bad thing. It's not what governments should do. In this case, they had to but it was absolutely the last resort...One accepts completely that it had to happen but it was obviously regrettable and not something that governments should do as a matter of course. I don't think that's a party political point or even a philosophical point, it's just common sense. (Damian Reece, *Telegraph*)

At the *Mail*, a former reporter explained that the views of the editor reflected the Conservative viewpoint on state ownership which had solidified in the 1980s:

You have to remember that Dacre and many of the other people who were in charge of the *Mail* at the time were people who would have grown up – they're weren't Thatcher's children but you know what I mean – they came to positions of authority in newspapers and media during the late 70s and 80s when privatisation was deemed to have been a very good thing... and all the industries that were perceived to have been laggards, the car manufacturing industry was in the doldrums and then you had privatisation and you had new investors, new owners coming in and that was seen as being a good thing and seen as having revitalised large parts of the economy. (Former *Mail* reporter)

Yet the same source argued that although the *Mail* was opposed to state ownership it didn't necessarily follow that it was an unconditional friend of big business. Instead, he argued, the *Mail* had a similar 'tenor' to the *Guardian* of wanting to hold business to account and generally being quite suspicious of the corporate world. This view was also expressed by the *Mail on Sunday*'s Economics Editor who argued that 'the free market was just one priority, which was always having a wee bit of a tussle with social conservatism and with nationalism'. He also argued that 'both nationalism and social conservatism tend to trump the free market if there were a conflict' and that partly because of its readership base corporate Britain could not rely on the *Mail* as an unconditional supporter:

Dan Atkinson: If you look at the *Mail* titles, their commitment to the free market is a lot more qualified than, say, the *Telegraph* or *The Times* would be. They're social conservatives and pro small business and so on, but when it comes to corporate Britain, they can't rely on the support of those titles. Whereas the *Telegraph* or *The Times* – certainly the *Telegraph* – will always say we support free enterprise. You don't tend to get that in the *Mail*. Never have done.

Interviewer: Is that because they're seen to be reflecting the views of its audience?

Dan Atkinson: Yes, probably. Also they don't have a big executive readership. The old joke was its read by the wives of the people who run the country and there is that feeling. It's quite a strong female paper, it's quite a provincial paper, it's not like *The Times*, it's not read by high flying corporate executives. In the main it's just not for them.

However, Atkinson argued the GFC offered the *Mail* the opportunity to argue for the cutting of social welfare, an objective that reflected both its social conservatism and dislike of some of the roles that the state had taken on:

> Gordon Brown as Chancellor seemed to have found a way of affording things they didn't like. So they didn't like them whether we could afford them or not, and now that we couldn't afford them, they had the perfect excuse to get rid of them, whatever that may be – public health campaigns, or childcare, or anything where they think the state has no proper business. (Dan Atkinson, *Mail on Sunday*)

If support for the free market was not always the primary driver for *Mail* coverage it was a crucial issue for the *Sun*. In fact, the paper's political editor argued that it was because the newspaper was such a strong supporter of the free market that it was so critical of those—such as the bankers—who had abused it:

> The *Sun* does embrace [the free market], very much so but it embraces the free market when prosecuted, as it were, in a fair and balanced and responsible way and it is precisely because the *Sun* upholds the principles of the free market that when actors are found to be abusing that market, or taking predatory advantage of it or abusing it, that the *Sun* feels it is its role and duty and right to be way more aggressive about those people than anybody else who had a mild interest in defending the free market. So it's precisely because the *Sun* believes in it so much that the *Sun* cares so much about anybody abusing it. (George Pascoe-Watson, *Sun*)

However, there was also a degree of concern over whether the *Sun*'s attacks on the bankers might weaken support for the free market and an awareness that the newspaper had a very important and influential voice in the debate:

Interviewer:	Did you ever worry though by attacking the individual bankers you might weaken support for the free market?
George Pascoe-Watson:	I did, yes. I was writing editorials at the time as well, the sort of *Sun* says, and I was acutely conscious that you couldn't throw the baby out with the bath water and that the *Sun*'s influence on this debate was important, because the *Sun* is listened to by Prime Ministers, and particularly

Gordon Brown in those days and Alistair Darling, and it was very, very important to realise that you had to calibrate and be very specific in what you were saying so as not to demonise the entire banking industry. All *Sun* readers have a bank account on the retail side, so that's important and there needed to be continued trust in banking as an institution for the smooth running of the economy. And also, as you say, profoundly because the *Sun* believes in the market and believed in capitalism and banking.

The second key issue for the *Sun* was the desire to maintain 'small government'. This manifested in concern over the part-nationalisation of the banks. It also was a factor in the position taken on the deficit. George Pascoe-Watson argued that public spending cuts were inevitable because 'at the time, the economic circumstances were such that there seemed no other realistic way of tackling Britain's economic problem' but also that Labour's 'handling of public spending and growing the size of the State was a major cause of anxiety to the *Sun* and its editorial stance'. This concern was also a driver of criticism of state spending in the years leading up to the crisis:

Interviewer:	One of the key things we noticed in the period after 2001 when there was a very, very large increase in public spending, the reaction of a lot of the right wing papers was to argue, effectively, that this extra spending was being wasted.
George Pascoe-Watson:	Yes.
Interviewer:	So that wasn't just a kind of coincidence, it was a deliberate strategy, you wanted to get that point of view across.
George Pascoe-Watson:	Yes, very much so. Our intellectual view had always been small government, minimal public spending, more *Sun* readers can keep more of the money they earn and in 2001 when they increased the health budget by whatever it was, £12 billion overnight, don't forget we also knew the background to that decision which was basically taken on the back of a cigarette packet. It hadn't been long plotted out and modelled. It was a political act and we knew, therefore, that the chances of competent spend to increase productivity in the Health Service were minimal. And don't forget, when you have as many readers as the *Sun* used to have in those days, it's your readers' money that's being spent

here. It's not some mythical figure which is Government money, it's your readers' money. So it really mattered that we were going to try and extract value from that expenditure.

Political Partisanship and Personal Relationships

Much of the British press has been fairly consistent in its endorsement of the same political party during the post-war period (Guardian Datablog 2010). The *Mirror* has backed Labour in every election since 1945 whilst the *Telegraph* and the *Mail* have always supported the Conservatives. The *Express* has been resolutely Conservative aside from 2001 when it supported New Labour, whilst the News International titles have consistently backed the Conservatives apart from during the period when Tony Blair was Labour leader (*The Times* supported labour in 2001 and 2005, the *Sun* 1997, 2001 and 2005). The *Record* switched its allegiance from the Conservative Unionist Party to Labour in 1964 and has supported the party ever since.

How significant was this as an issue in reporting of the GFC? Certainly for Labour supporting titles it appeared to be an important factor. For instance, Kevin Maguire argued that the *Mirror* did see Brown and Darling as being partly culpable but that ultimately the GFC was a crisis of a capitalist system most strongly supported by the Conservatives and their allies in the press:

> *Mirror* readers vote Labour. The *Mirror* is a Labour supporting paper. Not a Labour Party paper but a Labour supporting paper. There's this huge crisis, who do you blame? Do you blame the Government or the bankers? Now, of course, both of those other papers took their cue from the Conservative Party which they were backing and they turned their fire on Brown and Alistair Darling. Brown and Alistair Darling deserve some blame and culpability as accessories, but ultimately it was a capitalist system that was championed particularly by the Tories and defended by those papers. We've never been big supporters of the banks so it wasn't a problem for us and, of course, we were a Labour supporting paper so that wasn't a problem. (Kevin Maguire, *Mirror*)

Kevin Schofield at the *Record* also recognised the importance of the newspaper's stance as a Labour supporting title but argued that support for

Gordon Brown went beyond 'blind faith' and reflected a belief in his leadership during the crisis:

> We were big fans of Gordon Brown and we thought he'd been dealt a very difficult hand and was doing his utmost. I think actually, to be fair, there wasn't just a blind faith in the guy. I think there was genuinely a lot of evidence actually backs that up, the stuff that he did to bring together world leaders at a special G8 or G20 in London not long after Obama became President. So he organised that massive summit in London which was completely at Gordon's behest and they managed to agree a deal to prop up the global economy with billions and billions of pounds of public money. So I think Gordon, he certainly was worthy of praise but we were certainly more than willing to give him praise, given that we were a Labour paper. (Kevin Schofield, *Record*)

Schofield also argued that the banking crisis had also become entangled in the politics of Scottish nationalism, with the Brown government using the collapse of the banks to argue that an independent Scotland would not have been able to provide a backstop for a huge institution like RBS. At the right of centre newspapers there was less acceptance of the argument that political partisanship drove coverage. For instance, Damian Reece at the *Telegraph* argued that in setting up the Tripartite Authority, Labour had 'created that environment which allowed the banking crisis to go undetected because no one had full responsibility in the right areas, so... they needed to take their share of the blame'.

What also came through in some of the interviews was that it wasn't just a question of whether a title backed a party, coverage was also influenced by the struggles within parties. This was particularly the case at the *Guardian* where the newspaper's conflicted stand on austerity policies reflected the struggle between Brownites and Blairites over the issue:

> It was happening inside the *Guardian* because there were two camps inside the Government and it depends who your contacts were. So there was a big struggle going on between the Gordon Brown/Ed Balls faction and the Alistair Darling/Peter Mandelson faction. The Peter Mandelson and Alistair Darling faction thought that the budget deficit was the major problem and that Labour should go into the election with a clear commitment to bringing down the deficit... and Gordon Brown/Ed Balls camp said, 1) economically this is not the right way to go forward and 2) politically it's a very bad place for Labour to be in because we can't outbid the Tories in an aus-

terity war if people want a Government who's going to be clamping down on public spending and capping the budget deficit... they'll choose the Tories. I was part of the Gordon Brown/Ed Balls camp but there were people on the *Guardian*, former Blairites or people who always hated Brown, of whom there were many on the *Guardian*, who were quite willing to take the Alistair Darling/Peter Mandelson line. So that's why you got different views because Labour was at war with itself on this issue. (Larry Elliott, *Guardian*)

The *Sun* had reportedly been very close to Tony Blair while he was prime minister. The late journalist Hugo Young spoke of Blair and Rupert Murdoch as having a close 'collaborative' relationship and that 'Downing Street seldom makes a big move without weighing carefully what the *Sun* will think' (Cited in King 2015: 161). In a 2008 Radio 4 documentary, the New Labour spin doctor Lance Price had suggested that 'his [Rupert Murdoch's] presence was almost tangible in the building [10 Downing Street] and it was as if he was the 24th member of the Cabinet. In fact more than that. In some areas of policy [he was] more influential on the Prime Minister and on the direction of government's policy than most of the other 23' (Cited in Dean 2013: 6). The *Sun*'s political editor suggested that in explaining why the newspaper had been critical of Gordon Brown there was a 'discomfort' in how Brown had 'moved Blair aside':

George Pascoe-Watson:	You can't divorce what was happening also on the political track, which was the *Sun* had been very close to Tony Blair. He was very close to Gordon Brown but it had been very close to Tony Blair and there was still a lot of discomfort, I suppose, in the way that Brown had forcibly moved Blair aside.
Interviewer:	So that was something that...
George Pascoe-Watson:	It was a residual burning in the background.

Conversely at the *Mail*, the relationship between the newspaper's editor, Paul Dacre and Gordon Brown was seen to be much closer than the one Dacre had shared with Blair. Responding to a question as to whether the reported closeness between Brown and Dacre had been a factor in why the *Mail* had been less critical of Brown than many of the other right-wing newspapers, Dan Atkinson commented: 'Yes, it probably did and so did the fact that he was genuinely thought to be a man with good values, a vast improvement on his slick predecessor and again a friend. So I think it all added up to leaving off him, to a very large extent.'

Sourcing, Advertising and Morality

As the data in the content chapters demonstrated there were some fairly predictable patterns in coverage. Broadsheets featured a much wider range of sources than tabloids and the three main parties and City sources tended to be well represented across the press. It was also clear that Labour politicians tended to be more heavily sourced in Labour supporting newspapers. When I asked a *Mail* reporter who were seen as the key sources at the time of the banking crisis he provided a list of financial and political elites which tend to dominate reporting at both the broadsheets and BBC:

> There was a variety of people. Economists, Treasury people. The Treasury were very active at the time which they're less so now. You had UKFI, Bank CEOs, you had a variety of people you had the Treasury Select Committee, politicians it was a wide range of people that informed the view. (Former *Mail* correspondent)

Conversely, Damian Reece argued that the people he trusted most were the *Telegraph*'s own internal experts. He argued that City, Treasury and academic economists had 'been behind the curve' in the lead up to the crisis, failed to foresee the GFC and underestimated its impact. In contrast, he argued 'some newspapers were very well resourced with experts who knew what they were talking about and could translate it into simple English … they were technically brilliant when it came to analysing the growing debt problem'.

Larry Elliott commented that the complex and fast evolving nature of the banking crisis meant that journalists were drawing on a wider range of expert views than normal which was reflected in the high incidence of joint bylines. He argued that many articles drew on his political contacts in government—who could provide the macro picture—as well as sources within the major banks who had links to the paper's finance specialists—Jill Traynor and Philip Inman. Elliott also argued that the sources he drew on depended on the type of story he was constructing. For 'spot news stories' City economists would be the first port of call because of their availability and ability to deliver quotes that were user friendly. In contrast, he suggested, academics were often 'difficult to get hold of' and 'long winded'. However, he said that if he was writing a column 'then academics are really useful I think because they've thought through a subject a lot more carefully than some talking head from the City has and they've probably got something original to say and they'll send you a paper and you think—that's interesting'.

Both Larry Elliot and Robert Peston argued that a reliance on advertising from the FIRE sector had shaped coverage, particularly in the period leading up to 2008. Peston argued that 'there was a vested interest in the media in not seeing the bubble in the housing market because the bubble in the housing market was paying people's salaries and generating big profit... so that was a very clear conflict of interest [and]... too many journalists were, if not consciously, subconsciously part of the same unsustainable gravy train'. However, Elliott argued that unlike other newspapers the *Guardian*—because of its ownership structure—had 'no vested interest' in pushing a certain line on the economy or the stock market:

Larry Elliott: I think that some papers and some journalists had a vested interest in keeping the system going. From the *Guardian* we have a different ownership structure, we don't have people owning us who've got some reason for keeping the stock market...

Interviewer: Were you not so reliant on property supplements and all of those things?

Larry Elliott: We do have ads from those people but they are kept at arm's length. I think one of the many good things about the *Guardian* is that no one ever comes up to you and says actually that's not the sort of piece we want in the *Guardian*, however difficult it might be for advertisers. Not once in my near 30 years on the paper has anybody ever said that's the wrong story or the wrong line. I'm sure that does happen on other papers.

Research has suggested that a desire not to offend real estate advertisers had been a key reason why the Irish media failed to warn about the GFC (Fahy et al. 2010). The *Telegraph* has also seen one of its most high profile commentators, Peter Oborne (2015), resign amidst claims that the newspaper suppressed stories about tax evasion committed by HSBC because of a fear that it might jeopardise advertising.

Another issue that was raised by Dan Atkinson at the *Mail on Sunday* and the BBC's Evan Davis were journalists' sense of 'morality' in that there had been a perception that the country had to face a reckoning because it had been living on borrowed money. Atkinson commented that its 'partly psychological…that we'd had it coming for years because we'd been living beyond our means… and we'd had good years. Indeed, if you take it back a bit further to, say, the second Thatcher election victory we'd had a quarter of a century when things had been pretty okay and we've had this one coming to us. The British are very moralistic in some ways'. This view of how print journalists saw the deficit was very similar to the perspective of the middle-class homeowners in Stanley's (2014) focus groups who believed austerity was 'reaping what we'd sowed'.

Labour's Turn to the Right and the Weakness of Left Civil Society Voices

A very striking finding in reporting of both the banking crisis and the debate over the deficit was the lack of coherent left-wing or social democratic alternatives. Due to both its political legitimacy and structural access, Labour would traditionally have been the key voice making such arguments. However, according to Kevin Maguire, Labour was unable to contest the Conservative narrative on austerity for two reasons. First, he argued that Labour was split and involved in internecine fighting that prevented the production of a unified narrative. Second, he suggested that the crisis had happened in a period when Labour was in a weak position and unable to mount a credible fightback because they were on the back foot over a series of policy failures on Iraq and the banks:

> It [the GFC] happened in a period when Labour had dirty hands and Labour had compromised. Ed Balls had made a City speech absolutely praising it to the hilt. Labour hadn't regulated the City fully or better and the political mood music was very different. It was coming after more than a decade of Labour rule. It was coming after Iraq. It was coming after confidence in Blair had plummeted. Trust in politics was low. It could be exploited by the Conservatives. It happened on Labour's watch. (Kevin Maguire, *Mirror*)

Larry Elliott also commented that because Labour had accepted so much of the Thatcherite settlement it was in no position to row back: 'Blairism had actually conceded all that ground. 20 years earlier there would have been much more of a traditional social democratic response.' Elliott suggested this was part of a broader problem that the left was completely unprepared for the GFC—in sharp contrast to how the New Right had been ready for the breakdown of the social democratic model in the 1970s—and the extra-parliamentary left, in particular, was stymied by a lack of coherence and factionalism:

> I think that tragically the left was completely unprepared for the crisis in 2007/8 and had no real remedy for it... there was a Marxist analysis and there was a Green analysis and there was sort of Keynesian analysis, but it never coalesced into a fully thought through alternative to neoliberalism, in the way that neoliberalism was a fully thought through programme ready to be implemented in the mid-1970s when the social democratic model broke down... much less seriously as it happens I think, but the thinktanks of the right and the politicians of the right had actually got a complete manifesto of what they wanted to do. They'd analyse what was going wrong and they knew what they wanted to do from their liberal right wing perspective... where in the West, the political parties of the left, the Labour Party, the Democrats in the US, Social Democrats in Germany, Socialists in France, none of them were prepared...You got it at the edges ...but it never really caught on...there are a number of reasons why not. I think one was that so much of the left had been captured by neoliberalism. It's partly because the left is quite sectarian ... everybody just splintered off and did their own thing and that left a big vacuum which the right filled. That's broadly what I think happened. By late 2009/10 the initial, let's go back to Keynes....that was stamped on. (Larry Elliott, *Guardian*)

Groupthink, Institutional Capture, Speed, Geography and the Reactive Nature of Journalism

An issue that emerged in the interviews with both press and journalists was the question of how a very strong consensus could stymie the range of issues or views that journalists could cover. Once a position had become widely accepted by key agenda setters then journalists struggled to be able to challenge it. In trying to understand why the GFC wasn't predicted Larry Elliott remarked that journalists were 'insufficiently curious' but also taken in by the consensus set by powerful actors:

> I think some journalists were insufficiently curious or were just a bit blinded by the orthodoxy... there was an orthodoxy really and Mervyn King talked about the NICE decade and the IMF reported even a couple of months

before the crisis about how everything was great and how all these new financial instruments were making the world a safer place. It's kind of hard sometimes to go against the consensus and you can make yourself look a right idiot if you're not careful...people talked a lot about a groupthink thing and there was a massive, massive groupthink thing. It's hard to remember now just what it was like back in 2006, early 2007 when it was all about M&A [mergers and aquisitions] and takeovers and hedge funds and stories about Mayfair being... and all that stuff and it was just everywhere and people were completely taken in by it. (Larry Elliott, *Guardian*)

The notion of the consensus having an ability to shut down debate was also invoked by Kevin Maguire in explaining how difficult it became for the *Mirror* to challenge some of the false ideas about the deficit that came to dominate television and the press:

It was an incredible frustration. Hopefully it's recorded in the *Mirror*, you've seen that there was no true appreciation of the deficit and debt under the Labour period and, in fact, as a proportion of GDP, it was lower than had been inherited in 1997. There had been a couple of years when actually some had been paid off and it went haywire because of the crash, which dragged down the economy. Fewer taxes came in from the City, which was an important part, dragged down the [inaudible], public spending had to go up to compensate for the private collapse. That's why... but that was not represented in most papers and we used to battle with it because you were always fighting... you very rarely saw full appreciation of it on TV or heard it on radio and you felt you were running uphill in heavy boots whenever you made the argument. (Kevin Maguire, *Mirror*)

Another issue that was raised in the interviews was the lobbying power of the City and how this had captured powerful political elites. This had a number of effects. One was to create the lax regulatory system that contributed to the crisis. Another was that the key political voices in the Labour party who would previously have served as a counterweight to those from the financial sector were now acting as its boosters. The close City-politics 'nexus' also meant that the financial sector could lie low during the crisis, confident that politics would not challenge its hegemony, before regrouping to argue for the economic benefits of finance:

One of the problems with the banks and the Government and the nexus is that there's been institutional capture of government by the financial sector.

Why was it that only the City had a test when it was the five Euro test? There was one separate test for finance. There wasn't a test for manufacturing or a test for retailing but there was a test for finance? Why was it that whenever there was an attempt at a European level or any level to have a financial transaction tax or a withholding tax, the Government would be over it like a rash? Because it was being lobbied very heavily. Why was it that the City was more deregulated than pretty much... it became like a wild west of finance in the run up to the crisis because the City was such a powerful lobbying force. That didn't end with the financial crisis, it just went quiet for a bit and then gradually you heard them say all the things like we export a lot, we account for a lot of jobs, we're very high value added, blah-blah-blah. (Larry Elliott, *Guardian*)

One of the most challenging aspects of reporting the GFC was the fast moving pace of the story—particularly during the September/October 2008 period. A number of journalists—both print and broadcast—discussed how this made it very difficult to provide a full account of what was happening. The seriousness and speed of the crisis, one journalist argued, also meant that key issues such as the debate over whether the government should have gone further and fully nationalised banks wasn't really covered as comprehensively as it could have been. This was problematic he suggested because not fully nationalising the banks had negative consequences:

[The part-nationalised banks] did some pretty terrible things to its private sector customers and things like funding for lending, which really just ramped up the housing market, would have been much more effective if it would have been channelled through a state owned bank, I think. I'm not an expert on banking but it just strikes me that that was an opportunity missed. Why it wasn't taken up more, I don't know why really. As you say, I mentioned it but probably not at the time it was all going on, there was just so much happening. The question in 2008 when the banks nearly went bust was – were they were going to survive or not. Perhaps we should have been a bit more vigorous about it. (Larry Elliott, *Guardian*)

In the introduction I discussed how the financial sector had become one of the key engines of growth following the 'Big Bang' but that the rise of the City had contributed to Britain's extreme levels of economic polarisation. These issues were rarely covered in broadcast news or in newspapers, except at the *Guardian* which one journalist attributed to the paper's regional roots: 'The *Guardian*'s always been a slightly different animal that's been more willing to think about these things. Remember it was the *Manchester Guardian* and that's still in its DNA. So regional interests, what's happening outside London, the *Guardian* takes that more seriously' (Aditya Chakrabortty, *Guardian* and the BBC). However another journalist stressed that journalism was largely led by the actions of key elite agenda setters which meant that covering structural issues—even during crises—could be difficult unless raised on a consistent basis by powerful sources. This could mean the economic, social and demographic shifts that drive historic events like Brexit could be missed by a journalism that was not attuned to deeper structural processes.

> Much of the media is pretty reactive day to day and sometimes those big fundamental questions get overlooked and they probably don't get the scrutiny they require. So if politicians aren't doing it or think tanks aren't doing it, there's some politicians who were trying to, some trade unions were trying to, some think tanks were trying to but it was like you know the media is really day to day fire fighting, that's what it is rather than a larger reconstruction period. You'll get the odd column, you'll get the odd feature ... you're unlikely to get a media which is out every minute, every hour, every day looking at those big strategic decisions further ahead. ...If politicians aren't leading that debate, it may be unreasonable to expect the media every minute, every hour, every day to be somehow leading that. You need people to say things to report them. (Kevin Maguire, *Daily Mirror*)

THE PRODUCTION OF BROADCAST COVERAGE OF THE GFC

Perceptions of the Audience and the Challenges of Reporting an Unprecedented Crisis

Whilst broadcast journalists shared with press journalists a strong mission to simplify and explain the complexities of the GFC, one noticeable difference was that the BBC was prepared to devote resources to audience research. As one journalist explained the BBC 'do all sorts of focus groups to test knowledge... I was in a focus group when you sat with members of the public about terms such as GDP. I'm not sure they keep it uppermost in their minds but they do do the work, that's something they are committed to' (Aditya Chakrabortty, *Guardian* and BBC). Another journalist explained that he normally pitched his broadcasts with a particular listener in mind as well as a 'fuzzy idea about the need to pitch it at slightly different levels' for different programmes:

> So I think of my audience as probably understanding the word equity but probably not understanding the word bond. That's sort of where I would be and I wouldn't expect them to understand the notion of bank capital. I would expect them to know what a fixed rate mortgage is. So this is the kind of level I'm aiming at. In my head I'm aiming at someone who knows less than my father…So *Today, Newsnight* I think of as materially the same… on the main BBC One… I would think that comes down another notch. (Evan Davis, BBC)

The challenge of explaining the banking crisis, in particular, to a mainstream news audience was magnified by both the speed and unprecedented nature of the crisis. As one Editor put it: 'It was all moving so fast. Parliament didn't really know what was going on. This was unprecedented. This was huge. This was not something where a journalist would go "oh yeah I remember it was like that". Nobody had any memory bank to fall back on' (Hugh Pym, BBC). Hugh Pym suggested that this was compounded by the structure of the news industry which tended to discriminate against journalists gaining deep specialist knowledge of an area. Robert Peston, he argued, 'was a rarity, it's quite hard to adopt a specialism and remain in that for a lengthy period and hope that you'll find an employer who is prepared to pay for it'. This challenge was further magnified by the fact journalists were having to explain policies such as part-nationalisation which were new and unfamiliar to audiences. However, although both broadcast and print journalists clearly saw themselves as on a mission to explain, there were limits on what they thought the public needed to know in order to understand economic debates. For instance, one editor explained that he didn't think that the public needed to know the broader contours of public spending in order 'to have an entry ticket into any debate or discussion', and that adding too much context didn't necessarily help people:

Evan Davis: There are huge amounts of divergence in levels of knowledge but a lot of it doesn't matter. So you can say God, people know nothing, they don't know the difference

	between a million and a billion which quite literally is probably the case for a lot of people and you can ask them what's the education budget and they'll say oh it must be like £100 million. No, it's actually £70 billion. But I don't think that matters if you don't know the education budget to within…
Interviewer:	Would it not help people even if they knew what the size of the pie was, the public spending pie?
Evan Davis:	I think it would be very nice but I don't think you need to know that to be able to get quite a long way to making decisions. So of course it would be nice if people were more economically and financially literate or numerate, but what I don't want to do is say basically you have to know all of that to have an entry ticket into any debate or discussion about these issues. You don't. Our job sometimes is to make sure they're getting enough but you're not overloading them and if you start saying, let me explain now the GDP is £1.5 trillion and then Government is about £700/800 billion of that and then departmental expenditure is this and [inaudible] is that, you're not helping people. You've got to dumb down to make comprehensive. (Evan Davis, BBC)

But not providing information about the contours of public spending has important consequences. One is that it doesn't equip audiences with the information they need to understand or evaluate announcements or debates about public spending. For instance, if a government minister were to announce an extra £500 million for the health service, that might sound like a significant sum but it actually represents less than 0.5 per cent of total health expenditure. It is not possible for audience members to evaluate such an announcement without some contextual knowledge of the broader picture of health spending. Another problem as our focus groups—as well as polling (Ipsos-Mori 2016)—demonstrate is that if people have little understanding of the relative size of the different constituent elements of public spending they tend to hugely overestimate the contribution of items with high press visibility such as unemployment benefits, welfare payments to migrants, EU contributions or foreign aid. Such misunderstandings can have powerful impacts on public attitudes and political choices as Brexit so clearly demonstrated. The BBC has the potential to act as a public educator in this regard but to do so it must provide sufficient context.

Agenda Setting the 'Conversation' and Political Pressure

The question of who sets the agenda for news reports is a core interest for journalism studies. Previous research has pointed to the centrality of political and other institutional elites whose actions and statements are seen as a key news value (Wahl-Jorgensen et al. 2013; Harcup and O'Neil 2001). These elites tend to drive the news agenda but also to set the range of legitimate debate on particular issues (Hallin 1986). Other research has pointed to the importance of the news diary in allowing journalists to plan ahead and fill schedules in a fast moving environment (Manning 2001). One of the interviewees pointed to four sets of actors who set the agenda for BBC economic news:

> A lot of it's diary stuff around announcements by the Bank of England, the Office for National Statistics, the Treasury and a smaller extent, political parties or policies, particularly at times of election. So call that diary stuff. Then there is a second category which I would say are the kind of commentariat, the CBI and much, much lesser the trade unions but not insubstantially the thinktanks. The Resolution Foundation is the big new one that's come really from nowhere to 60mph in little time. The thinktanks, Adam Smith, these people are bunging out press releases and they do sometimes get our attention. Two honourable mentions among the thinktanks, the Institute of Fiscal Studies and the National Institute of Economic and Social Research, Jonathan Portes's lot. So that's a big second category and I think they do move us. A third category is what I would call the City, the City economists. I don't think they set the agenda but they're the ones who push the default key and they pop up and say something on demand. So they're useful commentators... Then the fourth category is all the other media. Robert [Peston] did set out and pick the right wing ones, the *Telegraph*. I think the *Mail* is important. I think probably no single thing is read more than the *Mail* and I would think maybe the *Guardian* up there but not quite as much, at the BBC at least I think *Mail* and *Guardian* are both very widely read. (Evan Davis, BBC)

One reason why the *Mail* and *Guardian* were seen as significant was because of their 'very good' open access online presence. Davis also argued that the *Mail* was 'closer to the public than a lot of us who work at the BBC. So there's a kind of sense that you might be getting more insight from them about what's interesting people'. These newspapers weren't necessary taken a barometer of public opinion but more an indicator of what might be of interest to the public at any particular moment:

> I just think that you're always just trying to keep across where everyone else is, and the *Mail* is good at twanging the right little string to get a story and it's always interesting to see which string they're twanging. The *Guardian*'s basic journalism is very good and is very available. So I didn't quite agree [with Robert Peston]. I wouldn't quite pick out the *Telegraph*. Maybe the *Telegraph*. I don't think the *Telegraph* quite as much actually as the *Mail* or the *Guardian* but people have different impressions from the people they mix with. (Evan Davis, BBC)

This theme was also picked up on by one of my other interviewees who spoke about the notion of 'the conversation'. This was seen as the mix of issues dominating public debate which was in part set by newspapers. A big worry, he suggested was that BBC reporters might miss some part of 'the conversation' which was being highlighted in other parts of the media:

> News organisations like to feel in some way that there representing the conversation and that the worst verb for any news desk is miss. Why did we miss that? Why didn't we miss that? Why have they got that line and we haven't?... I used to find that infuriating but that's as true of any newspaper as it is of the BBC so literally what they say about the *Today programme* being agenda setting is true. The things you notice when you walk in the BBC, and I'm sure you've seen it is you go round the newsrooms they've got papers on their desk and certain papers feature more heavily than others. The *Mail* is one of them not because they love the *Mail* but because they're checking it because they want to see they haven't missed anything. (Aditya Chakrabortty, *Guardian* and BBC)

In terms of which newspaper was most influential this interviewee also pointed to the *Guardian* and also *The Times* and 'sometimes the *FT*'. He also suggested that there was an elite version of the conversation which was structured by a small number of political and financial sources:

> You are economics editor at the BBC you go and see the BOE governor on a one-to-one basis every four to six months. You also go the inflation report every three months. You also go to the Treasury stuff and you probably also go to Philip Hammond's Christmas drinks. God help you. And John

McDonnell's Christmas drinks which might be a bit more lively but the point is that's where you're really picking stuff up. So the Governor's having a private word with you and saying 'well there's a couple of things on our mind' and you'll go away and you'll think about that and you'll talk to other economists as you're going about or reading stuff and you'll think, Steven King at HSBC is a classic case or Roger Bootle where he was at the time. These people are big serious conventional macroeconomists who talk about the world but they do have interesting stuff to say, they're not useless these people, they're good. So they're the sort of people you'd be in contact with. What you're not in contact with is Mark Serwotka. (Aditya Chakrabortty, *Guardian* and BBC)

Whilst previous studies and some theoretical models have emphasised the role of political pressure or 'flak'—particularly during times of conflict—this wasn't an issue that was raised often by my interviewees (Philo and Berry 2004, 2011; Glasgow Media Group 1985; Herman and Chomsky 1995). The only person to discuss this at length was Robert Peston who spoke about it in relation to two issues. One was the pressure he and the BBC were put under when he had tried to warn about problems in the banking system prior to the crash. Peston stated that 'I got savagely attacked for about a year until RBS and the rest went down, and people recognised that I was not a scaremonger'. These attacks he said came from 'politicians, regulators, economists…[and] went all the way up to the Director General' but that despite this the 'BBC stood by me'. The other instance where Peston argued he had been subject to pressure was over the bank bailouts when 'right wing MPs' had contacted him to ask why he was not featuring the 'Hayekian' view that the banks should be allowed to go bust:

There were a group of people who took what you might call the Hayekian view, who were of the view that it was wrong to the save the banks at all and that they should be allowed to go bust and although there would be a shock to the economy, that the best way to basically rebuild is to write off the debt. I have to say the political consensus was that this would have been appalling because it would have led to many, many more companies going bust and a massive rise in unemployment. But there were quite a lot of right wing MPs getting in touch with me and saying why aren't you reflecting this view? Your coverage is biased because you are taking it as a given that it is better to save the banks. (Robert Peston, BBC)

Sourcing, the 'Consensus' and the Weakness of Left Counter-Narratives

Closely related to the idea of the 'conversation' is the notion of the consensus and how this is structured around the views of a particular section of elite opinion. As the content analyses in Chaps. 2 and 4 demonstrated a key source category during both the banking crisis and the debates over the deficit were people from the City such as bankers, stockbrokers, hedge fund managers and analysts. These were accorded the status of experts whose opinion on the bailouts, nationalisation plans, bank reform proposals—and later the deficit and macroeconomic policy—were prominently featured in news accounts. A number of interviewees stressed during the banking crisis there was no choice but to rely on people from within the sector because of their inside knowledge and technical understanding of modern finance. As Hugh Pym argued 'during the crisis nobody else knew what was going on...your sources had to be people in the Treasury or the Bank of England or the banks, by definition that had to be in the City because it was all happening there'. Evan Davis argued that prior to the crisis the BBC had consciously tried to avoid relying on City sources but had to turn to them during the crisis despite an awareness that they came with a 'taint':

> At the time of the financial crisis, although they come with taint, they are more knowledgeable about the workings of the financial sector than most other people who commentated. So there was a relevance to them in the financial sector. I will actually tell you something – when Peter Jay was the Economics Editor, Peter more or less forbid us using City commentators and when I took over from Peter Jay as Economics Editor, I strived very hard not to use City commentators and that kind of all went out the window when the crisis came along, when actually you kind of needed... when finance became a much bigger part of the story, you needed people who were kind of more inside and informed on finance. (Evan Davis, BBC)

However, other journalists argued that the structural access granted to City sources wasn't just a function of their specialist knowledge it also reflected the fact that in the years leading up to the crisis they had made it much easier for the journalists to access their perspectives by installing cameras on their trading floors. These reinforced a reciprocal relationship where City institutions reduced the ease of BBC newsgathering—a form of information subsidy (Gandy 1982)—in exchange for publicity:

The bank people were installing cameras on their trading floors. They were thinking about what would make the best shot for the likes of the BBC. This was a reciprocal arrangement…It's clear what they were after…Credit Suisse First Boston, UBS you can see it the language is not disguised they've got a backing with UBS behind them, that's what they want. Bear in mind this is early to mid 2000s, we've just gone through the second great wave of globalisation and attempted democratisation of asset ownership. People want to day trade, or they want to own ISAs or whatever. These guys want to be able to retail it to them that's what they're thinking. (Aditya Chakrabortty, *Guardian* and BBC)

Chakrabortty also suggested that the move to feature more business news reflected the organisational belief that the BBC was 'too sniffy, too ignorant and too willing to omit business news'. He suggested that there was 'truth in that' citing the example of the AOL-Time Warner merger which wasn't sufficiently covered. However he argued that this had led to the 'Bloombergisation' of business news with too much time devoted to 'talking heads from the City talking about macroeconomics and often times political risk' which could lead to economics being reduced to little more than statistical indicators:

How can we have a unit [the BBC's business unit] which is simply taking City voices and treating economics as if it's all about statistical indicators and not think about the bigger picture, the economic processes which in the middle 2000s we were part of. So there were lots of big arguments about globalisation, about immigration about what the British consumer spending too much and borrowing too much but you would not have found those things on the news programmes. (Aditya Chakrabortty, *Guardian* and BBC)

Other elements of the consensus included the spectrum of dominant opinion within the main three parties at Westminster and the opinion of key financial elites such as the Governor of the Bank of England and major think tanks like the IMF and OECD. Evan Davis argued that the BBC tended to operate within a broadly 'mainstream' perspective which excluded 'oddball' views from a 'radical left' or 'radical green' perspective. This notion of the consensus shared by powerful sources also appeared to be an important reason why in the years prior to the crisis the BBC hadn't raised some of the arguments—most prominently voiced by Will

Hutton—that an overreliance on the City had created an unbalanced economy:

> Yes I think that [Will Hutton's perspective] is an important perspective and I think yes I can see we probably didn't give enough of a voice to those views before Northern Rock then the collapse of Lehmans. I'd go back to what I said last week there was a consensus, I don't mean anything sinister, a very, very broad consensus as I said right across Parliament, right across mainstream economic debate and of course including the City – I think very important right across Parliament which is there for views to be aired, that we had growth, we had low inflation, we had relatively low interest rates, you know low unemployment. We were into some kind of virtuous circle which seemed to be delivering for people and therefore to sort of say there were flaws in it and the banks were not doing the right things I would say was not a view very widely expressed at the time beyond people like Will who is you know a very respected economist in his own right so I don't think we were actually guilty of actually ignoring something I think we reflected a very, very wide view that things were sort of ticking along OK. (Hugh Pym, BBC)

This consensus, Evan Davis argued, meant that during this period economic issues that might have seemed important in the past—such as rising consumer debt or Britain's persistent balance of payments deficit—were now seen as potentially much less significant. However not all journalists accepted that BBC reporting worked within a particular consensus which excluded these kinds of broader critiques. Robert Peston, in particular, argued strongly that in the aftermath of the banking crisis the BBC had featured structural critiques of the City's role within the broader economy:

> Interviewer: That having such a very large banking sector is problematic in some senses. It raises exchange rates, it damages manufacturing. It tends to move investment towards kind of short termism rather than long term patient finance but we didn't find that perspective represented very much on the BBC and I wondered why...
>
> Robert Peston: We did... We did. We had all of that on. It absolutely fuelled our coverage for something like 18 months. We had all those voices saying all those things. I completely disagree with what you're saying here. I don't understand where you get this idea from. I don't even believe that Will would say that we didn't

cover those arguments. Will was on all the time. Lots of people
were on all the time saying precisely that.

It possible that these kinds of arguments were made outside the sample
period I examined—the fortnight around the bank bailouts and the first
seven months of 2009 when the Turner Report and Government White
Paper on Reform were published—but I did not find them reported on
the *Today programme* during this period. There were reports talking about
the damage the banking crisis had done to the economy and public
finances, calls to increase lending and arguments in favour of reducing the
size of *individual* banks or ring fencing their 'casino' operations. However,
the broader argument about the *aggregate size* of the City, its structural
relationship with the rest of the productive economy and the argument
that the British model produces 'the wrong kind of finance because the
circuits from finance produce asset price inflation not productive transfor-
mation' (Engelen et al. 2011: 190). These kinds of arguments weren't
featured.

Another one of my interviewees suggested that in general the BBC
struggled to cover these kinds of broader 'process problems' in economics
and needed to think harder about to report structural issues:

> What I would have done if I was the editor is say these are the people who
> called it [the banking crisis] right. Let me see the world through their eyes.
> Did they do that – no because the BBC never does stuff like that. What is
> does is 'you think one thing they think another thing let's get you on and
> we'll have a six minute debate and that's a debate and that'll be the issue
> tucked away. It's what I call the kind of cutesification of big issues. So we can
> have a really massive issue like 'what the fuck are we going to live on for the
> next 10 years' and it's like oh the UK's got a productivity problem and
> here's two economists they argue about it for five minutes – done. Here's
> Trump's tweets. It's rubbish. It's rubbish they need to think a lot harder
> about how to represent these harder process problems and economics is a
> process problem not a big news event story. (Aditya Chakrabortty, *Guardian*
> and BBC)

In relation to the question of the deficit and the introduction of austerity
policies as the analysis in Chap. 4 demonstrated, the BBC featured a number of very serious warnings about the dangers created by the deficit—particularly the threat of a bond strike—with the dominant solutions being to
cut public spending and/or increase regressive taxation. Hugh Pym sug-

gested that this kind of coverage reflected the kind of consensus that prevailed at the time amongst key elite sources, particularly in early 2010, which Labour failed to contest robustly:

> I think in the UK in the spring of 2010 there was a pretty wide view that if there was an unsettled period in British politics that could create a bond buyers' strike. And I think that might, might sort of entered our consciousness, maybe we could have challenged it but to be fair if the head of the civil service Gus O'Donnell is warning about it and the Lib Dems and the Tories and I don't think Labour were massively challenging it at the time actually you know it would have been different now you know Jeremy Corbyn and John McDonell have taken a much stronger line on the need to go out and borrow at low interest rates to invest. At the time under Gordon Brown and then Ed Miliband and that view the conventional view wasn't challenged so much by Labour. (Hugh Pym, BBC)

The strong focus on the deficit and the advocacy of austerity policies was not just a function of the prominence of party political and City voices but it also a product of the heavy presence of the IFS. The IFS was the key source for fiscal analysis but also a prominent voice on what the appropriate policy response should be. Our interviewees were clear that the IFS represented a very important and authoritative voice in the debate over the deficit. Hugh Pym commented that 'The IFS are always important because they are seen as resolutely independent and not beholden to any financial interests...I think they're seen as very robust, very robust indeed'. However although all my interviewees agreed that the IFS were independent and not beholden to a political party, one press journalist expressed the view that they did have a particular economic perspective that favoured 'balanced budgets'. The journalist argued that when 'the IFS starts to delve into macro issues, I don't think actually they should be taken at all seriously' because of their aversion to Keynesian policies:

> Sometimes I take what they [IFS] say with a pinch of salt because they do have a world view. They're not quite as...impartial. They do believe in tax [inaudible] and low tax and they have a world view... they believe that having a big budget deficit is a bad thing and you wouldn't find the IFS coming up with a Keynesian style argument... that you deal with the problem of low growth and high unemployment first and then that helps you deal with the deficit...that basic Keynesian principle...raise spending or cut taxes, you'll get the economy going and that's going to lead to high levels of revenue,

their world view would dispute that. They would say our model would show that... whereas I would say that actually we tried the alternative. We tried the IFS rigidly orthodox view of the world and it's been a complete disaster. (Press journalist)

As noted in Chap. 4, some macroeconomists argued that the media tended to overestimate the dangers of deficits and underestimate the risk posed by fiscal cuts when the economy was still very weak. Wren-Lewis (2015) argued that this was in part a consequence of an overreliance on City economists. This critique drew a mixed response from my interviewees. Hugh Pym commented that 'I think he's got a point that there might have been people of his type of view challenging some of these assumptions that we could have given a bit more space to. So I don't think there was anything systemic but for various reasons—not because we didn't want to hear their voices but we didn't quite give them the sort of voice that we could have done'. However others argued strongly that the size of the deficit meant that the BBC had a duty to emphasise its dangers. For instance, Robert Peston argued 'a 10% deficit is, by all peacetime standards, a very, very, very high deficit and it would have been utterly irresponsible of the BBC not to have mentioned that...I agree with you when you say that there's arguments to say it was cut too fast but the notion that we should not have captured on the BBC the idea that a 10% deficit is unsustainable is bonkers'. Evan Davis took an even firmer line in pushing back against the critique:

Evan Davis: I think the deficit was a very big problem in 2010. When you have a projected deficit of 11% of GDP, I think it's important that the public know that is unlike anything we have experienced outside wartime, that the national debt is going to double in the course of a Parliament at that kind of level of borrowing. I think it's absolutely relevant for the public to be told that the highest ever deficit post-war that we've had are this year, last year, next year and the year after, the five highest deficits all occurring within one five year period. We'd have been mad not to have alerted the public to the seriousness of the fiscal deterioration. Simon Wren-Lewis is not somebody who comes and looks at that issue with detachment. Simon Wren-Lewis comes with a very strong Keynesian view, which is I think incidentally perfectly sensible, that we shouldn't be worrying about deficits when the economy's flat on its back. Fine, that's a perfectly good argument and a perfectly logical place to be, but that's quite different to saying that we should just blithely come and just say don't worry about the deficit. That would have been beyond our remit. There were clearly people who were worried about the deficit. There clearly were people who weren't worried about the deficit.

Interviewer: Do you think you represented all of those opinions, because he thinks you focused far too much on...

Evan Davis: Yes, but he's on one side of the argument. I think it's very easy... I know very few Israelis who think we're biased in favour of Israel and I know almost no Palestinians who think we're biased in favour of Palestinians. By and large, people who hold a very strong and rigid position on an issue find it very difficult not to see that we're biased against them on anything, and Simon Wren-Lewis is in that...

However as the analysis in Chap. 2 demonstrated during the sample period in 2009 when the deficit became a major political issue there were no sources—outside of Labour—who were given space to put the Keynesian view in comparison to the range of sources who put the case for a faster pace of fiscal consolidation. Also it wasn't just macroeconomists who felt that the BBC coverage lacked balance. One of the press journalists I spoke to stated that they were 'outraged' by what they saw as 'reactionary' and 'pro austerity' BBC coverage. The Conservatives, he argued, 'must have loved it' and 'it was absolutely manna from heaven for George Osborne':

> So Stephanie Flanders I thought was... her coverage was really, really pro austerity in a way that I thought was....her coverage was just, this is what everybody thinks, this is the orthodoxy, there is no alternative to this, this is what it is and I thought it was outrageous because the BBC ...has a reputation for being impartial and should give both sides of the argument and you never ever heard the argument, just the basic Ed Balls argument at the time which was that cutting too soon and too far would actually lead to lower growth and a higher deficit which proved to be absolutely 100% right.

However this journalist thought the idea that BBC journalists had been captured by their sources from the City was wrong. Instead the journalist argued that the City sources were included because they backed up the 'orthodox' economic views of some BBC journalists:

I think Simon's [Wren-Lewis] wrong. If he thinks Stephanie [Flanders] had just been hobnobbing too much with City economists and that's why she thinks the way she does... I think that's just because that's what Stephanie thinks. Stephanie is a mainstream... she was just an orthodox economist. She did believe all that orthodox shit. She'd grown up in an environment where that's what she was taught...Deficits were bad. That's what people are taught in university these days. They're taught neoclassical economics. Big government bad, small government good. Budget deficits bad, budget surplus good. I think she was just a very mainstream thinker.

Some interviewees suggested that the flipside of a dominant orthodoxy was that economists who believed in concepts such as an interventionist state or the benefits of public ownership had been marginalised within the profession—and consequentially the media too. Aditya Chakrabortty argued that 'There isn't a thriving left economic base and to some extent within economics itself they exiled all the heterodox economists they've destroyed their career prospects'. This view was supported in discussions with economists such as Michael Hudson and Panicos Demetriades, the former Governor of Cyprus's Central Bank, both of whom argued that access to the most prestigious economics journals—and hence career advancement—was closed off to papers which challenged a dominant free-market perspective. Hudson commented that 'It's well known that Chicago-style libertarians have gained veto power over all alternative opinions submitted to refereed journals. They're smart enough to realize 'free market' economics requires totalitarian control of the academic media' (personal email, 22 April 2012). Although a survey (Chu 2015) conducted in 2015 found a majority of economists believed the turn to austerity had been a mistake, Chakrabortty argued that during the crucial period in 2009–2010 few economists publicly challenged the policy:

> The economics faculties were not exactly spilling over with people saying this is wrong. They were actually pretty quiet – I remember this. There were some people who were saying actually it's a good thing. Chris Pissarides who won the Nobel Prize at the LSE he was saying this is actually a pretty good thing. There were some who were pretty anti it. What happened three years later as it became clear it was falling apart they then got involved and said this thing's wrong. (Aditya Chakrabortty, *Guardian* and BBC)

The concept of balance is central to the BBC's organisational ethos though it is usually defined in relation to political opinion. However, I was interested in how this worked in relation to economic reporting. Is there a sense that journalists should be balancing left- and right-wing perspectives on the economy?

Evan Davis: I think it's more complicated in economics than in politics, as someone who's been mildly involved in both. What's the reason for that? The different factions are more diffuse and more difficult to define. So politics, you kind of have to stick with your... essentially there's a kind of left and right. Now, economics is a bit more complicated than that because there is quite a lot of left and rightism but in a lot of things, left and right are sharing the same assumptions. That growth is good. So it's not that the parties have come together, the politics has come together. There's a lot of shared assumptions. There are a lot of other factions.

Interviewer: What would you say are some of those shared assumptions?

Evan Davis: I think they're essentially assumptions about the working of a mixed economy, broadly speaking, the kind of way we want to structure our society. So they may differ. Let's take the broadest range within the mainstream of political thinking. You're talking about Government being maybe between 35% of national income and Government being 45% of national income but that's quite a big difference...

I then raised the issue of how this question of balance in economic reporting worked in relation to public ownership where in some areas public opinion tended to be quite strongly in favour of nationalisation:

Interviewer: So do you think that kind of argument about what should be in the private and what should be in the public is relatively settled now?

Evan Davis: I think it's less exciting than it used to be. We're not at the edge now, we've done most of it, there are the last few stragglers.

Interviewer: So there's a consensus roughly on that?

Evan Davis: No, I don't know if I'd say there's a consensus on the public. The public are overwhelmingly in favour of nationalisation I think.

Interviewer: But if they're in favour, shouldn't some of those views then be represented more in coverage?

Evan Davis: Potentially, yes. But equally they continually elect people who want to privatise these things. I think if the issue is a big one and if there's disagreement on it, then I think it should be debated, yes. If we didn't debate it, then I think that's a bit of an issue. It didn't feel to me like it [privatisation of the Post Office] was as controversial as I'd expected it to be because it really had been talked about for decades and never happened, chose not to do it and then up it pops and no one really says anything.

We are back again at the notion of the consensus set by Westminster politicians and key elite financial sources, and how difficult it is for opinions outside of that framework to be represented within broadcast news. The journalist commented that no one had really objected to the Royal Mail privatisation but the trade unions had run a long running campaign against it and much of the public were opposed. However, as we saw in Chaps. 2 and 4 the trade unions were almost completely excluded as commentators on the banking crisis or the debates around austerity. When I asked why this part of civil society was given so little space in broadcast news my interviewee struggled to provide an answer:

Evan Davis: Well, if I'm honest, I think it's that… it's a difficult one. I'm not sure. I think it's because they probably haven't had as much to say as the CBI. There's just a crucial mass in the CBI. I think it's also fair to say… it's kind of not clear who they're representing, the trade unions. They're not representing that big a proportion of the labour market. I can't remember the figure but what is the figure for private sector employment represented by unions? I think we're down to below 20%.

Interviewer: I don't know. Overall it's about six to seven million I think.

Evan Davis: That's lower than I thought overall.

Interviewer: It's obviously less than it was

Evan Davis: It's very heavily concentrated now in the public sector.

Interviewer: How does that affect the kind of…

Evan Davis: It's a very important group but in a way, I suppose it's a bit narrow. I'm thinking aloud, I'm trying to help you in why I don't think they would take much notice.

Interviewer: Is their research not seen as being up to scratch?

Evan Davis: No, I don't think so. I think maybe they're just not that big and so there's not much coming out of them. I don't want to exaggerate the weight we give to the CBI. I don't think the CBI get as much weight as they used to.

However another interviewee was able to point to a number of reasons why the unions had disappeared from broadcasting. These included the loss of manufacturing, the decline in industrial action and disappearance of labour beats and subsequently the 'slightly troublemaking' journalists who had close links to the union movement. The interviewee also suggested that the unions were partly to blame because they weren't proactive enough: 'I don't think the TUC pick up the phone to me very often. You know I write a lot about worker's rights, zero hours, I write a lot about the gig economy and I write a lot about precariousness. They don't pick up the phone' (Aditya Chakrabortty, *Guardian* and BBC). He contrasted this with the activities of think tanks like the New Economics Foundation, citing the example of their report on 'ghost towns' which 'got a lot of pick up across the BBC'. The weaknesses of the unions the interviewee argued was symptomatic of the weakness of civil society more generally in terms of constructing alternatives in relation to 'banks, finance, upstream economics'. He noted that the much of the financialisation literature available at the time of the GFC had come out of America rather than Britain and that people who were arguing for left alternatives to the economic system were 'lone wolves' who didn't have the 'strength in numbers' to make them part of the 'conversation':

> From the point of view of the BBC thinking what is the conversation, there's not like loads and loads of people pumping out stuff about the banking sector and what's wrong with it. And afterwards there's not a concerted effort by left civil society groups to think about what's wrong with finance…There wasn't a cluster of people who were putting out stuff at that time. Will [Hutton] was pretty much out on his own, the *Guardian* was pretty much the only place that was running these sort of critiques at length. (Aditya Chakrabortty, *Guardian* and BBC)

The BBC's Organisation Structure, Location and Recruitment Policies

One of my interviewees also spoke at length about a range of other factors that influenced the production of economic news. One was the internal layout of the newsroom at Television Centre where the business programmes unit was based until 2013. This created a situation where City voices who had originally been interviewed for business slots found their way onto the main mass bulletins to discuss macroeconomics:

We worked all in one giant room and that's meant to be the business expertise unit. So there were guys who do the *Today programme*, business [inau-
dible] and guys who do the breakfast and there's [inaudible] Evan Davis or
whatever and there's the internet people behind us. What you noticed especially in the business programme in the bit where I began was there was a
straightforward equation you're doing something on finance you want to go
to the City, you're going to do the latest economic indicator you're going
to go straight down the line from Credit Suisse First Boston and those banks
will have downline cameras for them and all the rest of it. That sounds
innocuous enough but when it then comes to the point of view of what goes
on in the day to day hurly burly of trying to get a two minutes on air for one
o'clock or six o'clock often times people are directly using those same guests
from the business programmes unit in the main outputs. Why the business
programmes unit so straightforwardly sees the equivalence between what
the banking sector says and what's going on in the economy, I think is a
really good question. I think by the time it gets to the main outputs it's a
much less contested question. So almost by logistical process some guy
whose already been recorded talking down the line fairly fluently about what
GDP for first quarter 2014 means it's very easy to use him again for the one
o'clock or six o'clock news. The onus is on the 10 o'clock news to do something different and normally they will do. (Aditya Chakrabortty, *Guardian*
and BBC)

As well as the geography of the newsroom it was also suggested that the
location of BBC News—which at the time of the GFC was located in
Shephard's Bush—was also important. Chakrabortty spoke of how 'her-
metically sealed the BBC was…at the end of the Westway miles from the
centre of London and even further away from Canary Wharf'. This, it was
argued, meant that contact building wasn't great—to have lunch with
contact was seen as 'exotic'—which amplified the reliance on 'downline'
City voices.

Another issue that Chakrabortty raised was how the metropolitan location of the BBC and the class and ethnic backgrounds of its staff produced
a journalism that favoured the 'smart over the real' and which subsequently wasn't attuned to issues of inequality and regional polarisation.
The journalist spoke of how difficult it had been to raise inequality and the
possibility of Brexit with 'liberals' because 'mankind cannot bear too much
reality' and that 'if you write the kind of stuff I do or if you were to do that
for the BBC you'd be seen as bleak. Ooh you're very bleak. You're… writing social commentary rather than economics commentary'. Part of this,

he suggested, was down to the 'narrow social classes from where people are drawn. It's still overwhelmingly white. It's still overwhelmingly middle class blah-blah-blah. Part of it is also as you say if you're stuck all the time in London where all the power and money is concentrated that's what you're going to get back'. All of these factors, he suggested, coalesced to produce an economics journalism which struggled to capture the lived economy:

> I think there's a problem in economics reporting more generally—not just at the BBC—which is there's not enough sense of what the lived economy's like and much more sense of what the headline statistics are. But the difference between the two is what's at the heart of what's wrong with economics now...so when I write my report [about regional perspectives on the economy] that's seen as not being economics. that's seen as being social... There's a certain kind of journalism which I don't like but which is kind of journalism which privileges the smart over the real and the smart is someone turning up on *Newsnight* and giving you an eight minute clever thing with clever people talking about these numbers and giving you different interpretations of the numbers whereas the real thing to do is to go off and say actually you've heard about these numbers but [inaudible] what matters is these people are being treated, the cleaner in our studio is working for a different agency – why is that and what [inaudible] that's part of what's gone wrong in the labour market. It doesn't come up. (Aditya Chakrabortty, *Guardian* and BBC)

CONCLUSION

This review of the production of GFC journalism demonstrates that a wide variety of factors structured the process of news gathering. These included issues that have consistently been identified in the literature on the sociology of news production such as the ideological preference for free markets and small government traditionally favoured by many newspaper owners (Davies 2008; McKnight 2012; Curran and Seaton 1997); elite sourcing (Galtung and Ruge 1965; Sigal 1973; Tuchman 1978; Gans 1979; Clausen 2004; Lee et al. 2005; Wahl-Jorgensen et al. 2013; Berry 2013, 2015, 2016) and public relations, information subsidies and source strategies (Gandy 1982; Schlesinger 1990; Davis 2000; Philo and Berry 2004, 2011). However, as the interviews here show, there are major differences in how the matrix of factors work in broadcast and press journalism—and even within different newspaper titles. The analysis also demonstrates that although there are a number of general processes at work grounded in political economy and the routines of news production, there are also other factors that are much more organisation, subject and time specific. These include shifting patterns of personal and political allegiances, the geographical locations of news organisations and the constraints imposed by having to report unfamiliar or fast moving stories. Ultimately as Sparks (2008) notes, grand totalising theories of news production (e.g. Miliband 1969; Herman and Chomsky 1995) take you only you so far in explaining the content of media. A more comprehensive understanding of how news is produced needs a much more granular analysis that recognises the myriad and shifting complexities grounded in news production at specific times and places.

NOTE

1. Journalists who were contacted via Twitter or email who didn't respond to requests for interviews were Edmund Conway (*Telegraph*), Philip Aldrick (*Telegraph*), Bendict Brogan (*Daily Mail*), Sam Fleming (*Daily Mail*), Steve Hawkes (*Sun*), Clinton Manning (*Mirror*), Peter Cunliffe (*Express*), Stephanie Flanders (*BBC*). Paul Mason (*BBC*) initially agreed to an interview but was later unobtainable.

REFERENCES

Berry, M. (2013). The Today Programme and the Banking Crisis. *Journalism, 14*(2), 253–270.

Berry, M. (2015). The UK Press and the Deficit Debate. *Sociology, 50*(3), 542–559.

Berry, M. (2016). No Alternative to Austerity: How BBC Broadcast News Reported the Deficit Debate. *Media, Culture and Society, 38*(6), 844–863.

Chu, B. (2015, 1 April). Two Thirds of Economists Say Coalition Austerity Harmed the Economy. *Independent.* Available at: http://www.independent.co.uk/news/business/news/two-thirds-of-economists-say-coalition-austerity-harmed-the-economy-10149410.html. Accessed 9 July 2018.

Clausen, L. (2004). Localizing the Global. *Media Culture and Society, 26*(1), 25–44.

Curran, J., & Seaton, J. (1997). *Power Without Responsibility.* London: Routledge.

Davies, N. (2008). *Flat Earth News.* London: Random House.

Davis, A. (2000). Public Relations, Business News and the Reproduction of Corporate Elite Power. *Journalism, 1*(3), 282–304.

Dean, M. (2013). *Democracy Under Attack: How the Media Distort Policy and Politics*. London: Policy Press.

Engelen, E., Eturk, I., Froud, J., Johal, S., Leaver, A., Moran, M., Nilsson, A., & Williams, K. (2011). *After the Great Complacence*. Oxford: Oxford University Press.

Fahy, D., O'Brien, M., & Poti, V. (2010). From Boom to Bust: A Post-Celtic Tiger Analysis of the Norms, Values and Roles of Irish Financial Journalists. *Irish Communications Review, 12*, 5–20.

Galtung, J., & Ruge, M. H. (1965). The Structure of Foreign News. *Journal of Peace Research, 1*, 64–91.

Gandy, O. H. (1982). *Beyond Agenda Setting: Information Subsidies and Public Policy*. New York: Ablex Publishing.

Gans, H. (1979). *Deciding What's News: A Study of CBS Evening News, NBC Nightly News, Newsweek, and Time*. New York: Pantheon.

Glasgow Media Group. (1985). *War and Peace News*. Oxford: Oxford University Press.

Guardian Datablog. (2010). *Newspaper Support in UK General Elections*. Available at: https://www.theguardian.com/news/datablog/2010/may/04/general-election-newspaper-support. Accessed 13 July 2018.

Hallin, D. (1986). *The Uncensored War: The Media and Vietnam*. New York: Oxford University Press.

Harcup, T., & O'Neill, D. (2001). What Is News? Galtung and Ruge Revisited. *Journalism Studies, 2*(2), 261–280.

Herman, E., & Chomsky, N. (1995). *Manufacturing Consent: The Political Economy of the Mass Media*. London: Vintage.

Ipsos-Mori. (2016). *Perceptions Are Not Reality*. Available at: https://www.ipsos.com/ipsos-mori/en-uk/perceptions-are-not-reality. Accessed 9 July 2018.

King, A. (2015). *Who Governs Britain?* London: Pelican.

Lee, C., Chan, J., Zhongdang, P., & So, C. (2005). National Prisms of a Global 'Media Event'. In J. Curran & M. Gurevitch (Eds.), *Mass Media and Society* (pp. 320–335). London: Hodder Arnold.

Manning, P. (2001). *News and News Sources: A Critical Introduction*. London: Sage.

McKnight, D. (2012). *Rupert Murdoch: An Investigation of Political Power*. Sydney: Allen & Unwin.

Miliband, R. (1969). *The State in Capitalist Society*. London: Weidenfeld and Nicolson.

Oborne, P. (2015). *Why I Have Resigned from the Telegraph*. Available at: https://www.opendemocracy.net/ourkingdom/peter-oborne/why-i-have-resigned-from-telegraph. Accessed 9 July 2018.

Philo, G., & Berry, M. (2004). *Bad News from Israel*. London: Pluto.

Philo, G., & Berry, M. (2011). *More Bad News from Israel*. London: Pluto.

Schlesinger, P. (1990). Rethinking the Sociology of Journalism: Source Strategies and the Limits of Media-Centrism. In M. Ferguson (Ed.), *Public Communication the New Imperative* (pp. 61–83). London: Sage.

Sigal, L. V. (1973). *Reporters and Officials.* Lexington: D.C. Heath.

Sparks, C. (2008). Extending and Refining the Propaganda Model. *Westminster Papers in Communication and Culture, 4*(2), 68–84.

Stanley, L. (2014). We're Reaping What We Sowed': Everyday Crisis Narratives and Acquiescence to the Age of Austerity. *New Political Economy, 19*(6), 895–917.

Tuchman, G. (1978). *Making News: A Study in the Construction of Reality.* New York: The Free Press.

Wahl-Jorgensen, K., Sambrook, R., Berry, M., Moore, K., Bennett, L., Cable, J., Garcia-Blanco, I., Kidd, J., Dencik, L., & Hintz, A. (2013). *BBC Breadth of Opinion Review: Content Analysis.* Available at: http://downloads.bbc.co.uk/bbctrust/assets/files/pdf/our_work/breadth_opinion/content_analysis.pdf. Accessed 10 July 2018.

Wren-Lewis, S. (2015). The Austerity Con. *London Review of Books, 37*(4), 9–11.

CHAPTER 8

Conclusions

Introduction

This concluding chapter pulls together the results from research on all three elements of the circuit of communication (production-content-reception) highlighting how my research reveals the media's role in representing the process of bank reform and the policy shift to austerity in public discourse. I then reflect on the implications of the research findings for debates in three areas: (1) media influence, (2) the priorities of public service broadcasting and (3) the strategic communication policy of the Labour party.

Putting It All Together: The Production, Content and Reception of GFC News

The Banking Crisis: Toothless Media Meets Protégé Industry

The banking crisis was arguably the most important economic crisis in the post-Second World War era. It revealed with alarming clarity major weaknesses in the British economy, including an overreliance on finance to the detriment of other sectors of the economy, household and corporate leverage as unstable core motors of economic growth and a country chronically unable to pay its way in the world. This could have been a point where questions were asked about the British economic model and new pathways explored. As one of my interviewees put it 'this is a moment

© The Author(s) 2019

M. Berry, *The Media, the Public and the Great Financial Crisis,*
https://doi.org/10.1007/978-1-137-49973-8_8

which the hood is up you can see the workings we can't go on pretending. This is our moment' (Aditya Chakrabortty, BBC Producer). Yet within a few months the finance sector began to return to business as usual and the possibilities for major systemic reforms receded. What role did the media play in this process, and what does this say about its ideological and political power?

The analysis of press reporting in Chap. 2 showed that coverage—particularly in the mass circulation tabloids—primarily concentrated on telling a morality tale focused on greed and bankers' bonuses. In the right of centre newspapers—and to a lesser degree the *Guardian*—this was coupled with heavy criticism of Gordon Brown and the regulatory system he created. The broadsheets told a more developed story which highlighted the culpability of a range of different actors and institutions. The quality press also explored a wider range of potential reforms and—unlike the tabloids—continued to report in some detail the reform process as it developed in 2009. In terms of how the bank bailouts themselves were reported there was unanimity across the press that the bank bailouts represented the only possible solution to the crisis. Whilst there were regular complaints in the right of centre press about the costs of the bailouts, the damage they would do to shareholders and the general undesirability of the state getting involved in running banks, there was a consensus that there was no alternative. Arguments in favour of public banking appeared as tiny scattered fragments whilst the case against public banking was made in a series of editorials and comment pieces in the right-wing press. This part of the press also tended to present 'worst case scenario' estimates of the costs of the banking crisis which were then linked to long-standing criticisms of the public sector and arguments for cutting public spending.

Reporting on the *Today programme* shared many similarities to press accounts but there were some significant differences. Criticism of the finance sector in October 2008 was much more subdued than it was in any newspaper, with bankers not subject to the kind of censure that was common in the press. In terms of causes, the *Today programme* featured a range of explanations that were similar to those that appeared in the broadsheets whilst on the question of the bailouts, sources on the *Today programme* shared the consensus that united the press—that the government rescue plans were the only viable solution. Almost all the sources on the *Today programme* gave a positive assessment of the bailouts with criticisms being less pronounced than those seen in the press. In October 2008, arguments in favour of alternatives such as temporary or permanent full nationalisation were completely absent from the *Today programme*. Every time these options were mentioned they were dismissed by an interviewee (reflecting the particular ideological range of interviewees invited onto the *Today programme*). Discussion of long-term reforms in the first sample (October 2008) were sparse with the great bulk of coverage given over to the three solutions being pushed by leading politicians—restrictions on bonuses/dividends in the part-nationalised banks, the need for a new 'global financial architecture' and vague calls for more regulation. In 2009 debate widened to include some calls for temporary full nationalisation of some banks. This period also saw structural reforms come more to the fore particularly from the most heavily featured political source, Vince Cable.

It is also worth highlighting one further finding that stretched across press and broadcasting. This was that almost no accounts—outside of a few articles in the *Guardian*—stepped back to discuss the larger structural issues—notably the broader role of the finance sector in Britain's unbalanced economic model. The consequences of not addressing these problems were later highlighted by Ashoka Mody, the IMF's former deputy-director for Europe:

> Professor Mody, who led the EU-IMF Troika rescue for Ireland, said the pound had been driven up to nose-bleed levels from 2011 to 2015 by global property speculators and the banking elites acting in destructive synergy, causing serious damage to Britain's manufacturing base and long-term competitiveness. The role of the City as the unrivalled financial centre of Europe made it a magnet for speculative property flows from Russia, China, the Mid-East, and the wider world, a bubble that was further leveraged by cheap dollar credit though global banks operating in London. "It was essentially a bank-property nexus, and the rest of the economy was left to suffer. It is stunning that just 1.4pc of all loans were going to the manufacturing sector," he said. The country was suffering a variant of the "Dutch Disease", although in this case the problem was over-reliance on finance rather than commodities. "Britain was borrowing 5pc to 6pc of GDP a year to buy imports and live beyond its means. The strong pound was great if you wanted to buy a Mercedes Benz or take a holiday in Spain, but the prosperity was an illusion, borrowed from the future," he said. (Evans-Pritchard 2016)

The interviews with journalists reported in Chap. 7 provide some explanations as to why the banking crisis was covered in this way. Some factors such as the speed and unprecedented nature of the crisis or the difficulties in explaining complex and unfamiliar financial products created challenges for both press and broadcasting. Other issues were specific to particular news organisations. The heavy focus across the tab-loid press on bankers' bonuses and the lack of interest in the nitty gritty of reform in 2009 reflected specific news values and beliefs about what would appeal to particular audiences. They also reflected—as a former *Mail* jour-nalist explained—a desire to generate public outrage because this is seen as an effective way to win brand loyalty. Across the press, ideology was also important. For right-wing newspapers support for the free market and small government drove their attacks on the bankers and their intense antipathy to public ownership. Other key issues included political parti-sanship, personal relationship between proprietors, editors and politicians, and a reliance on advertising from the finance sector.

At the BBC, a central issue was the notion of the consensus shared by a group of key political and financial elites. In the period leading up to the crisis this consensus had been that the model of light touch regulation was all that was necessary and the increased financialisation of the British econ-omy was a benign development. During the crisis, the consensus was that public ownership was a bad thing but unavoidable in the circumstances and that the banks should be returned to the private sector as soon as feasible—a view also endorsed by some journalists who editorialised about their preference for private over public banking. Two source groups were key in building this consensus. One was representatives from the City, such as bankers, hedge fund managers, private equity partners and ana-lysts. Because of their specialist knowledge and insider status they were the dominant sources used for explaining the crisis, evaluating the bailouts and discussing plans for reform. Although the research showed that cover-age in 2009 did have a more critical edge, representatives from the finance sector were still heavily featured—especially in prestigious interview slots. The second important group were senior Labour politicians. Traditionally this would have been the group that would have contested the dominance of finance and argued for social democratic alternatives, but having embraced financialisation, they were incapable of offering a coherent alter-native. This lack of alternative perspectives on the role of finance within the broader economy also reflected the weakness and fragmentation of left-leaning civil society voices in the trade unions, academia and think tanks. Although it was possible to point to a range of individuals or groups, they didn't operate as a critical mass and so were not seen as part of the 'conversation' by BBC journalists.

The consequence of the patterns of news reporting could be seen in the responses of audience groups in Chap. 3. The explanations in press and broadcast news accounts were frequently reproduced within focus group discussions, especially when—as with the perception that the banking crisis was a consequence of the overextension of credit—these chimed with participants' experiences. Nowhere was this clearer than on the issue of the bank bailouts, where despite many people expressing unhappiness about the rescue plans, almost all participants agreed that there was 'no alternative'. In fact, some participants were surprised to hear that the option of full nationalisation existed and felt that *public service broadcasting, in particular, had a responsibility to discuss all the options that were available*— even if they didn't form part of the policy offerings of the two main parties at Westminster. The narrowing of the public's awareness of arguments in favour of an interventionist state reflects the disappearance of social democratic voices from the press and broadcasting. At a broader level it is part of the atrophy of organisations and political cultures which previously offered alternative perspectives on how the economy could be managed. At the same time, as Davis (2017: 600) notes, a 'professional econocracy' has come into existence comprised of elites who dominate a wide variety of sectors including business, politics and the civil service, whose ideology represents a 'post-Keynesian neoclassical economic consensus'. Finally, the lack of discussion of long-term reforms across most of the press and broadcasting was also reflected in the low levels of public awareness about what could be done to reform finance so that the sector was more focused on investment to the productive economy. Instead public anger was channelled into relatively peripheral issues—such as bonuses—whilst leaving the structural dominance of finance unexamined and unaddressed.

In considering the role of the mass media during the banking crisis it is first important to recognise the limits of media power. The media can raise awareness of issues, it can embarrass and even destroy politicians. The media can also be used to build support for particular policies. However, it is very difficult for the media to force politicians to enact policies when there is a strong political consensus opposed to those policies. In the case of the banking crisis, there existed both a media where arguments in favour of structural change were not prominent and a political consensus across the main two parties that the British finance sector needed to be shielded from systemic reform. The City was effectively seen as a 'protected' or 'protégé' industry, as one academic expert on finance put it to me, drawing an analogy with the treatment of the German car manufactures in Europe in the wake of the diesel emissions scandal where—unlike in America—not a single executive has as yet been prosecuted (Karel

Williams, Skype Interview). Ultimately, this meant that the bankers could lie low during the crisis aware that they could later influence the process of reform, as the media spotlight moved on to other issues.

The Deficit Debate: Singing from the Same Hymn Sheet

Despite the fact that one led to the other, the deficit 'crisis' represented a very different kind of media event to the collapse of the banks. Whereas the bankers may have felt uncomfortable with the censure and abuse they received in the media—and sent their representatives and lobbyists out onto the *Today programme* to argue for the social and economic benefits of the sector—they were aware that, protected by the political class, they didn't have to win a media struggle for public legitimacy. In stark contrast, the Conservatives and Labour would have been only too aware of the challenge facing them in their attempt to introduce austerity policies. Shortly before the 2010 General Election, Mervyn King was reported to have commented that whoever won the election would be forced to enact austerity measures so severe that they would be out of power for a generation (Elliott 2010). Whereas the process of bank reform would be invisible to almost the entire population, the cuts that both parties were planning would be highly visible and painful—and so would need a great deal of ideological work to justify.

Reporting in much of the media helped in this regard. The right of centre press told a dramatic story of a country facing bond strikes, interest rate rises, a falling currency, visits from the IMF and even national bankruptcy. Readers were provided with incorrect information on the UK's public finances as well as misleading international and historical comparisons. Such narratives were then linked to arguments in favour of accelerated deficit reduction and strong advocacy of severe cuts to public spending. Central to the case for cuts were attacks on migrants and welfare recipients, who were routinely represented as symptomatic of an over generous 'soft touch' welfare state. The right of centre press also attacked what it described as the 'bloated' and 'parasitic' public sector and attempted to drive a wedge between private and public employees by arguing that state sector workers were 'featherbedded' and provided with 'lavish pensions'. As the analysis in Chap. 6 demonstrated, these narratives did not suddenly appear in 2009. Instead their resonance and power derived from the fact that they had been used in thousands of newspaper articles in the years leading up to 2009.

The left of centre press did not engage in the kind of scaremongering that was common in parts of the press. However, the *Guardian* did feature many of the warnings common in the rest of the media, partly as a consequence of the media visibility of pro-austerity elite agenda setters like Conservative politicians and Mervyn King, but also because they were endorsed by some of their own journalists. Nonetheless, it also featured counter-arguments at a higher level than other newspapers. It was the only newspaper to occasionally broaden the debate by suggesting alternatives such as pro-growth policies or taxation directed at the wealthy or those on high incomes. The two Labour supporting tabloids in general took the view that cuts were inevitable—at some point—but only Labour could be trusted to make them in a humane and fair manner.

Reporting on the BBC's News at Ten on the whole provided accurate explanations as to the origins of the deficit and its scale. In this sense, it didn't engage in the kinds of alarmism common in parts of the press. However, it did prominently feature warnings about the consequences of a rise in the deficit such as interest rate rises or a potential bond strike. These warnings were endorsed by journalists while economists who contested these views were not featured in coverage. When it came to how to respond to the rise in the deficit the BBC concentrated almost entirely on cuts to public spending or regressive tax increases. Alternatives such as pro-growth policies or levying wealth, property or transactions taxes were invisible as public policy options. Furthermore, the potential negative aspects of an accelerated pace of deficit reduction were not explored by journalists.

It is clear that ideology was a key driver in explaining how newspapers reported the rise in the deficit. For the right of centre press this involved a belief in 'sound finances', 'fiscal discipline' and an aversion to the growth of the public sector to a level comparable to European neighbours such as France and Germany. At the *Mail,* this policy option offered the opportunity to argue for cutting parts of the 'nanny state' such as childcare provision or public health campaigns that clashed with its social conservatism. For the left of centre newspapers coverage was also shaped by ideological beliefs but in this case these were more likely to be based around social democratic ideas. At the *Guardian* in particular it was clear that the Keynesian views of its economics editor and some of the newspapers' leading commentators were crucial in setting the tone of much of its coverage. Despite this, the newspaper's reporting also featured advocacy of austerity reflecting—like other titles—struggles within the Labour party.

For the BBC coverage reflected the consensus set by powerful institutional sources. In 2009, these argued that the deficit represented a major threat and needed to be addressed quickly—primarily through cuts to public spending. These included the Conservative and Liberal Democrat parties, the Bank of England, City sources, the Treasury, the IMF and the OECD. This consensus also included the most heavily featured and prestigious non-political source—the IFS. Finally, it worth noting the weaknesses of sources who might have contested the turn to austerity. The Labour party was initially split on the issue before accepting the need to enact austerity policies. Despite the fact that a majority of economists later saw austerity as a mistake, most of the economics profession did not protest strongly against the policy at the time—and some of its leading lights publicly backed it (Chu 2015). Furthermore, there wasn't an organised left-wing civil society grouping ready with a thought through economic alternative in the way the pressure groups and think tanks of the New Right had been ready for the breakdown of the social contract at the end of the 1970s.

The findings from the audience groups in Chap. 5 demonstrated that the media had a significant impact on the public acceptance of austerity, through both short- and long-term patterns of influence. In the short-term press and broadcasting helped establish the belief that the deficit represented a major economic threat which had to be addressed urgently. The press and broadcast news were also crucial in establishing the belief that addressing the deficit would inevitably mean cuts to public services—even if the legitimacy of some of those cuts was resisted by some participants in our audience groups. By contrast, alternative measures which were invisible in the media—such as pro-growth policies or taxation focused on the better off—were rarely raised by audience groups, even though they were greeted with a generally positive—if slightly sceptical—response when mentioned by a moderator.

In terms of long-term impacts the press was important in establishing key strands of audience belief that helped justify the implementation of austerity policies. These included the view that much of New Labour's extra public investment had been wasted on a 'bloated', 'inefficient' public sector riddled with managers, 'non-jobs' and public servants living off 'gold-plated' pensions. This influenced the belief—reinforced by Labour's own messaging—that cuts could be made without impacting frontline services or would fall on groups who were being unfairly privileged with taxpayers' support. The second way that long-term patterns of media socialisation operated was by portraying groups such as welfare claimants and immigrants as a strain on state resources, despite evidence suggesting that immigration was a net benefit to the UK economy. This provided both a rationale for cuts to public spending and an opportunity for Conservative politicians to boost their popularity by attacking stigmatised groups (Stanley 2016). In this way politicians were able to harness the ideological power of press accounts—identified through qualitative polling—for political gain. Commenting on his time as a part of the 2010–2015 Coalition government, the former Liberal Democrat leader Nick Clegg remarked that 'welfare for [George] Osborne was just a bottomless pit of savings, and it didn't really matter what the human consequences were, because focus groups had shown that the voters they wanted to appeal to were very anti-welfare, and therefore there was almost no limit to those anti-welfare prejudices' (cited in Asthana and Hattenstone 2016). This is of course, not to say that the media were the only factor in the rise of anti-welfare, anti-state and anti-immigrant sentiment but they were an important contributor.

IMPLICATIONS FOR DEBATES ON MEDIA, THE BBC AND LABOUR PARTY

Media Influence: Then and Now

As this book has demonstrated, print and broadcast media were key factors in the development of public understanding and attitudes towards the GFC. The media influenced who was held responsible and it shaped the range of options—that people were aware of—for addressing the banking crisis and the deficit. It also influenced viewer attitudes towards issues such as the legitimacy of different aspects of public spending and whether certain social groups were seen as deserving or undeserving. Some of these effects were likely to have been particularly powerful because often viewers were encountering consonant messages—for instance on the dangers of the deficit or the view that part-nationalisation of the banks had been the 'only option'—coming from both the press and broadcasting.

What the research also shows is that the press were more significant than television news in influencing public knowledge and attitudes towards the GFC. This goes against a common strand of public commentary which sees broadcasting as having a greater impact than newspapers (e.g. Daley 2013). Commentators point to the higher penetration of the BBC and the fact that polls consistently find it is considerably more trusted than the press—and especially the red-tops (e.g. Greenslade 2014; Cox 2016). However, just because someone says they don't trust a newspaper doesn't mean they are not influenced by its content if they are a regular reader. In fact, the idea that readers regularly consume a newspaper whose content they automatically discount as false—and that what they consume has no effect at all—is implausible. As the results reported in Chap. 5 demonstrated, in explaining the source of their beliefs focus group participants often pointed to the content of articles from newspapers which regularly feature at the bottom of trust indexes. Furthermore, polling shows that on a range of issues people regularly overestimate the prevalence and cost of issues that have a sustained negative presence in the right-wing press (Ipsos-Mori 2016). In a sense this shouldn't be surprising. Newspapers are not bound by impartiality regulations so are free to take positions with no restraint except the pressure of market forces. They can develop arguments over many years in thousands of news articles, comment pieces, editorials and cartoon strips. They employ highly skilled professionals who are proficient in techniques such as 'card stacking', 'fear appeals', 'ad hominem attacks' and 'demonisation' that are not available to television journalists (Jowett and O'Donnell 2011).

What the results of this study therefore show is that the dominant strand of thinking in political science which is sceptical of media influence or primarily concerned with the media's potential role in reinforcement or (usually short term) attitudinal change misunderstands how media power and influence operates. It is through the daily repetition of themes and arguments over many years that climates of opinion and ways of seeing are shaped, which favour certain interests. As Greenslade (2016) noted it is through this long term 'drip, drip, drip' process that 'newspapers have an impact on readers who never think about, let alone question, the propaganda they consume'.

If another financial crisis happened today would the press and broadcasting still be the key information sources influencing public knowledge and understanding? Newspaper print circulation is certainly in a period of sustained long-term decline. Since the 2008 banking crisis the print circulation of all the newspapers analysed in this book has roughly halved (Press Gazette 2008; Mayhew 2018). This picture of traditional media rapidly losing its power and influence appeared to be reinforced by research from the Reuters Institute for the Study of Journalism which found that in 2016 the internet finally overtook television to become the single most popular news source (Newman et al. 2017). The report also noted that social media was an increasingly important news source especially for young people.

However, television is still a weekly source of news for about 70 per cent of the population though its audiences are shrinking—particularly for younger viewers (Nielsen and Sambrook 2016). Furthermore, the shift to online news sources has not overturned the dominance of print and broadcast media since it is traditional news organisations such as the *BBC*, *Mail*, *Guardian* and *Sky News* which tend to top the list of most popular online news sites—with the *BBC* in particular having a commanding lead over the rest of the field (Newman et al. 2017). The decline in newspaper print circulation also masks the wide reach of their online editions. In 2017, daily multi-platform readership for the *Sun* was 7.3 million, for the *Mail* 7.26 million, and for the *Mirror* 4.14 million (PAMCo 2018). Multi-platform readership for the two broadsheets analysed in this book was also substantial—for the *Guardian* it was 4.58 million and for the *Telegraph* 3.54 million (PAMCo 2018). For the short to medium term at least, the threat to press organisations is not a decline in aggregate readership but the erosion of their business model as (a) digital advertising cannot compensate for the loss of revenue from declining print editions and (b) advertising is increasingly shifting to search engines and social media providers (Edwards 2017; Greenslade 2017). As for the popularity of social media as a news source, more often than not the news that people are sharing and reading on comes from traditional news organisations (Newman 2011; Mayhew 2017). For instance, in July 2017 the Mailonline was the 'most engaged website' on Facebook with 'over 26 million interactions' (Newsmedia Association 2017).

As Chadwick (2017) has persuasively written, over the last decade a 'hybrid' media system has developed where new and old media interact and interpenetrate in a variety of complex ways. This has destabilised and transformed news production and dissemination and revolutionised traditional notions of the 'news cycle'. It has also transformed the consumption of news as audiences increasingly access their news from platforms such as Youtube, Facebook, Twitter, Google, Yahoo as well as mobile phone apps. However, what it hasn't done is radically change the profile of the organisations that produce the most widely consumed news. There are very good reasons for this: traditional news organisations can command trust and brand loyalty—which is particularly important in an area where—as this book has demonstrated—public understanding is very limited. This means it is likely that economic news produced by the press and broadcast media will remain the most important factor influencing public knowledge and attitudes for the foreseeable future.

Public Service Broadcasting: Comprehension, Impartiality and Representation

As the audience research in this book, as well as polling and other research, has demonstrated much of the GFC was poorly understood by audiences. Furthermore, it wasn't just the details of esoteric financial products such as credit default swaps or collateralised debt obligations—that confused audiences, it was also the far more mundane issues like the difference between debt and deficits or how recessions impact the public finances. Journalists at the BBC worked hard to try and make the complexities of the crisis intelligible, which was a challenging task since news audiences were composed of people with different degrees of economic knowledge and understanding. Although a number of interviewees stated that the BBC have carried out qualitative audience research in the past this is an area where more systematic work could be conducted. Key to these efforts could be examining how to explain macroeconomics in a way that is easily grasped. How, for instance, might the 'fiscal multiplier' be explained in a way that most people could understand? Another issue that could be examined is how journalism might dispel some of the myths that surround the working of the economy. As the research in this book as well as other studies have demonstrated there is widespread public acceptance of a series of economic fallacies—often spread by politicians—such as idea the 'government can't spend money it doesn't have' or 'government spending is analogous to household expenditure' (Skidelsky 2013). Journalists cannot stop politicians spreading these falsehoods but they can point out that this is not how economies function. Another area where research might help is fiscal spending. At the moment the composition of state expenditure is a 'black hole' of public understanding which warps public discourse and hinders a rational debate on spending priorities.

A second issue to emerge from this research concerns the impartiality of BBC economic reporting. The BBC is committed to 'due impartiality' as one of the cornerstones of its journalism. Just prior to the GFC the BBC Trust (2007) produced a new policy document titled 'From Seesaw to

Wagon Wheel: Safeguarding Impartiality in the 21st Century'. Written by John Bridcut, the report attempted to rethink impartiality in the digital age. It's core conclusion was that impartiality needed to go beyond a simple left-right binary to take in a 'wagon wheel' of diverse perspectives more appropriate to the changing social, technological and political environment. However, these aims are difficult to reconcile with the patterns in reporting found in this book. Rather than a diverse wagon wheel of views, reporting of the GFC was centred on a narrow consensus set by front bench Westminster politicians, the City, the Treasury, the Bank of England, IFS and IMF. Excluded from coverage was a spectrum of mainstream Keynesian and left of centre economic opinion, which meant that the BBC featured almost no arguments in favour of public ownership, an interventionist state or the benefits of deficit spending. It was also the case that the City's structural relationship to the rest of the economy tended to be presented in a mostly positive light. But there is a long-standing alternative perspective that was highlighted in a Bank of England report written just after 'Big Bang'. This report argued that the're may be 'disadvantages to hosting a major financial sector' in that 'regional disparities may be exacerbated' because of monetary policy geared to needs of the City, and that 'some argue' that 'the finance sector merely preys on the rest of the economy, adding to costs and distorting other markets' (Davis and Latter 1989). BBC reports didn't include these perspectives but they did feature a range of City and business sources who made the case for the finance sector's contribution to the economy. The BBC's discussion of deficit spending was also unbalanced with journalists repeatedly endorsing the perspective that high debt/GDP ratios were unsustainable and a danger to the economy. However, even the IMF, the organisation arguably most associated with the austerity doctrine, has recently released a working paper that fundamentally challenges this view. The paper found that governments in good standing—like the UK—don't generally repay debt but refinance it and the key to debt sustainability is that interest rates should be less than nominal GDP over the very long run. The paper found that this was true for the UK and concluded that 'unless governments can commit to infinitely large deficits, they can issue as much debt as they like without becoming insolvent' (IMF 2018 cited in Coppola 2018). As Coppola (2018) notes, the paper concluded that a more significant issue than debt to GDP ratios was the maturity profile of government debt—an issue that wasn't mentioned in BBC coverage:

> Barrett [author of IMF paper] finds that the term structure of government debt matters considerably…The U.K., which is the principal test country in

this paper, has a median debt maturity since 1960 of 8–10 years, which is long by advanced country standards. Using this as a parameter, Barrett estimates a safe debt/GDP level for the U.K. of 140%. Barrett concludes that in practice, governments probably do have limits on debt issuance, but those limits are unlikely to stem from affordability constraints. They are more likely to arise from rollover risk.

Why did the BBC tend to endorse a very negative view of deficit spending? One of my press interviewees suggested that the BBC's coverage reflected the perspectives of its journalists who had been trained in 'neoclassical economics'. In this, he argued, they represented 'a great swathe of British intelligentsia' for whom 'the acid test of how right on you are' is 'social liberalism' rather than 'what you would once have believed in 40 years ago, which is that full employment should be the main task of Government, and governments can influence the course of the economy through macro policy, that budget deficits are not always a bad thing'. Another reason for the disappearance of alternative perspectives on the economy was the decision by Labour to accept the Thatcherite economic settlement which removed the most powerful institutional source who would traditionally have opposed the free market. There is also the issue of the relative weakness of organised left-wing economic policy making with many traditional left of centre think tanks like the Fabians having largely accepted Gordon Brown's economic model—at least up until 2008. Whilst it was possible to identify those warning about the unbalanced and dysfunctional nature of the British economy—people like John McDonnell, Ann Pettifor, Graham Turner, Steve Keen, Larry Elliott, Will Hutton or academic researchers at the CRESC research institute at the University of Manchester—these people were seen by the BBC as 'lone wolves'. Despite this, the BBC could have done more to actively seek out a wider diversity of voices in its economic reporting rather than relying on a merry-go-round of familiar political and City elites. On the day that the bank rescue plans were unveiled, discussion of the bailouts during one segment on the *Today programme* was conducted between Sir George Cox, described by a BBC journalist as 'someone with a liberal, free-market economic background, Institute of Directors and from perhaps the more right end of British politics', and Patrick Minford who was introduced as 'one of Mrs Thatcher's chief economist supporters' (*Today programme*, 13 October 2008).

A third point about the BBC coverage concerns the issue of representation. Here I don't mean representation in terms of how different groups are portrayed on television—but instead whose interests and concerns are represented in the reporting of economic news. The BBC as a national broadcaster with a public service remit has a responsibility to represent the economics concerns of all parts of the population. However a major problem with BBC economics news is that it fails to connect with the lived economy experienced by most British people—particularly outside of London and the home counties. As Davis (2017) notes economic news prior to the 1980s used to be far broader. It dealt with macroeconomic debates, industrial and labour issues. There was more plurality in news sourcing with trade unions having a major presence to voice the concerns of workers. However, with the turn to neoliberalism in the 1980s and the increasing financialisation of the economy the contours of economic news narrowed. Reporting on industry declined whilst economists working for the trade unions or in academia disappeared from the media. As both main parties embraced the free market debates over macroeconomic policy largely vanished. Meanwhile, financialisation created a new core nexus of dominant news sources centred on a small group of political and financial elites who defined the economy in narrow financialised terms:

> Economic news came to reproduce an economic elite discourse of what the 'UK economy' is, based on the perspectives of financial, corporate, central bank and treasury sources; a discourse that, in many ways was divorced from that experienced by most of the public. This focuses on a series of headline macroeconomic indicators... Every day UK news operations quote changes to the FTSE 100 index as an indicative snapshot of the UK economy – but many FTSE 100 companies are based in other countries and do their dealing in other currencies. Their rise and fall often relates more to speculative activities that bear little relation to the actual health of the economy...The most quoted defining measure of the UK economy (as with many economies) is GDP growth. This aggregate measure is problematic in that it does not record large inequalities and differences across the economy. More importantly, it is usually presented as GDP rather than GDP per capita. So, economies such as the UK can be recorded as growing, even though a large proportion of that growth results from population rises, often linked to immigration. Another commonly quoted figure is the inflation rate – something key to monetary policy, interest rate setting and pay rise negotiations. But the Consumer Price Index (CPI) used excludes housing costs and mortgage interest payments, as well as many financial services, and certainly not the trillions in value of exotic financial products being created and circulated. So, inflation may be officially low, but as housing costs usually rise well above inflation and wage rises, personal income can easily be dropping in real terms. Another figure is levels of unemployment, recently often presented in terms of either employment or unemployment benefit claimant

counts. These figures all say little about the rise of low paid, temporary, part-time and zero-hours employment, all of which have increased (Davis 2018: 166).

As the interviews in Chap. 7 indicated most journalists didn't raise too many questions about the major problems in Britain's economic model in the years leading up to the crash in part because they were blindsided by the consensus which focused on a narrow range of elite sources and aggregate indicators. It was the 'NICE' decade with low inflation and strong growth. Regional imbalances, inequality, destruction of the manufacturing base, weakness of labour and consequent build up of consumer debt were not regular topics of news reports. In the period since the crash the BBC has continued to focus primarily on aggregate measures—such as GDP growth—despite the fact that much of this growth has been concentrated in London and the South East with some areas barely growing at all (Davis 2018). This disconnect between the way the economy is seen by elites and experienced by the public was captured brilliantly in an exchange between a professor and a heckler at a debate on the EU referendum in Newcastle. Invited by the professor to imagine the fall in GDP that a Brexit vote would bring, the heckler shouted 'That's your bloody GDP. Not ours' (Chakrabortty 2017).

There are other consequences of this style of disconnected reporting. One is how it may have contributed to the rise of populism and demagoguery and weakened the credibility of experts (Davis 2018; Davis 2018). If politicians and the news media ignore or fail to provide explanations for personal and regional economic problems, then other people will—and they are unlikely to be the kind of people that liberals approve of. Another is how this approach carries risks for the long-term survival of the BBC. The Corporation has many powerful enemies in politics and the press. Its main defence is public loyalty. Unfortunately economic reporting is part of a broader problem where BBC reporting—sometimes driven by an insular and narrow consensus—is not connecting with the experiences and concerns of large parts of its audience. This is especially problematic in relation to young people who will be integral to the future of the BBC in the coming years and are already deserting the Corporation (Nielsen and Sambrook 2016). George Monbiot (2017) points to the example of the rise of Jeremy Corbyn and some of the BBC reporting of the no-confidence vote against him by much of the Parliamentary Labour party: 'One report on the BBC News at Six finished with the words 'This is a fight only one side can win. The others face being carted off to irrelevance. The place for political losers'. The accompanying shot showed a dustbin lorry setting off, painted with the word Corbyn. As Monbiot noted such reporting is unlikely to have gone down well with the large number of young people who are Corbyn supporters:

> The net result is that the most dynamic political force this nation has seen for decades feels alienated by the media, and not just by the Tory press. Those who have thrown so much energy into the great political revival, many of whom are young, have been almost unrepresented; their concerns and passions have been unheeded, misunderstood or reviled. When they have raised complaints, journalists have often reacted angrily, writing off movements that have gathered in hope as a rabble of Trots and wreckers. This response has been catastrophic in the age of social media. What many people in this movement now perceive is a solid bloc of affluent, middle-aged journalists instructing young people mired in rent and debt to abandon their hopes of a better world. Why has it come to this, even in the media that's not owned by billionaires? (Monbiot 2017)

The Brexit results appears to have made some journalists think about this disconnect. In a *Varsity* interview, Robert Peston stated that he had thought because he attended a state school he was aware of how his fellow citizens lived but 'it turns out I have not really been living in the United Kingdom but in a privileged metropolitan bubble' (Day 2017). Peston commented that 'job security has been more eroded over the past 20–30 years' and that 'the most extraordinary thing is that people put up with stagnating and declining living standards for so long. Some of these people, their stagnating living standards and the erosion of their way of life, massively predated the crash'. However, reflexivity on the part of individual journalists is unlikely to produce the kind of structural changes necessary to make economic journalism relevant to the lives of most people.

One potential solution is to recruit journalists from more diverse regional, ethnic and class backgrounds and encourage them to escape journalism's 'hall of mirrors' (Monbiot 2017). Debates on economics and policy making could be broadened to include a much wider range of expertise. Left-wing, Keynesian and environmental perspectives on the economy, in particular, deserve much more representation. Another area where improvements could be made is the use of statistical indicators. One simple change would be to include measurements of GDP per capita alongside GDP. This would provide a better indicator of living standards but would also help to dispel myths about the economic impact of immigration by revealing the boost to growth from migration. The range of economic indicators that the BBC reports on could also be expanded to capture key measures of inequality and sustainability. For instance, the Commission on the Measurement of Economic Performance and Social Progress, chaired by Joe Stiglitz and Amartya Sen made 12 recommendations on possible new metrics to better capture the health of the economy and human welfare (Stiglitz et al. 2008). These included focusing on consumption rather than production, having a greater emphasis on the distribution of income, wealth and consumption and looking more closely at multi-dimensional measures of well-being which include indices of environmental, social and political health. Others have suggested major structural reforms to democratise the BBC and improve diversity in its news delivery (e.g. Freedman 2016; Freedman and Goblot 2018; Media Reform Coalition 2018; Hind 2018).

The Labour Party: Economic Messaging and Strategic Communication Priorities

As the content analyses chapters demonstrated once the New Labour economic model imploded in 2008, the party found itself ideologically beached with little coherent to say about the economy. Having embraced the free market and financialisation it had no answers for the problems they had created—though some New Labour figures such as Peter Mandelson seemed to have a sudden conversion to the benefits of a regional industrial policy. The current leadership have been clear that a more interventionist role for the state is essential to address the imbalances in Britain's economy through measures such as a state investment bank and the support of strategically important sectors of the economy.

Such policies have to be sold. To do this Labour will need to develop distinctive ways of seeing the economy which can be condensed into phrases that can easily be grasped by audiences. These will need to encapsulate both what is wrong with the current economic settlement and what Labour will do to fix it. As Philo (1995) notes, one of the key factors in Mrs. Thatcher's three consecutive election victories was her government's ability to develop perspectives on the economy which made sense and appealed to key voter segments, particularly in South East. Phrases such as 'there is no alternative', 'right to buy', 'share owning/home owning democracy', 'enterprise culture' and 'popular capitalism' entered public consciousness and became templates through which people interpreted their own experiences and new information they encountered in the media. The Conservatives also developed a series of negative messages which were used to encapsulate what was wrong with Labour's policies, such as 'lame duck' nationalised industries and 'winter of discontent' which as the analysis in Chap. 2 showed could be deployed at opportune moments in later crises.

Labour's response to consecutive election defeats was to retreat into image management and abandon the key terrain of economic contestation. In the 1987 and 1992 elections little was said on the economy and no significant attempt was made to develop a critique of the damage wrought by Conservative policies on Britain's economic base and social fabric (Philo 1995). This process continued through the New Labour period with an ever increasing retreat from ideology and greater reliance on professionals from the world of advertising and public relations. One of the most striking aspects of pollster Deborah Mattinson's (2010) memoirs of her time working for New Labour is how much attention was focused on the image of individual politicians—and how little was directed towards arguments around economic policy. This is not to say that how the public perceive leadership is unimportant. Recent elections show that how the public perceive political leaders can be crucial—especially if they haven't produced a clear, distinctive and coherent policy platform. However image management can never be a substitute for winning ideological arguments, especially on the core issue of the economy. This should be fertile territory for Labour since the Conservative economic policies are marginalising large parts of the population. The challenge is to craft messages on the economy that will resonate and unite a new electoral block.

A second issue for Labour concerns their strategic communication and in particular how to manage a perennially hostile press. New Labour's approach in the lead up to the 1997 election was to make deals with parts of the press. Support from News International titles was exchanged— according to some accounts—for favourable cross-media ownership policy or particular stances on Europe (Abrams and Bevins 1998; Macshane 2015). Whatever the truth of these claims—and they have been denied by some of the protagonists—the agreement did not stop those newspapers from attacking the party when it took positions they disagreed with. The role that News International titles played in Labour's 1997 victory is subject to debate (Curtice 1997; Norris et al. 1999; Newton and Brynin 2001; Ladd and Lenz 2009). What is less controversial is how damaged

Labour were by the reporting of some of issues examined in Chap. 6 such as immigration, welfare and public investment. Whilst some titles may have been officially endorsing Labour, *their day to day reporting was systematically destroying the party's support on core issues.*

As the interviews in Chap. 7 demonstrated any Labour party that seeks to raise public spending to a level comparable with Western European will inevitably come into conflict with the parts of the press that support a small state and low public spending. This calls into question any policy that attempts to co-opt this part of the media. An alternative strategy could be to develop a much more sophisticated system of media and public opinion monitoring together with a proactive and robust system of rebuttal. The party should be constantly commissioning research to examine which arguments work in response to media attacks. Then it could utilise its mass membership to use such arguments in face to face conversations, social media and in the more open spaces in broadcast and print media such as phone ins and letters pages. This will be very challenging but the alternative—triangulation and shadowy deals with press magnates—is unlikely to succeed.

REFERENCES

Abrams, F., & Bevins, A. (1998, February 11). Murdoch's Courtship of Blair Finally Pays Off. *Independent*. Available at: https://www.independent.co.uk/news/murdochs-courtship-of-blair-finally-pays-off-1144087.html. Accessed 9 July 2018.

Asthana, A., & Hattenstone, S. (2016, September 2). Clegg: Osborne Casually Cut Welfare for Poorest to Boost Tory Popularity. *Guardian*. Available at: https://www.theguardian.com/politics/2016/sep/02/nick-clegg-george-osborne-cut-welfare-poorest-boost-tory-popularity. Accessed 9 July 2018.

BBC Trust. (2007). *From Seesaw to Wagon Wheel: Safeguarding Impartiality in the 21st Century*. Available at: http://downloads.bbc.co.uk/bbctrust/assets/files/pdf/review_report_research/impartiality_21century/report.pdf. Accessed 9 July 2018.

Chadwick, A. (2017). *The Hybrid Media System: Politics and Power*. Oxford: Oxford University Press.

Chakrabortty, A. (2017, January 10). One Blunt Heckler has Revealed Just How Much the UK Economy is Failing Us. *Guardian*.

Chu, B. (2015, April 1). Two Thirds of Economists Say Coalition Austerity Harmed the Economy. *Independent*. Available at: http://www.independent.co.uk/news/business/news/two-thirds-of-economists-say-coalition-austerity-harmed-the-economy-10149410.html. Accessed 9 July 2018.

Coppola, F. (2018, April 17). Everything You've Been Told About Government Debt Is Wrong. *Forbes*. Available at: https://www.forbes.com/sites/france-scoppola/2018/04/17/everything-youve-been-told-about-government-debt-is-wrong/#66e7f7da314f. Accessed 9 July 2018.

Cox, J. (2016, December 6). Survey: 18 Per cent Trust National Press to Tell the Truth, Tabloids Less Trusted than Estate Agents. *Press Gazette*. Available at: http://www.pressgazette.co.uk/survey-18-per-cent-trust-national-press-to-tell-the-truth-tabloids-less-trusted-than-estate-agents/. Accessed 9 July 2018.

Curtice, J. (1997). Is the Sun Shining on Tony Blair? The Electoral Influence of British Newspapers. *Harvard International Journal of Press/Politics, 2*(2), 9–23.

Daley, J. (2013, October 13). The BBC Foists on Us a Skewed Version of Reality. *Daily Telegraph*. Available at: https://www.telegraph.co.uk/finance/newsby-sector/mediatechnologyandtelecoms/media/10374036/The-BBC-foists-on-us-a-skewed-version-of-reality.html. Accessed 9 July 2018.

Davis, A. (2017). The New Professional Econocracy and the Maintenance of Elite Power. *Political Studies, 65*(3), 594–610.

Davis, A. (2018). Whose Economy, Whose News? In L. Basu et al. (Eds.), *The Media and Austerity* (pp. 157–169). London: Routledge.

Davis, E. P., & Latter, A. R. (1989, November). London as an International Financial Centre. *Bank of England Quarterly Bulletin*. Available at: https://www.bankofengland.co.uk/-/media/boe/files/quarterly-bulletin/1989/london-as-an-international-financial-centre. Accessed 15 Oct 2018.

Davis, W. (2018). *Nervous States: How Feeling Took Over the World*. London: Jonathan Cape.

Day, L. (2017, November 30). Robert Peston: 'This Was a Chance for Them to Kick the Establishment'. *Varsity*. Available at: https://www.varsity.co.uk/news/14208. Accessed 16 Oct 2018.

Edwards, J. (2017, February 20). For Every £154 Newspapers Lose in Print Revenue, They Gain only £5 on the Digital Side. *Business Insider*. Available at: http://uk.businessinsider.com/statistics-smartphones-print-newspaper-revenues-2017-2. Accessed 9 July 2018.

Elliott, L. (2010, April 29). Mervyn King Warned that Election Victor Will Be Out of Power for a Generation, Claims Economist. *Guardian*. Available at: https://www.theguardian.com/business/2010/apr/29/mervyn-king-warns-election-victor. Accessed 9 July 2018.

Evans-Pritchard, A. (2016, October 10). Britain Should Embrace Weaker Pound and It Needs to Fall Further, Says Former BoE Governor and Currency Guru. *Daily Telegraph*. Available at: https://www.telegraph.co.uk/business/2016/10/10/currency-guru-says-pound-slide-liberates-uk-from-malign-grip-of/. Accessed 9 July 2018.

Freedman, D. J. (2016). *A Future for Public Service Television: Content and Platforms in a Digital World*. Project Report. Goldsmiths, University of London. Available at: http://futureoftv.org.uk/report/. Accessed 15 July 2018.

Freedman, D. J., & Goblot, V. (2018). *A Future for Public Service Television*. London: Goldsmith Press.

Greenslade, R. (2014, November 27). BBC and (Some) Newspapers are More Trusted than Politicians. *Guardian*. Available at: https://www.theguardian.com/media/greenslade/2014/nov/27/bbc-and-some-newspapers-are-more-trusted-than-politicians. Accessed 9 July 2018.

Greenslade, R. (2016, February 11). The Brexit Drippers: How Eurosceptic Papers Wage Their Propaganda War. *Guardian*. Available at: https://www.theguardian.com/media/greenslade/2016/feb/11/the-brexit-drippers-how-eurosceptic-papers-wage-their-propaganda-war. Accessed 14 July 2018.

Greenslade, R. (2017, January 24). Winning Back Advertisers Is Key to Saving the Newspaper Industry. *Guardian*. Available at: https://www.theguardian.com/media/greenslade/2017/jan/24/winning-back-advertisers-is-key-to-saving-the-newspaper-industry. Accessed 9 July 2018.

Hind, D. (2018). *Owen Jones Versus the British Media*. Available at: https://thereturnofthepublic.wordpress.com/2018/04/21/owen-jones-vs-the-british-media/. Accessed 9 July 2018.

Ipsos-Mori. (2016). *Perceptions Are Not Reality*. Available at: https://www.ipsos.com/ipsos-mori/en-uk/perceptions-are-not-reality. Accessed 9 July 2018.

Jowett, G. S., & O'Donnell, V. J. (2011). *Propaganda & Persuasion*. London: Sage.

Ladd, J. M., & Lenz, G. S. (2009). Exploiting a Rare Communication Shift to Document the Persuasive Power of the News Media. *American Journal of Political Science, 53*(2), 394–410.

Macshane, D. (2015). *Brexit: How Britain Left Europe*. London: I.B.Taurus.

Mattinson, D. (2010). *Talking to a Brick Wall*. London: Biteback.

Mayhew, F. (2017, September 7). News Websites Account for Nearly Half of All Social Media 'Engagements' with UK Content, Analysis Shows. *Press Gazette*. Available at http://www.pressgazette.co.uk/news-websites-account-for-nearly-half-of-all-social-media-engagements-with-uk-content-analysis-shows/. Accessed 9 July 2018.

Mayhew, F. (2018, February 15). National Newspaper Print ABCs: Daily Star Overtakes Daily Telegraph for First Time in Over a Year + Full Figures for Jan. *Press Gazette*. Available at: http://www.pressgazette.co.uk/national-newspaper-print-abcs-daily-star-overtakes-daily-telegraph-for-first-time-in-over-a-year/. Accessed 9 July 2018.

Media Reform Coalition. (2018). *Draft Proposals for the Future of the BBC*. Available at: http://www.mediareform.org.uk/wp-content/uploads/2018/03/MRC_flyer_20180312_WEB-1.pdf. Accessed 9 July 2018.

Monbiot, G. (2017, June 13). The Election's Biggest Losers? Not the Tories but the Media, Who Missed the Story. *Guardian*. Available at: https://www.the-guardian.com/commentisfree/2017/jun/13/election-tories-media-broad-casters-press-jeremy-corbyn. Accessed 9 July 2018.

Newman, N. (2011). Mainstream Media and the Distribution of News in the Age of Social Discovery. *Reuters Institute for the Study of Journalism*. Available from: https://reutersinstitute.politics.ox.ac.uk/sites/default/files/2017-11/Mainstream%20media%20and%20the%20distribution%20of%20news%20in%20the%20age%20of%20social%20discovery.pdf. Accessed 9 July 2018.

Newman, N., Fletcher, R., Kalogeropoulos, A., Levy, D. A. L., & Nielsen, R. K. (2017). *Reuters Institute Digital News Report 2017*. Available at: https://reutersinstitute.politics.ox.ac.uk/sites/default/files/Digital%20News%20Report%202017%20web_0.pdf. Accessed 9 July 2018.

Newsmedia Association. (2017). UK *News Media Journalism Powers Social Networks*. Available at: http://www.newsmediauk.org/News/uk-news-media-journalism-powers-social-networks/181674. Accessed 9 July 2018.

Newton, K., & Brynin, M. (2001). The National Press and Party Voting in the UK. *Political Studies, 49*(2), 265–285.

Nielsen, R. K., & Sambrook, R. (2016). What Is Happening to Television News? *Reuters Institute for the Study of Journalism*. Available at: https://reutersinsti-tute.politics.ox.ac.uk/sites/default/files/2017-06/What%20is%20Happening%20to%20Television%20News.pdf. Accessed 9 July 2018.

Norris, P., Curtice, J., Sanders, D., Scammell, M., & Semetko, H. (1999). *On Message: Communicating the Campaign*. London: Sage.

PAMCo. (2018). *Daily Multi-Platform Readership*. Available at: http://www2.newsworks.org.uk/readership.pptx. Accessed 9 July 2018.

Philo, G. (1995). Political Advertising and Public Belief. *Media, Culture and Society, 15,* 407–418.

Press Gazette. (2008, February 8). *January ABCs: Sun Sales Back Above Three Million*.

Skidelsky, R. (2013, November 21). Post-crash Economics: Some Common Fallacies about Austerity. *Guardian*. Available at: https://www.theguardian.com/business/2013/nov/21/post-crash-economics-austerity-common-falla-cies. Accessed 10 July 2018.

Stanley, L. (2016). Legitimacy Gaps, Taxpayer Conflict, and the Politics of Austerity in the UK. *The British Journal of Politics and International Relations, 18*(2), 389–406.

Stiglitz, J., Sen, A., & Fitoussi, J. (2008). *Report by the Commission on the Measurement of Economic Performance and Social Progress*. Available at: http://ec.europa.eu/eurostat/documents/118025/118123/Fitoussi+Commission+report. Accessed 10 July 2018.

Index[1]

---

[1] Note: Page numbers followed by 'n' refer to notes.

Printed by Printforce, the Netherlands